GEORGE'S WAR

GEORGE'S WAR

GEORGE HILL

First published in the United Kingdom in 2010 by
Bank House Books
PO Box 3
NEW ROMNEY
TN29 9WJ UK
www.bankhousebooks.com

© George Hill, 2010

The Author hereby asserts his moral rights to be identified as the Author of the Work.

All rights reserved. No part of this publication may be reproduced, stored in a retrieval system, or transmitted, in any form or by any means, electronic, mechanical, photocopying, recording or otherwise, without the prior permission of the publisher and copyright holder.

British Library Cataloguing in Publication Data
A catalogue record for this book is available from the British Library

ISBN 9781904408727

Typesetting and design by Chandler Design

Dedication

To my comrades in the 151 Light Field Ambulance,
Royal Army Medical Corps.

Acknowledgements

To my very good friends Terry Miller and his wife Pat for their tremendous help and encouragement in the preparation of this story of my experiences in the Second World War. As Terry so aptly put it, they kept nudging me in the right direction!

Also, Terry's Italian neighbour, Adriano, who is an internet enthusiast. He was able to contact a lady doctor, Cecilia Deni, who actually knew Signora Maria Luis Bernardi – the Crocerossina Sorelli Maria whom I met on the Hospital ship *Toscana*.

Unfortunately Signora Maria died a couple of years ago, but her married daughter Emmasofia Donini possesses a photo album of Maria's wartime experiences, and, with the help of Dr. Cecilia's husband Gianfranco, was able to transmit some photos of Maria and also the *Toscana* received with grateful thanks.

Introduction

My name is George Hill. I was born on 21 July 1918 and it is now 2009, meaning that I am ninety-one years of age. I now live in a retirement home and have outlived two wives; long lines of children, grand-children and great-grandchildren now form my family.

However, this story is not just about me. It tells how four other young men, the same age as myself, met on our journey to join the Armed Forces during the Second World War, became firm friends, remained together during practically the whole of the war, and kept in touch until their deaths.

Before I begin my wartime story I must properly introduce myself. I was born in Hanley, Staffordshire, and in 1919 when I was ten months old my father and mother brought me to Bradford in Yorkshire to live in a cottage at Headley, just outside Thornton, because my father, a highly skilled foundryman, had obtained the position of foreman at the brass foundry of an engineering workshop at Fairweather Green, partway between Thornton and Bradford. Although our cottage was old and rather primitive, with no mains water, electricity, gas or inside toilet, I grew up to love the countryside that surrounded it. My father took me for long walks at the weekends when he was home from work, telling me the names of the plants and animals we encountered, while mother stayed at home preparing our greatly enjoyed Sunday dinner.

However, shortly after the First World War ended my father caught the dreaded influenza which swept the country and caused many deaths. He had always kept fit and managed to survive, but the illness left him with a weak chest that deteriorated into asthma. In those days there was no treatment to relieve the breathing difficulties, so he grew progressively weaker, having to take long spells away from work. Finally the strain affected his heart, and he died when I was eleven years old. Our savings were wiped out by the funeral expenses. During Father's absences from work my mother had earned money from cleaning jobs at nearby farmhouses, and that and the small widow's pension was all we had to live on, so we had to tighten our belts.

I attended the local Thornton school and passed my scholarship examinations with quite high marks. The headmaster urged my mother to apply for a charitable grant to kit me out for the grammar school where I could be educated until I was sixteen, but she turned this down, saying she did not wish to beg for charity. I agreed with her that it would be better for me to stay at the local school, leave at the age of fourteen and get a job to help keep myself.

This I did. I went to see the manager of the firm where my father had worked, and he agreed to take me on and train me in engineering. I took to this work with interest, and when I reached my twenty-first birthday and had completed my training he promoted me to the position of time and motion controller, with quite a good wage – which made life a lot easier at home.

It seemed however, that I was pleased with myself too soon. During the few previous years Hitler had succeeded in becoming the leader in Germany, and one of his first actions was to re-arm the German army. In the later 1930s his actions became quite belligerent, as he marched his tanks and troops into the neighbouring Sudetenland, claiming that it had always belonged to Germany anyway. This caused much unease among other European countries, particularly when German armour was seen to be gathering near the Polish border. Our prime minister, Neville Chamberlain, made a hasty trip to Berlin to warn Hitler that any further invasions of foreign territory would lead to a swift reaction from Britain, and Hitler assured him most faithfully that he had 'no further territorial ambitions in Europe'. Mr Chamberlain returned home in high glee, proclaiming that there would be 'no war in our time'. Some of our political leaders were not completely convinced and the minister for defence, Mr Hore-Belisha, managed to persuade the government to pass a motion that required all young men who became twenty-one years old in 1939 to attend a military training camp for six months, to help to build up our much depleted armed forces. So in early 1939 young men began to receive notices to report to local centres. I knew about this, of course, because it was in all the newspapers and on the radio, and sure enough within a few days of my birthday a buff envelope popped through the letter box, instructing me to register at a local office in Bradford. I took some time off work and presented myself. After submitting to the usual physical examination (the one where you are asked to cough!), I was interviewed by an army officer who wanted to know my general state of health, what my employment was, and whether I had any preference for a particular military unit. He also asked whether I could attend training immediately. I answered to the best of my ability, and asked if, as I was hoping to sit an examination in mid-August, my attendance could be deferred until after that date. He agreed, handing me the form to sign. I left the office much lighter of heart, certain that the six month break would be like a working vacation from my usual job.

Herr Hitler had other ideas, however, and when in late August 1939 his armies swept into Poland our country was plunged into war, having pledged our support to the Poles if they were attacked. This altered things immediately. The men aged twenty-one who were attending training camps were immediately transferred to military units, and I knew it would not be long before I was called up – as all deferments had been declared null and void.

Sure enough, towards the end of September 1939 a buff envelope arrived containing instructions to catch a particular train from Leeds to Newcastle-upon-Tyne on 4 October 1939, with an accompanying railway voucher to show at the ticket office. And so, early that morning, having said my farewells to a sad mother and a distraught girlfriend – Edna Chambers, with whom I had been going out for the last six months, I made my way to Bradford Exchange station, showed my ticket voucher and climbed aboard the local train to Leeds, beginning my journey to Newcastle and an unknown future.

CHAPTER 1

I dashed out of the smaller Leeds station, where the line from Bradford terminated, and hurried up the main street to the Central station where, my documents informed me, I was to board the train to Newcastle-upon-Tyne, where further instructions would be given to me.

I happened to catch a glimpse of my reflection on a shop window as I passed. It was of a smart young man, well built but not overweight. My earlier medical examination had recorded me as 'Weight – ten stone eleven pounds. Height – five feet eleven inches' and my reflection confirmed this, but it gave no indication of the turmoil going on in my head, where sheer panic vied with tremulous excitement at the idea of being involved in battles. I had listened many times to the tales of First World War veterans: the trenches thick with mud, and shells blowing you to pieces. Was I about to experience this for myself? The document I was clutching gave no indication of the kind of military unit I was joining. With a shrug I realised that the only way to find out was to get on with it.

I hurried on and entered the forecourt of Leeds Central station. An elderly porter glanced at my proffered railway warrant and pointed me towards the ticket barrier. 'Through there, lad,' he said. 'Show 'em your warrant an' go to platform six – there's a train waiting there.' He added, with a grin, 'So you're one of that lot, eh? Hurry up – they've been hangin' on for you!'

Clutching my small suitcase with the few personal items I had been told I could take with me, and my civilian gas mask in its square cardboard box, I leapt aboard the last carriage of the train, which had two old-fashioned coaches – just plain carriages with two long seats, one either side, and no connecting corridors. As I jumped in, the guard, who had been standing by his van, blew his whistle, waved his flag and stepped aboard as the already moving train, with a great blast of steam and an answering whistle, began to gather pace. I threw my suitcase and gas mask on to the rack above my head and looked around at the only other occupant as I sat down, who was smiling broadly at me. 'Only just in time!' he chuckled. He was probably two or three inches taller than me, lean of body and fit looking with a head of dark brown hair, he spoke with a pleasant, well-educated voice, with only the merest trace of a Yorkshire accent. 'I bet you're on your way to join our Armed Forces at Newcastle,' he added.

'How did you guess that?' I countered. He laughed, and replied, 'That was easy: this is a special train commandeered by the military authorities to pick up young chaps like you and me. It started off somewhere further down south and it's only going as far as Newcastle, so there you are. I'd better introduce myself: Arthur Copley, living in Wakefield, age twenty-one. I worked in the Town Hall there until I got this.' He held up a set of documents similar to mine. 'So that's me: how about you?'

'I'm George Hill,' I replied, 'from Bradford. Time and Motion bloke in a local factory. I haven't the faintest idea what branch of the forces they have in mind for us; have you?'

Arthur shrugged. 'Haven't a clue, but I'm sure we'll find out very soon.'

We carried on chatting about our lives in 'civvy street', and it seemed no time at all before the train was grinding to a halt at York. A few more young men came clambering aboard. One of them, a sturdily built chap with curly jet black hair, opened our door and stepped into the carriage as a middle-aged porter handed up his case and admonished him, 'Now just you think on, our Alan, don't get into any trouble, and do what your officers tell you!'

With a grin our newcomer sank into the seat beside us. 'My uncle,' he explained. 'Works for Great Northern Railway, same as I do – or did till I got this.' He waved a set of documents just like ours. 'He insists on looking after me like a mother hen. My name's Alan Wright, on my way to Newcastle, which I guess you are as well.'

We introduced ourselves as the train rattled its way northward, and it was not long before we were stopping again, this time at Middlesbrough, where a lanky young man with a thin lugubrious face joined us.

'Billy Hough,' he announced, 'lately of Redcar where my father owns the local betting shop. I help him – or I did until this morning, when I was required to locate myself in pastures new.' He waved his papers at us, looking around at the aged carriage and murmured, with a cheeky grin, 'Not exactly Pullman class, is it?'

We chatted amicably as the train continued its journey. It halted again at Durham station, where another bunch of young men joined the train. One of them opened our door and climbed in. He was a well-set tallish young man, dark haired and with a serious expression on his face.

'Morning, gentlemen,' he said, as he stowed his case on the rack and sat down opposite us. 'I'm John Hill. I worked with my father in his chemist's shop here in Durham until this morning.' He waved his documents at us with a faint smile.

'Any relation to George here?' asked Billy. 'His name's Hill too.'

'Never seen him before in my life!' exclaimed our newcomer, his serious expression illuminated with a beaming smile,' but I guess we'll soon know all about one another.' He cheerily joined in our conversation, and we all got along very well together, as if we had known one another for a long time.

In the meantime our train was speeding on its way to our destination, and quite suddenly we were slowing down as the Newcastle platform appeared. With a squeal of brakes, and a tremendous sigh of escaping steam, our train seemed to be saying, 'Well – that's my job done!'

We scrambled out, dragging our suitcases and gas masks with us, to discover that we were part of a group of forty or so young men. We did not have to wait long before two lance-corporals in khaki uniform strode up. The first, a shortish thin man, ordered us in strident tones to form up into three ranks. I really hadn't any idea what that meant, but by watching the others we five joined the three lines and waited expectantly. The thin NCO introduced himself as Lance-Corporal Andy Kilgour, and announced that he and the other NCO, Jack Benson, were going to march us a mile through town to Sandyford Road Drill Hall, where we would be allotted to the units that were expecting us. With the barked command 'By the left, quick march!' we set off out of the station and through the centre of Newcastle.

Unaccustomed to proper marching, we must have appeared a pretty rough and ready bunch as we wearily struggled up the hill. It was with great relief, and short of breath and sweating profusely, that we espied the board bearing the words 'Sandyford Road Drill Hall' on the end of a long low stone building. Here, our guiding NCO ordered us to line up in single file in the courtyard, from which two steps led up to an open door. One at a time we were to enter and display our paperwork to the sergeant at the desk. After we had done this we were directed to form up in two lines, one each side of the long hall.

A rather mature, stern-looking Senior NCO with a crown on his jacket sleeve came from the back of the hall, and barked 'Squad – attention.' We stopped muttering to one another, and attempted to stand upright and straight. He looked around with a gimlet eye, shook his head somewhat sadly and announced, 'You lot on this side. You're about to be taken into the Royal Army Medical Corps.'

I was rather taken aback at this, having been trained as an engineer, and I exclaimed, 'Hey, Mister, I don't know anything about medicine.'

He turned, fixed me with a glare that rooted me to the spot and, with his jaw jutting out like a bulldozer, growled, 'Laddie, if we in our superior knowledge deem you to be suitable for our medical unit, then that is where you will be! Furthermore, if you ever speak to me again, or to any other NCO wearing this crown on his sleeve, you will address us as "sir" and nothing else. IS THAT CLEAR?'

Shivering in my shoes, I answered meekly, 'Yes sir', and made up my mind to keep my mouth shut in future.

Moving back to address our whole line, he said, 'Your NCO will now march you to the rear of the drill hall where you will be given some fish paste sandwiches and a mug of tea, before marching back to the railway station for a short trip to Malton in North Yorkshire where you will become part of the 151st Cavalry Field Ambulance.' He turned to Lance-Corporal Kilgour, who had been standing patiently at the end of the line. 'Take them away, Corporal. Feed them and get them where they have to go!'

Our diminutive NCO marched us out through the rear of the building, where a trestle table bore plates of sandwiches and steaming mugs of hot tea, which two soldiers in dirty white overalls were handing out to us five and the fifteen other young men who were now on their way to join the Medical Corps.

Billy approached Lance-Corporal Kilgour and said, 'Hey, Corp, what's with this Cavalry Field Ambulance carry-on? Does it mean we'll have to ride around on horseback to bandage up casualties?'

The NCO replied with a serious frown, 'Why aye man – did they not tell ye about getting up at dawn to groom and feed your horses?'

Seeing the devastated looks on our faces he burst out laughing. 'The 151 unit was attached to a cavalry regiment during the last war and continued afterwards as a Territorial unit, training part-timers in case of any future war. The men we left in the drill hall are going for training in the Royal Army Signal Corps, to learn how to drive our ambulances, large and small trucks and staff cars, and how to repair and service them. Then they'll rejoin us.'

CHAPTER

2

We were marching uphill again – all right, perhaps 'marching' is too imaginative a word to describe the progress of the straggling bunch of twenty conscripts that had stepped down from the train at Malton station and was now being urged by Lance-Corporal Kilgour to 'Keep in step – heads high, shoulders back, left, right, left, right, left, right. Keep it up now, we'll soon reach oor camp on the hilltop.'

Arthur grinned at John, who was next to him, and panted, 'It's a pity Billy's notion of horse riding wasn't true – I haven't done this much walking in ages, and I'm just about jiggered.' I was just behind them and I wasn't feeling too worn out, having lived most of my early life in a very hilly part of West Yorkshire, where I had enjoyed walking with my father.

We followed the narrow winding road. I could see a few scattered cottages set back from the road, with gardens where the flowers were now beginning to wilt in the October coolness. Eventually we passed a fairly large detached house with no curtains at the windows and an air of neglect about it; weeds flourished in the walled garden. Immediately after this we came to hedgerows, bordering open fields on either side, and even I gave a sigh of relief as we came to the top of the hill. On the right a wire fence enclosed a large grassy area where tents were pitched, together with a large, semi-circular corrugated iron-roofed hut and three strange circular objects like large metal dustbins on legs, which had pipes reaching up from the rear from which acrid smoke billowed.

Bill sniffed the air appreciatively. 'That's what I call a grand smell!' he exclaimed.

'What, the smoky chimneys?' I asked.

'No, George, the stew – they've got a lovely stew cooking there somewhere. It's my favourite meal, and just now I could eat a horse!'

One of the others, a tall ginger-haired lad named Eric, muttered, 'Don't worry, you could quite easily be doing that!'

Lance-Corporal Kilgour led us through an open gate and brought us to a halt outside a large tent, where a notice-board bore the title 'Orderly Office'. He addressed us. 'Now then, lads, just pay attention. In a few moments our Senior NCO 'Twitchy' Menham will be coming out to greet you, so when I call yer to attenshun just try to do it a bit smart like. Give 'im a good first impression!'

A moment later I saw a small wiry figure approaching; his upper sleeve had three stripes and a crown on it. Our lance-corporal rapped out the command 'Squad – Squad Attention,' which we carried out to the best of our ability. Staff Sergeant Menham gazed at us rather sadly, and with a shake of his head he said to the lance-corporal, 'I think you'll have to really work hard with this lot, Corporal, to bring them up to our standard.'

Lance-Corporal Kilgour answered, 'Yes, Staff, but divn't fret – me an' Benson will lick 'em into shape!'

Staff Sergeant Menham peered keenly at our little group. I noticed that his right shoulder appeared to be twitching up and down at irregular intervals, and he winked at us with his right eye every few moments. 'Welcome to the One Five One, he said. 'You may wonder why you've been chosen to become part of this rapid response medical unit, particularly as it would appear that none of you has any real medical experience. The answer is that we're a Territorial unit, and we need a few strong, healthy, reasonably intelligent young men like you whom we can quickly train to fill the present vacancies and bring us up to full strength, ready for active service.' He eyed us keenly, as if daring us to contradict him. This was followed by a quick wink. He turned to our lance-corporal. 'Right, Corporal, have them go through the orderly office here, for documentation, then march them off to the quartermaster's store to get them kitted out. By that time the evening meal should be about ready.'

Lance-Corporal Kilgour barked, 'Squad – Shun,' and with a gigantic wink Staff Sergeant Menham strutted away.

Our NCO said, 'Right, you heard that. One at a time through the office here, then line up to march to the QM stores.'

Bill was looking puzzled. 'I say, Corp. Does the staff sergeant think this is all one great big joke? He kept winking at us all the time he was speaking!'

Lance-Corporal Kilgour turned on him fiercely. 'Divn't let me hear ye makin' snide remarks about oor staff sergeant, bonny lad! I'd like ye to know that he was a stretcher bearer in the First World War, an' as he an' his partner were rescuin' a casualty in No Man's Land an enemy shell burst right beside them, blowin' 'em all off their feet. His mate an' the casualty were killed outright an' he was badly wounded – left him with shell shock it did, and hence his nickname Twitchy. But let me tell you he's a very brave man, an' we all think the world of him!'

Later that evening, having been issued with our individual pay books and allocated our own personal number, which we were instructed to memorise for life, we had marched off to the QM stores to be issued with our uniforms, eating utensils, groundsheet and three blankets each. Then we had eaten our evening meal in the corrugated roofed hut we had noticed as we entered camp. I had to admit that in spite of the smoke-belching cooking boilers the stew we were served was very tasty, as was the rice pudding that followed.

Now, we five friends and Lance-Corporal Kilgour lay wrapped in our blankets on top of our groundsheets, with only the grassy earth beneath them. The six of us lay in the pitch dark like the spokes of a wheel, heads towards the outer tent wall, feet pointing towards the central tent pole. I felt the rough khaki shirt scratching my shoulders and the thick woolly long-johns tickling my legs: all our civilian belongings had been stuffed into our suitcases, which were now to be returned to our home address – as per the label issued to us, which we had duly filled in. The earth was hard beneath my groundsheet, and I was beginning to feel just a little bit sorry for myself. Faint night sounds echoed around outside – the sigh of the wind, the hooting of an owl, the distant barking of a dog, the muted rustling of who knows what nocturnal insects, the breathing of my comrades – and despite my discomfort I soon fell asleep.

Suddenly there were hundreds of people clapping – I must be at a concert! As I abruptly woke I realised that the clapping was the sound of heavy raindrops beating on the canvas over my head, and then there were other sounds from my friends – as they realised that water was starting to trickle across the floor of our tent. Lance-Corporal Kilgour got to his feet with a lighted candle in his hand, a strange sight in his khaki shorts and long-johns, and urged us to get up, grab our kit and blankets, and make for the dining room: with its raised wooden floor it should offer a safe haven from the water. Hastily we grabbed everything and dashed through the rain, to find the rest of our group of twenty had also taken refuge inside. We slung our bedding down alongside them and were soon fast asleep.

Next morning, when it was barely daylight, we were awakened once more. This time, though, it was not the sound of the rain but the strident voice of the night guard bawling 'Wakey, wakey'. We struggled to open our eyes and sit up, to find that he was accompanied by the duty sergeant, a Sergeant Ross, one of the Territorial NCOs, a sturdy figure of a man with a squarish face. He grinned at us and spoke with a Scottish twang. 'Right, come on, get yerrselves dressed sharpish, grab yer kit, wrap yerr bedding in yerr groundsheet, and pile everything into the big van outside!'

Billy was quick off the mark as usual. 'What are we doing now, Sarge?' he asked.

'It seems like you chaps had a personal swimming bath installed last night, and we can't be doing with that. Our CO has arranged to take over the empty vicarage just down the lane as a billet for you twenty new recruits. Come on then, sharp's the word if ye want to get back here in time for yerr breakfast!'

Lance-Corporal Kilgour was the first to be dressed, and hurried around helping the others to roll up their bedding and load it into the big van – a hired vehicle which, with its civilian driver, seemed to be doing most of the fetching and carrying round here. We didn't need to be told twice, and as the sergeant had allowed us to jump aboard the van along with our belongings we were soon bumping down the hill. Soon we pulled into the walled yard of the empty house we had spotted the previous day. We clambered down, clutching our kit and bedding. Our lance-corporal produced the key Sergeant Ross had given him, opened the side door and said, 'Right – three upstairs bedrooms – sort yourselves out.'

We five managed to lay our equipment down in the first room, and as our lance-corporal joined us Arthur asked, 'What made them change their minds? About fixing us up down here, I mean.'

'It seems that when the lads put the extra tents up for you lot they didna' know that after very heavy rainfall a spring bubbled up an' ran down the hill just there – or at least that's what they said. Anyway, we'll be more comfortable here. Come on, back in the van. Let's get oor breakfast before it's all eaten up.'

Back in the dining room we joined the queue to the serving table, collected porridge, bacon and egg and a mug of tea, and were about to tuck in when Sergeant Ross entered and rapped out the command 'Orderly officer! Any complaints!' He was followed into the dining hall by a tall officer with three pips on his uniform shoulder.

I was amazed at the transformation. Everyone fell silent and sat upright as the fair-haired captain approached the man at the head of the table and enquired, 'Any complaints?' to which each time he received the answer 'No complaints, sir.' Having completed his round, he said, 'Tell them to carry on, Sergeant,' and left the room. Immediately normal conversation returned and the food was rapidly consumed.

I turned to our lance-corporal. 'What would have happened if I'd said I had a complaint?'

He grinned at me. 'I think you might have ended up on cookhouse fatigues, bonny lad – peelin' lots o' taties!' he chuckled.

As soon as we had finished the two lance-corporals lined us up on the small square of concrete and quickly brought us to attention as the wiry figure of Staff Sergeant Mallen approached. He gazed at us keenly, shook his head and remarked, 'Lot of work to be done with the drill, eh, Corporals.' He turned back to us 'This is what will happen. For the next fortnight myself and my two lance-corporals are going to march you up and down, giving you all the drill commands, and keep on doing it until you're absolutely perfect – and tired out, I may say. In the afternoons we'll go on route marches with your full kit. I think by the end of that you may be fit and proficient enough to join the rest of our Territorial unit.'

Our feet hardly touched the ground! We sweated and strained on the parade ground, polished our buttons and boots every night, and by the end of the fortnight we were fitter, and lighter, as well as fully alert; to all commands we reacted like a unit.

After our fortnight was completed we lined up as usual. As the staff sergeant came towards us we noticed that there was an officer with him.

He was tall, thin and older than the other officers, and his uniform had two pips and a crown on the shoulder tabs. As they approached Lance-Corporal Kilgour rapped out the command, 'Squad – Attention,' which we obeyed with alacrity.

Staff Sergeant Menham beamed with delight. 'Good for you. You've done extremely well, and our Commanding officer, Lieutenant-Colonel Swindale, would like to have a chat with you.'

The CO gazed around our little parade and smiled. 'Stand at ease, men. I've been hearing some very good reports about you from my staff sergeant, who assures me that you're proficient enough to join our main unit. However, there's just one more task I wish you to carry out.' He noticed the anxious look on our faces, and said, 'No need to worry – it's not too strenuous. As the winter's approaching the prospect of camping out in the wilds of Yorkshire is not very appealing, and our controlling authorities have made available some more sheltered accommodation in Ludford, a small village in Lincolnshire. We shall be housed in proper buildings, but I understand that a certain amount of cleaning up needs to be done before we move there. I've therefore decided to send you twenty men in the care of Sergeant Ross and our two lance-corporals, under the control of Captain Pomfret, as an advance party. You'll have a full week to get everything tidied up and ready for the rest of us. I also wish to announce that Staff Sergeant Menham is taking a week's leave, and when he returns he's being promoted to the rank of regimental sergeant major, replacing our RSM whom you met at our headquarters in Newcastle – who's been offered a commission as a lieutenant and has moved elsewhere. So, Staff Sergeant, soon to be RSM Menham, I leave it to you to see that these men are prepared, along with Sergeant Ross and Corporal Kilgour, to move off tomorrow down to Ludford in our van, with Captain Pomfret following in his staff car.'

Lance-Corporal Kilgour called us smartly to attention and saluted as our CO walked away, then dismissed us to prepare for another journey into pastures new, and the prospect of getting to grips with our much-needed medical training.

CHAPTER 3

'It looks like a small country town,' murmured Alan, peering out of the open rear of the one ton truck – which had an upper structure of tubular steel bars covered by a waterproof canvas, camouflaged in the typical military style of brown, green and black patches.

There had been a change of plans since those issued by our CO the previous day, brought about by the arrival shortly after we had been dismissed from the parade ground of the first contingent of our long-awaited official unit transport, driven by our new Royal Army Service Corps drivers. For the time being it was only a small portion of the fleet we would need to make our unit fully mobile, but the sight of the two one ton trucks, two fifteen hundredweight smaller trucks and one ambulance was enough to make Lieutenant-Colonel Swindale alter his plans. Instead of sending twenty men to Ludford, he decided to send just ten of the new intake, five in the one ton truck and the other five in the ambulance, with Lance-Corporals Kilgour and Benson and Sergeant Ross sitting in front with the drivers. Captain Pomfret was to travel down as planned in his staff car.

So it was that the rest of the day was spent loading up the trucks with as much of the equipment needed at our new site as could be stowed away still leaving space for our own personal kit and bedding, and five travellers.

'It could be Market Rasen,' said Arthur. 'When I was a youngster my parents took me on holiday to Mablethorpe on the coast, and I remember going through a little town with a name like a raisin. If I'm right, Ludford should be only about six miles further on.'

We stared out of the open rear, and a minute or two later I cried out, 'Look, over there! That small shop with three windows – above the door it says "Market Rasen Co-operative Society".'

Arthur was right. Within half an hour our little convoy was pulling into a tiny village, little more than a hamlet. There was a general store also serving as a post office, a slightly more imposing building which was the Ludford District office of Lincolnshire County Council, a school, a square-towered church and a pub called the Golden Hind. There were several cottages scattered around, various farm buildings nearby, and, just back from the road, a large square field sporting what was quite obviously a cricket pavilion.

As our vehicles drove into the pub car park there it was, Captain Pomfret's staff car waiting for us. We scrambled out as our sergeant stepped out of the front of the small truck to be immediately joined by the lance-corporals, and we formed up, expecting the order 'Squad – Attention.' It didn't come; instead, Captain Pomfret said, 'It's all right – stand at ease. We're just a small group with a job to do, so let's dispense with the spit and polish for the time being. We've got a very busy week before us if we're going to get this place in condition for the rest of our unit in just a few days. I'd like you two lance-corporals and Sergeant Ross to join me in the pub here for a few minutes while we discuss what needs to be done, and how we're going to go about it. You men, just stretch your legs. You must be stiff after that long ride down.' So saying, he ushered the three NCOs into the Golden Hind.

He was right, of course; it had been a long bumpy road down, particularly for the five of us who had been perched precariously on the piled up kit and stores for some six hours. We had only stopped once, when our driver spotted a public park – where public conveniences dealt with a very necessary need. We had also managed to scoff the corned beef sandwiches handed out by Corporal Cook McCann before our journey commenced, and have a long-wished-for drink of tea, poured from the huge thermos that he had passed up to us. Then we were off again.

After we had hung around for what seemed like a long time, the three NCOs reappeared and motioned us to join them beside the ambulance. Sergeant Ross acted as spokesman. 'Right, men, this is the position. There are two large and one small empty barns close by, plus the cricket pavilion and two fairly large empty rooms in the schoolroom yard. The pavilion will accommodate some of the men, so for a start you five who travelled down in the large truck go along with your driver and the truck to the pavilion, drop off your kit and bedding there, then go along with the truck and off-load the rest of the stores at the smaller barn, which is going to serve as our quartermaster's store. The other five men will drop off their kit at one of the larger barns, which is going to be sleeping quarters for the rest of the unit, then go back to the QM's store to help with the unloading – apart from Privates Jennings and Miller, who we have decided shall be providing our meals until Corporal McCann and his gang arrive to take over. That will be at the other large barn, which is to be our men's mess hall and cookhouse. Your cookhouse equipment is in the small truck, so you go down there in the vehicle and get things cracking for our evening meal. Miller and Jennings started to mutter something but the sergeant silenced them with a scowl and barked, 'You're in the army now, so that's an order – get cracking!' Without another word the two newly appointed caterers climbed aboard the small truck.

Billy, never backward at asking questions, enquired, 'What about the officers, Sarge? Where are they going?' Sergeant Ross grinned and replied, 'They'll live in perfect comfort as guests in the Golden Hind, laddie. What else would you expect? Now, have you any more questions before we get down to business?'

'Yes, Sarge, who was that smashing bird I saw getting into Captain Pomfret's car this morning before we set off?'

'That smashing bird, as you call her, happens to be Captain Pomfret's wife, so don't you start getting any fancy ideas and making eyes at her. She came down with him for a few days' holiday', laughed Sergeant Ross, adding with a wry grin, 'Don't some people have all the luck?'

The week passed by much more quickly than I expected, and while Miller and Jennings prepared our meals the rest of us worked alongside Corporals Kilgour and Benson, freed from the stringent daily bouts of drill and discipline. We were able to get on well with cleaning up and clearing out the barns, which had a neglected appearance but seemed basically sound and weatherproof. Much of the clutter inside proved to be decrepit farm machinery and implements, which we dragged out and piled in a far corner of the surrounding field. Then we got to work with the brushes and shovels we had brought with us, and were delighted to discover that each barn had a cold water supply from a tap mounted on the wall, about two feet above the floor.

We had cleared the cricket pavilion on the day of our arrival. It had not been too difficult: it was comparatively clean, as it had been in use quite recently. There was a small spare room at one end, and a reasonably large toilet and washing facility at the other. Lance-Corporal Kilgour immediately collared this room, placing his kit and bedding firmly in place as a badge of ownership. As he came out of the room John asked him, 'What made Sergeant Ross decide to give Miller and Jennings the job of preparing our food?'

The corporal laughed and replied, 'Oh, that. He overheard them moaning about Corporal McCann's efforts at Malton, saying they could do better with their hands tied behind their backs. I guess he's giving them a chance to prove it.' It must have been an inspired choice on the sergeant's part because the two men served us with some very tasty meals from their makeshift kitchen outside the barn specified as our dining room.

Eight days after leaving Malton, with our task completed, we awaited the arrival of the rest of our unit. Captain Pomfret, accompanied by Sergeant Ross, had kept a sharp eye on our labours. When he informed us that the rest of our unit would be on their way that very day, he said, 'I don't want you chaps hanging around and getting anxious waiting for them, so I suggest that Sergeant Ross takes you all for a little route march – a little welcome exercise!' Seeing the looks of alarm on our faces, he grinned. 'Don't worry, I don't mean a strict left, right, left, right, march to attention kind of route march – more an orderly patrol through some of the local lanes here. Get to know the surrounding district!'

So we set off on our little voyage of discovery through countryside that was still green, although it was now the end of October, and returned not tired but refreshed to eat the corned beef sandwiches that Miller and Jennings had prepared in our absence. The two cooks were now anxiously supervising the big tureen of stew for the hungry travellers who would soon be with us. Arthur put his half-empty mug of tea down on the trestle table with a sigh of satisfaction, and murmured, 'I'm a lot happier being kept busy like we have been these last few days than doing all that strict drill every day. Don't you agree?'

I swallowed the last few crumbs of my sandwich. 'You're right, though I guess we've got a great deal more to learn – medically, I mean – before we're ready for real active service.'

John nodded. 'There doesn't seem to be an awful lot going on at the moment in France, where our expeditionary forces are. Mostly it's the odd German plane nipping over and dropping his bombs, like a few days ago when they duffed up our naval base in the Firth of Forth. But to be honest, I've got this sneaking feeling that Hitler's got something a lot bigger up his sleeve!'

Billy nodded and snorted. 'Huh! Yeah, and they tried to tell us it would be all over by Christmas. And pigs might fly!'

Our discussion was interrupted by the strident voice of Sergeant Ross. 'Come on you lot, line up by the roadside here to receive our guests.' We did as we were ordered, joined by Captain Pomfret and our two lance-corporals, just in time to see Lieutenant-Colonel Swindale's staff car come over the breast of the slight incline outside Ludford and descend towards the village, followed by the rest of the trucks, ambulances and staff cars, equipment and men of our unit. The CO stepped out, motioning his driver to park further along the road, and strode towards us as Sergeant Ross barked 'Squad – Attention!', an order that we carried out with precision as the sergeant presented an immaculate salute.

Captain Pomfret stepped forward and greeted our commanding officer. 'Welcome to Ludford Camp, sir. I hope you'll find everything fit and ready for you.'

Lieutenant-Colonel Swindale eyed our small advance group keenly. 'Stand at ease, men,' he said, smiling. 'If you've done your job as proficiently as you've practised your parade drill I'm sure everything will be satisfactory!'

The remainder of the unit vehicles drew into the village, and for the next few hours the area was a scene of seething activity as we advance party men guided each lorry to its assigned unloading place, then with the help of each section's personnel supervised the placing of kit and bedding, the storing of equipment, cookhouse tackle and the multitude of stuff that had arrived. Things were just about achieving a state of order when the sound of the old cookhouse bell (a two foot length of hollow steel tube dangling on a short rope, struck with an attached length of wood, which had been carefully shepherded down by Corporal McCann) sounded. In a very short time all the unit men were seated around the tables erected in the chosen barn, and murmurs of approval greeted the stew prepared by temporary cooks Miller and Jennings. When the orderly officer did his round asking 'Any complaints?' the answer of 'No complaints, sir' was entirely genuine.

Next morning, as the whole unit paraded, our CO announced that in our new location the training emphasis was going to be medical matters: treatment of wounds, care of the injured before their transit to a base hospital, treatment of short term illness and so on. 'We hope to produce, by a series of lectures and practical tests, a number of teams who can carry out the difficult and highly skilled task of caring for wounded or sick service men under conditions of extreme hardship and danger.'

During the next few days we attended lectures, given by our unit officers who had been doctors or surgeons, mostly in the Royal Victoria Infirmary at Newcastle or as local GPs, who all had first-hand experience of these matters. At other times we bandaged imaginary wounds or applied splints to supposed fractures. At other times we did stretcher drill, where a team of four men carefully lifted a supposed casualty on to a stretcher and loaded him into a waiting ambulance.

The five of us found these lectures and exercises particularly interesting, and Arthur commented, 'You were right, George: this is more like the kind of thing we ought to be doing.'

All this had been going on for about four weeks when our unit was called together at morning parade, for our CO to address us once more. 'We've made great strides forward with our training programme, and we'll eventually submit you all to a series of examinations, both oral and practical, to determine which of you are best suited to carry out the different tasks required in a rapid response medical unit on active service. However, as winter approaches real medical experience will be a great step forward. To this end I've made representations to our RAMC hierarchy, who have agreed that our unit may now return to its original base in Sandyford Road, so that those of you who've shown most promise in our local tests may have further "hands on" training at the Royal Victoria Infirmary, Newcastle. I'm also delighted to inform you that as Christmas is only a short time away you will all be granted Christmas leave. Those of you who come from outside Newcastle will get the week up to Boxing Day and our local men will take Boxing Day to New Year's Day. We'll be moving up to Sandyford Road in a couple of days' time.'

An excited murmur of approval swept through the ranks at this most acceptable turn of events, and as the parade was dismissed we went with light hearts to the task of preparing for our journey northward.

Never mind the hard work involved, it was all worth it as we could look forward to spending Christmas with our families and loved ones. I could hardly wait for the evening meal to be over so that I could write home to tell my mother and my sweetheart, Edna, the good news. I quickly scribbled a letter to each of them, adding more personal greetings to Edna's letter, then rushed off to post them before the day's final collection.

The two days passed like lightning, as the trucks were reloaded with stores and equipment, this time with a much lighter heart, particularly on the part of the original Territorials at the prospect of being on home ground once again, and for five of us the prospect of being home on leave over Christmas. Still, as Billy remarked, 'It's a pity they didn't come up with this idea before we came down here to get it ready for the rest of 'em!'

Lance-Corporal Kilgour happened to overhear him, and chuckled, 'Divn't let it bother ye, bonny lad, we s'll maybe have ti shift a sight quicker than this when the time comes!'

When the third day following our CO's announcement came round, the fleet of trucks, ambulances and staff cars, with all the unit personnel crowded into the trucks or ambulances, began their journey northward, after an early reveille and a quickly snatched breakfast. Our CO's car led the way, with the rest of our officers' cars interspersed at intervals between the trucks, with the cookhouse truck and the quartermaster's car bringing up the rear. Our departure was watched by a crowd of children from the local school, who lined up to wave us on our way with shouts of 'Are you off to deal with that Hitler chap?' to which one of our drivers shouted back, 'Yes – but not till we've had our lunch!'

And so it was that several hours later, after a couple of stops and a hasty munching of the sandwiches passed round from the cookhouse truck, we were rolling down Sandyford Road and turning into the yard of the drill hall where everything had begun just a few weeks before.

CHAPTER

4

Arthur, Alan, Billy, John and I were passengers on a train one more, but this time with a significant difference; we were travelling homeward in full uniform, the brass buttons on our greatcoats polished to shine like pure gold. Our webbing equipment had been blancoed to a spotless light green, as had the backpacks, side-packs and water-bottle carriers that we had tossed on to the luggage rack overhead, accompanying our gas masks in their khaki cotton carriers.

It was the week before Christmas 1939 and, as our CO had promised, we conscripts whose homes were more than twenty miles away from Newcastle were allowed seven days' home leave, returning to our unit the day after Boxing Day, with the rest of the unit going on leave from then until the new year.

Since our CO had announced our Christmas leave we had waited, with bated breath, the publishing of Part One Orders, which stated who would be in the first party and which day our leave would commence. I had written to Edna with the good news, promising I would let her know which day to expect me. However, the lists of names and travel instructions were not put up until the evening before our departure. It was as we returned from our evening meal at our mess hall that we spotted the lists on the orderly office notice-board, and to our delight there were our names. With slight panic we realised that we were off the very next morning – with no possibility of letting our families know: hardly any family possessed a telephone in those days. We handed in our kitbags at the QM stores for safekeeping, collected our leave passes and travel documents together with the forthcoming week's pay from the Orderly Office, and tried to get some sleep – not an easy thing to do in our excited state. In the morning the night guard came to rouse us early, saying that we were to take our greatcoats, gas masks and small kit, and a truck would run us up to the mess hall at Jesmond Dene for our breakfast, after which it would take us to the railway station.

As the train trundled on we were feeling pretty pleased with ourselves, and our return to the unit seemed ages away. The prospect of 'Civvy Street' and the delights of Christmas was almost too much to take in. Billy gave a whoop of laughter and asked, 'Did any of you lot manage to get word home about us turning up today?' We all shook our heads. 'Never mind,' he chuckled. 'It'll make it all the more fun us turning up unannounced.'

Alan joined in. 'Yes, I agree. I mean, it isn't as if there was much going on out there in France. There are no planes dropping bombs or firing guns at us – it's pretty much a stalemate.'

Arthur shook his head. 'I wouldn't call what the German U-boats are doing to our Merchant Navy a stalemate. I can't see Hitler just sitting there for long and not making a move. You know how he keeps going on about Germany being the "Master Race" – the cleverest and most advanced people on earth . . .'

John held up both hands. 'You're probably both right, but none of us really knows what the future holds, do we? So let's enjoy this leave while we can. That's what I intend to do.' Saying which, he lifted his kit down from the rack, donned it quickly and stepped down onto the platform of Durham station as the train halted, waving cheerily as he walked away.

After a few moments the train was moving again, rather slowly, as it had done all the way. The rolling stock had a worn and tired look about it, but we didn't mind: it was heading in the right direction – homeward. I said to Arthur, 'You know what you said about Hitler ranting and raving on to the people and soldiers of Germany about how their nation would soon lead the world?'

Arthur turned from gazing at the countryside, and gave a wry smile. 'Oh yes, it was on the newsreel at the cinema. Banging his fists, shouting and bawling – almost frothing at the mouth. You wouldn't see our lot going on like that!'

I nodded in agreement. 'When I was at work, our managing director often used to tell me about his trips all over the world, visiting our customers, and one of his favourite topics was the esteem with which Great Britain was regarded throughout the civilised world. We were respected for the quality of our products and for the honest, straightforward and friendly way we deal with other nations. It's a pity he can't give Hitler a bit of a lecture about it!'

Billy shook his head. 'He'd be wasting his breath,' he said as he buckled on his equipment. The train was slowing down once more as the platform of Middlesbrough appeared, and Arthur, Alan and I waved him *au revoir* as he stepped out, urging him 'not to do anything we wouldn't do'.

As the train moved away again, a little faster this time, Alan scrambled to his feet and stretched. 'I'd better see what sort of a mess they've got into at York station in my absence. See you in a week's time unless Hitler decides to start something before then!' With a broad grin he stepped down as the train ground to a halt.

The train was now rushing ahead, as if anxious to complete its journey. I was ready to step down as the train pulled into Leeds station, and wished Arthur a good leave and a Happy Christmas. As the train pulled away from the platform he shouted through the half-open window, 'Same to you, mate. Make the most of it. I'm sure this stalemate won't go on much longer!'

The train from Leeds to Bradford and the trolley-bus to Thornton were both there waiting. As I got off the bus in my home village I decided to call at Edna's first, knowing that she didn't usually work on Saturday afternoons. I knocked on the door. There was no answer! I knocked again, louder. This time I heard her mother, Clara, calling, 'Just a minute, please!' This was not the response I had expected. I heard her muttering as the key turned in the lock and the door opened a few inches. She gave a gasp, threw the door wide open, exclaiming, 'George! Oh, come in, George. We hadn't heard, so we thought you wouldn't be coming home today. We've had some gypsies around, knocking at our doors; I thought it was them again. Come in, take that heavy greatcoat off and dump all that webbing on the floor. Come and sit down by the fire. Have you been travelling a long time? I'm sure you must be tired out by now. Let me make you a cup of tea and get you something to eat.' She bustled off into the kitchen, and I heard the sounds of water running into the kettle and the gas ring being ignited with a plop.

I sank contentedly into the easy chair. 'Has Edna had to go to work today?'

Her mother laughed. 'No. When we didn't hear from you she decided to go up to your mother's house and stay there over the weekend. She's done that once or twice since you were called up so that your mother won't get too lonely. Edna sleeps in that spare bed in your mother's room, so don't you worry – your back bedroom's there waiting for you.' She gave a little chuckle. 'You'd better hurry up and drink this tea and eat these scones before you dash off up to Headley to give her the kiss she's been longing for! I expect you'll be spending most of your Christmas leave over at Headley, as we haven't got a spare room here, not even a spare bed. Horace Bingham, Edna's manager at School Green Co-op, said she could have a week off if you came home on leave, so make the most of it.'

'Where's Edna's dad today?' I asked.

'Still working on the buses, the late shift on the Thornton trolley-buses. He won't be home till 11p.m. And our Raymond's gone to the matinée at Thornton cinema with a friend who's in the same class at school. I hope we'll see a fair lot of both you and our Edna this Christmas. I'm just sorry we haven't a spare room here.'

I promised we would spend plenty of time with them, quickly finished my mug of tea and the delicious home-made scones, donned my greatcoat and webbing kit once more, and set off to complete my journey to Headley. Edna's mother said, 'I told her, "No news is good news", and I was right, wasn't I?' Edna's mother, short of stature, with a round and happy face, possessed a source of suitable sayings to match any occasion.

My kit getting heavier with every step I took up steep Headley Lane, by the time I reached the three cottages on level ground opposite Headley Hall I was sweating profusely. I walked along to number 1 at the far end overlooking the fields, taking care not to pass too close to the window. I knocked gently. After a moment the door opened and my mother peered out. As soon as she saw me her eyes and her mouth opened wide, and before she could speak I put my fingertips to my lips and spoke softly. 'Tell Edna there's a young lad who has an important message for her.' My mother's eyes twinkled mischievously, and because there was an inner porch door, I knew my words would not have been heard inside the room.

My mother called out, 'This young lad says he's got an urgent message for you!'

There was the sound of a chair being pushed sharply back, and Edna's voice growing louder as she hurried to the door. 'Oh my goodness! Is it a telegram? I hope nothing's happened to George . . .' She opened the inner door – and gave a little scream as she realised who the 'little lad' really was. I took her in my arms and hugged and kissed her. When she managed to get her breath back she burst out, 'Oh, you silly daft beggar – I thought something awful had happened to you! Why didn't you let me know? Ooh, don't tell me you can't stop and you've got to go away somewhere . . .'

I took hold of her hands and held them tight. 'Calm down, love. There's nothing amiss, and the important message is that I love you and for the next seven days I'm entirely yours. As for letting you know, I didn't find out I was coming on leave until late yesterday afternoon, much too late to send a telegram. And there's even better news! We've been told that some of us will be attending the hospital at Newcastle for special medical training for quite a few weeks. So how about that?'

Her eyes lit up with relief. 'So when do you have to be back with your unit?'

'The day after Boxing Day, and our special training doesn't start until some time in the New Year, so why don't we enjoy our wonderful Christmas?'

'It will be,' she chuckled gleefully. 'Oh – I feel as if all the Christmas bells have started ringing already.'

And that is as good a way as any of saying how much we both enjoyed every minute of that first leave. Those seven days went by like a flash of lightning, in a whirl of meeting friends, singing carols, opening presents and eating Christmas food – though this was not as sumptuous as before, on account of the shortages brought about by the sinking of so many of our supply ships by enemy submarines. It was wonderful to enjoy all this in one another's company, and eased for a while some of the tension caused by not knowing what was coming next. Horace kept his promise to allow Edna a seven day break, and we certainly made the most of it.

Like all good things my holiday had to come to an end, and by the afternoon of the day I had to return to the unit it all seemed like a dream. I had checked my train times, cutting it as fine as I dared. I had to be back in the drill hall by 11.30p.m., and according to the timetables I was due to reach Newcastle station by 11.00p.m. What if the trains were delayed? I didn't dare think about that! So here we were, Edna and I, on the forecourt of Bradford Exchange station, with about twenty minutes to spare before I boarded the train for Leeds.

Over Christmas we had discussed the idea of getting married, perhaps during my next leave, but Edna's dad was not enthusiastic about the idea of her marrying a soldier who might get killed or end up badly injured and crippled – and, as Edna said, there was talk of young unmarried women being called up to serve in the women's services – the ATS and so on: 'I might get sent away somewhere and we might never be able to see one another.' For the time being we put the idea on hold, promising that we would talk about it in our letters. As the engine whistle indicated imminent departure we clasped one another for a final hug and kiss before I hurried on to the platform, showing my travel document to the ticket inspector. I clambered aboard the old-fashioned carriage, lowered the window and stared back towards the forecourt, but the dividing partition was just too high to see her.

With another whistle and a mighty gush of steam the train was on its way. It was beginning to get dark outside, and the window blinds coupled with the partly blacked-out carriage lights presaged a very dingy journey. I began to feel just a little sorry for myself.

As I boarded the connection at Leeds station I kept a sharp look-out for Arthur, who would have got on at Wakefield, but there was no sign of him. I settled in a through coach with tables and seats on either side of the central aisle. It was not full. The occupied seats and tables were taken up by soldiers and airmen in uniform with their kit stacked beneath the tables, returning like me from Christmas leave. I was sitting by the window, and as we halted at each station I raised the corner of the blackout blind and peered out at the platform, trying to catch a glimpse of Alan, Billy or John, but ne'er a sight of them: they had decided not to risk being late back.

The servicemen in the coach were certainly not in a talkative mood. Some of them lounged in their seats, eyes closed, either asleep or dozing. A few were playing cards half-heartedly, but with very little of the laughter and banter that you would expect. A few were chatting amicably about their leave.

We were now on the last stage of our journey to Newcastle, and the train had made fairly good time. I glanced at my watch and realised a shade uneasily that it was now 10.50p.m. There was no clue as to how far we still needed to travel. I was beginning to feel distinctly worried. In a few minutes the train pulled up with a squeal of brakes alongside the station platform, by which time I had put on my greatcoat and webbing equipment ready for a speedy departure, as had the rest of the servicemen. We all dived for the door and out on to the platform, then on to the exit gate where the ticket collector was waiting to let us through. 'Cut it a bit fine, lads!' he exclaimed. 'Most of your mates were back an hour ago. You'll need to put your best foot forward if you've got to be in for half past eleven!'

As I dashed out of the station entrance I glanced at my watch once more. It was five minutes past eleven, and I had a mile's uphill trek to Sandyford Road's drill hall, fully laden. I puffed and panted as I struggled along, and my shirt was wet through with sweat, even though there was a touch of frost in the air. By the time I reached the man on guard duty I was just about at the end of my tether. As he charged me with the required 'Who goes there!' I gasped, 'It's me, Jim: George Hill.' He took a closer look, pulled a face and growled, 'You're late!' I was just about to start arguing with him when he burst out laughing. 'It's all right, George, I'm only kidding. Anyway, there's still two minutes to go. But you do like living dangerously, don't you?'

I stumbled in the semi-darkness, which the single lamp at the far end of the room could hardly penetrate, until I found my bed space, and as I unrolled my blankets on the groundsheet Arthur, whose bed space was five feet away, stirred and murmured, 'Hello there, George, had a good leave?

I replied in a whisper, 'Absolutely fantastic – tell you about it in the morning!' I quickly undressed to my underclothes, wrapped the thick woollen blankets around me, and within minutes was fast asleep.

CHAPTER

5

It was late January 1940, and we five friends had quickly been absorbed once again, along with our comrades, into the military routine. But that routine was beginning to expand. We still had our regular morning parades, followed by a short drill exercise – 'square bashing' as it was known in the ranks. At least twice a week the whole unit spent at least two hours route marching through the local countryside, wearing our greatcoats and webbing with backpack, but a large part of our training now consisted of lectures about the specialised treatment required for various types of injuries, and treatment for the ailments and diseases likely to occur on active service. These were presented by our officers who had come from a medical background, and ended with questions and answers. They were followed by practical exercises in the handling of various injuries. Again, one or other of us played the part of the stretcher-borne casualty, and was bandaged, fitted with splints and handled with the care that our tutors, the medical officers, had laboured to instil into us.

At first all this information seemed to be a lot to take in, but gradually it began to make sense. I said to the other four that this was something I felt I would be able to do: to help and to treat injured soldiers. They agreed that it was worthwhile. An added incentive to learn was given by Major Fawcett, who informed us that we would shortly be required to undergo individual spoken examinations about all these subjects, carried out by Captain Pomfret and himself, followed by practical demonstrations of our ability. Those of us who passed these tests with sufficiently high marks would be re-classified as nursing orderly third class, which would earn us an increase in pay. Further series of lectures and examinations would follow, allowing us to qualify as nursing orderly second class and finally nursing orderly first class, with further increases in pay. In addition our commanding officer, in talks with the senior medical authorities, had been able to arrange practical working sessions at the Royal Victoria Infirmary for those who passed the exams. All this made us even more determined to do our best, and as Arthur remarked, 'It's a lot more satisfying than doing drilling and marching and cookhouse fatigues.'

John nodded. 'Folks were saying it would be all over by Christmas, but it doesn't even seem to have started yet, apart from a few skirmishes on the eastern side of German territory.'

Alan exclaimed, 'I don't know about nothing happening. What about our merchant ships being attacked and sunk in the Atlantic by the German U-boats? Have you forgotten that food rationing was introduced earlier this month? All right, it was only for butter, sugar and bacon or ham, but you can bet your life there'll soon be a lot more items, and not just food, added to the list of "In short supply – only available through the ration book".'

Billy put his hand up. 'Hey, that's enough doom and gloom for the time being. Let's have another question and answer session.'

Alan turned to him with a grin. 'Right, clever clogs, Where's your patella?'

'On my knee', answered Billy, 'where I wish my girlfriend was!'

'Fair enough,' said Alan. 'So where's your coccyx?'

Billy loooked pained. 'There's no need to start talking dirty!'

'We're talking bones, you daft-head; it's a small triangular one at the base of your spine!'

'Of course I knew that,' said Billy, with a saintly smile. 'Whatever else did you think I was referring to?'

A small crowd was gathering around the notice-board where the orderly office clerk pinned up the daily Part One Orders, and a lot of discussion seemed to be going on. Eric, one of the lads who had been in our intake, came rushing across. 'Have you seen the notice?' he exclaimed excitedly.

'What notice?' asked John. 'Has Hitler decided to pack it in and call it a day?'

'No – it's a list of those who are to take the first exam. You five are on it, and I am and quite a few more. We have to report to Sergeant Ross after tomorrow's morning parade. He'll be responsible for sending us in batches of four to do our practical demonstrations under the watchful eye of Major Forsythe, then individually to the second office, where Captain Pomfret will expect correct answers to all his questions.'

We hurried across to the board, which confirmed everything Eric had told us, and Billy, with a slight attack of panic, exclaimed, 'Don't you think we ought to start revising right now, and doing our question and answers if we're going to be ready for tomorrow?'

I didn't agree. 'I think we'll do a lot better if we stop getting into a tizzy and just enjoy a relaxed evening, and start tomorrow with a clear head! How about going to the canteen for a mug of tea and a bun, and listening to Tommy Handley's half-hour on the radio. Then there's Billy Cotton's Dance Orchestra to put us in the mood for a good night's sleep.'

It proved to be a good idea. Tommy Handley's *ITMA* made us laugh, Billy Cotton's music lifted our spirits, and sleep came easily.

The following morning we, the named twelve, waited outside the orderly office as soon as the morning parade was dismissed, wondering how we would fare. Sergeant Ross was the first to arrive, and he quickly organised us into an orderly three ranks before Major Forsythe and Captains Clark and Pomfret appeared on the scene. We snapped to attention on Sergeant Ross's command and he executed an immaculate salute. Major Forsythe responded, and ran through our instructions again before the officers entered the orderly office buildings. Then Major Forsythe turned to us, and with a broad grin exclaimed, 'I hope you lot are all clued up for your exercises and answers! Good luck. Just do your best and you'll be OK.'

Sergeant Ross produced a list from his pocket, and ordered Arthur, Billy and two others to go in first. As they returned he sent John, Alan and another two in. As Arthur joined the ranks once more I raised my eyebrows to him in query, to which he grinned and stuck his thumb up. Soon it was my turn to go in along with the remaining three.

Captain Clark was standing beside a long table on which were laid various types of bandages and dressings, sticking plasters and splints; on the floor was a folding stretcher, as used in our training exercises. 'Right, nursing orderlies,' he announced, 'I want you each in turn to play the part of a casualty with a particular injury which I'll tell you about, and for which the other three will then carry out the appropriate emergency treatment. Do you understand?'

We answered 'Yes, sir,' and set about carrying out his instructions. We had been well trained, and he seemed satisfied with our performance; we were soon back outside with the others.

'Right, now comes the difficult part,' chuckled Sergeant Ross. 'Into the other office you go, one at a time as I call out your names. This time when you've answered all the questions you go out the other way straight back to the drill hall. OK?'

I was the last one to go in, and found Captain Pomfret sitting behind a table with Major Forsythe sitting to one side. The captain appeared a shade weary, and he spoke first. 'Good morning, Private Hill. Major Forsythe and I are going to put a series of questions to you, which we want you to answer as simply and as clearly as you can. No trick questions, just things we've spoken about in the lectures. Is that clear?'

I answered, 'Yes, sir', and the oral examination began, with the major asking the first question, Captain Pomfret the next and so on.

Finally the captain said, 'Now we come to the final question – and I advise you to think hard before answering it.' I nodded. 'What precautions would you consider it necessary to take if you were going to apply a tourniquet to an injured limb from which blood was flowing copiously?'

I thought hard for a few moments, then replied. 'I would regard the application of a tourniquet as a last resort, and would first have tried firmly bandaging pressure pads at the point of blood flow, as well as elevating the limb in question. A tourniquet, if not used with great care, could result in tissue damage and even gangrene. So if a tourniquet was the only way to stop the flow I would inspect the limb I was treating at very frequent intervals, checking that it was not becoming excessively pale and waxy looking or too cold. I would check for absence of pulse beats in the limb, and if this occurred I would immediately slacken the tourniquet for a time, while carefully watching for the resumption of bleeding from the wound.'

Major Forsythe, who had been listening intently, beamed and exclaimed, 'Excellent answer, Hill! Best we've had today!'

It was obvious that the questions were now at an end, so I plucked up my courage. 'How do you think we've managed this exam, sir?'

The Major's eyes lit up. 'Now then, Hill', he boomed, 'don't start getting too inquisitive. You'll have to wait for Part One Orders to find that out, like the rest, won't you?' And with that I stood up, saluted and left the room, to rejoin my comrades in the drill hall, all chatting and relaxing now the pressure was off.

If I thought we were going to have a quieter life once our first set of examinations were completed I had another think coming. In the next few days another batch of heavy trucks and ambulances turned up with their drivers, who had been undergoing some special training down in the Midlands and had been obliged to squeeze these new vehicles into the already well-occupied parking area outside the drill hall. At our morning parade our CO, announced that these extra vehicles were needed to transform us into a quick response medical unit, and that for the time being these new drivers would have to be accommodated in the already crowded drill hall – but we were not to worry because negotiations about extra billets were already going on. The RASC drivers now had an officer in charge of their detachment, Lieutenant Landon, and their NCO now held the rank of mechanised sergeant major.

Conditions in the drill hall were atrocious. There was hardly room to move when all the groundsheets and blankets were laid out, and by the middle of the night the air was hardly fit to breathe. Our mess hall, just a small hall in Jesmond Dene Gardens, had been adequate for our original company, but now, with the extra drivers, the meals were having to be served in two sittings, with the second complaining that the food was always cold.

A few days later, in the afternoon when Part One Orders were put up, Billy wandered over to find out if any of the five of us had been detailed for guard duty – as we were not studying for exams. He was away for quite a while and when he came hurrying back he was bursting with excitement. I said, 'What's up, Billy? Are we all on guard tonight?'

'No, it's nothing like that. There are sheets and sheets of notices with lots of new information. Come across and have a look for yourselves. But first of all let me tell you some very good news. The results of our exam are up – and we've all passed, all five of us!'

'What about the other seven?' asked Alan.

'Only ten passed. Big Johnny Morton and little Les Ableson didn't make it, but they'll be able to try again later.'

We hurried across and elbowed our way through the cluster around the board, and there they were, umpteen sheets of typed paper spread across the board. The first confirmed what Billy had just told us about the exams: we would now be paid as nursing orderlies third class. This was good news, and there was more to come on the further sheets. There was something about the cramped conditions in the drill hall, and news of a new influx of RAMC recruits in two weeks' time, the first in the founding of another field ambulance unit, larger and less mobile than ours.

John could contain himself no longer and burst out, 'And where do they think they're going to billet these new chaps? There isn't room to swing a cat as it is, never mind feeding them.'

'Calm down, John,' Billy interrupted. 'Just read on a bit further.'

We moved on to the next sheet, which announced that the Army Medical Authority had commandeered some extra accommodation in order to provide billets for all these extra personnel, and what was more, the huge banqueting hall in Jesmond Dene, next to the small hall we had been using as a mess, had also been commandeered and would now serve as our combined mess hall, with the smaller one now to be taken over completely by the cookhouse crew with extra equipment to prepare meals. 'And that's not all,' exclaimed an excited Billy. 'If you read on you'll see that one of the billets – a big detached house in Jesmond Dene Road, number twenty-seven, is ready for occupation now, and we five are among the first to move into it!'

'Hey – that's a posh area!' exclaimed John. 'Detached houses with their own gardens!'

Alan could hold out no longer. 'When do we move up there?'

'Read a bit further,' said Billy. 'Tomorrow morning, directly after morning parade. There are quite a few of us going, including one or two of the Service Corps drivers. The names are all there, and we have to put our bedding, kitbags and our other kit labelled with our name and number down by the drill hall entrance, ready for one of the trucks to take them to our new billet.'

'Bedding and kit being taken up,' Alan muttered suspiciously. 'What about us? Don't we get taken up as well?'

Billy eyed him sadly. 'How long have we been in this mob? Oh yes, we get taken up all right – on shanks's pony – our own two feet as usual!'

It struck me that perhaps we should be grateful we didn't have to carry our kit that way!

A few days later we were beginning to feel more settled in our new quarters, which were certainly a vast improvement on the overpopulated drill hall. Number twenty-seven was a detached house with four rooms on the ground floor, one of which was the kitchen, where a small coal-fired kitchen boiler was connected up to the cast-iron heating pipes that carried heated water around the other rooms. Our ration of coal proved to be just one bucket per day, so the boiler was lit only in the evenings. The other three rooms were empty and capable of accepting five beds each. On the first floor, reached by a wide staircase leading out of the kitchen, there was a narrow passage flanked on either side by two rooms, one of which proved to be a combined bathroom and toilet. The other three bedrooms were also capable of accommodating five people. Then a narrow wooden staircase led from the far end of the passage up to an attic room, capable of being used for storage – or emergency bed spaces.

In the end we didn't have to march all the way up there, because Eddie, the driver who had taken us down to Ludford and back again, caught up with us in the truck that was carrying the bedding and kit, and signalled us to jump in the back. We were first there, which meant we were able to choose our room, which was on the first floor overlooking the front garden, directly across the passage from the bathroom. What more could we ask?

All the windows were fitted with wooden framed blackout screens, which had to be put in place before dark and removed at first light, and each room was fitted with a single electric light bulb, only just bright enough for us to read or write our letters. Needless to say, the kitchen with its boiler was the favourite place to sprawl in the evening. The other rooms were soon filled up by the five who had passed the exam at the same time as we did, as well as the others who had joined the unit along with us and also some of the newly arrived Service Corps men.

One great advantage of our new billet was that our new mess hall was only four hundred yards away, which meant we could very easily stroll to it and be among the first to be served breakfast; and after our evening meal it was only a short journey back to our billet. Another good thing was our distance from the sergeants' mess. We were not such an easy target when they sought to detail men for the cookhouse fatigues!

CHAPTER

6

January drifted into February, and more medical lectures were the order of the day; classes of twenty or more of the RAMC trainees attended these under the tutelage of any officers from a medical background. As we ten had passed our third class exam we were called upon to act as make-believe casualties for the practical exercises.

It was following one such exercise that little Sergeant Gott, one of the original Territorial NCOs who loved to exercise his authority, approached us as we wandered in the direction of the canteen, and barked, 'Hey, you five! Orderly room, Major Forsythe's office, right away!' We hurried over to the orderly room in some dismay, wondering which particularly arduous fatigue duty we had been collared to carry out, or, even worse, if we were about to be punished for some minor misdeed. Sergeant Canning, the NCO in charge of the office, rose from his desk as we entered, and with a wry grin remarked, 'Hang around for a moment – the major's on the phone.'

'What does he want us for?' asked Alan nervously.

Sergeant Canning shrugged, and murmured. 'I wouldn't like to be in your shoes.' He shook his head sadly. 'I can't tell you too much – it's all top secret – special training – no, I daren't say any more, but I just wish you fellows best of luck and a safe return!'

By now we were beginning to get quite alarmed, and as Sergeant Canning opened the major's door we heard the officer saying, 'Can take the first lot tomorrow, you say? Fine. I'll be in touch later. Bye.'

The sergeant emerged a moment later. 'I've sent for Corporal Wallace, sir, and he's on his way.' Turning to us, he said, 'In you go. The major is ready for you now.'

We marched into the office, and stood nervously to attention. The major gave a fleeting smile and said, 'All right, stand at ease, men.' We must have appeared uneasy. 'There's no need to look so worried. I don't know what kind of yarn Sergeant Canning has been spinning, but what I'm about to tell you will, I'm sure, please you all.' As he finished speaking there was a tap on the door, and Corporal Wallace entered, saluted and stood beside us. The major pointed to a row of chairs along the rear wall of the office and boomed, 'Sit down, all of you, and I'll explain what this is all about.'

Corporal Wallace, one of the original Territorials, was a quietly spoken, medium height, dark-haired, bespectacled young man, who in peacetime had been a librarian in one of Newcastle's public libraries – a job that suited him to a 't'. He nodded to us, and we waited for the major to begin.

'Our CO has succeeded in arranging a series of six week long practical training sessions at the Royal Victoria Infirmary, where our men who have passed their third class exam can achieve some real hands on experience. You will do three weeks in the casualty department and three weeks in the operating theatres – the latter, of course, only as observers. You five and Corporal Wallace have been chosen to be the first group of six. Trail-blazers, you might say,' he said with a grin.

'Does that mean we'll be doing real bandaging and actually treating real casualties, sir?' I enquired eagerly.

'It means exactly that, Private Hill,' he answered, 'so I expect you to do your best.'

Corporal Wallace spoke up. 'What about guard duties and parades during that time, sir?'

'All taken care of,' answered the major. 'During your six week period you won't be called on for guard duties, and you'll be excused all parades – with the exception of the Friday Pay Parade, which I'm sure you wouldn't want to miss. You start tomorrow morning, and on your days at the RVI you'll have your breakfast and your evening meal as usual at the banqueting hall, but the hospital has kindly offered to give you lunch in the staff canteen there. When you first lot have done your three weeks in casualty, and move on to the operating theatres, the other five who passed the third NO at the same time as you, along with Corporal Winter, will begin their casualty session. By the time they've completed that we hope to have another lot of Third Class NOs ready to carry on up there.'

With this the major dismissed us, and we returned to our billet in Jesmond Dene Road, where we sat gleefully discussing this latest bit of good news – and the lack of any really good news from Europe. What we heard daily on the radio was mainly vague references to Russia attacking Finland, but Germany seemed to be concentrating on attacking our shipping with torpedoes fired by her U-boats, as well as dropping bombs from her aircraft on our ships, ports and manufacturing centres.

The following morning, after a hasty breakfast, Corporal Wallace marched the five of us up to the RVI. As we stepped into the main entrance a young lady seated at the reception desk called out, 'Are you the One Five One lot?' Corporal Wallace said we were. She picked up the phone on her desk, spoke briefly, then turned back to us and said, 'Staff Nurse in charge of the casualty department is coming to escort you into her office,' and even as she spoke a slim young lady in staff nurse's uniform opened the door and came hurrying towards us.

'Good morning, gentlemen. If you'll just follow me . . .' She led us through the door from which she had just emerged into a large treatment room, with cubicles down either side where examinations and treatments could be carried out. The room was filled with chairs, occupied by men, women and children all nursing some injury or disability and waiting their turn to be called into one of the cubicles. The staff nurse guided us to a smaller room with lockers around the walls and more comfortable chairs scattered around. 'Right, Corporal,' she said, 'this is our staff room. All of you choose an empty locker, where you can hang your coats. You'll each find a white cotton coat there, to wear while you're on duty here. Please put them on and report back to my office, which is half-way down the treatment room.' Saying which she swept out of the room.

We quickly divested ourselves of our greatcoats, gas masks and battledress tops and put on the long white coats. John remarked, 'Makes us look quite important, doesn't it?'

Billy responded, with a chuckle, 'Hey, she's a smasher that staff nurse – and did you notice that other nurse, the one who was doing some bandaging? She winked at me as we walked through. Oh, I think I'm going to be very happy here!'

Corporal Wallace gave him a stern look. 'Now just behave yourself, Hough,' he said sharply. 'Remember we have the good name of our unit to uphold' – but I did detect a faint twinkle in his eye.

Suitably attired for our duty, we made our way back to the staff nurse's office, and she signalled the other nurse to join us. 'This is Mandy, our second year nurse, who has been literally rushed off her feet because we're short staffed. But that's all about to change, isn't it, at least for a while, as you teams of RAMC nursing orderlies will carry out the required treatments – under her watchful eye, of course. She has a list of the people waiting in here, and you'll call them in turn into the treatment cubicles, where you'll assess their problems, decide what treatment you think is necessary, then confirm with Mandy that you're correct before going ahead and carrying it out. Each patient will have an official hospital form into which you must enter all details of ailment and treatment. I'll be here all the time to advise on any difficulties, and any very serious conditions will be seen by the doctor on duty, whom I can call upon at any time. Now, before we start we'd better introduce ourselves. I'm Staff Nurse Wilson, and this is Mandy, and you are . . . ?' She looked questioningly at us, whereupon Corporal Wallace made the necessary introductions, after which we took up our positions in the treatment cubicles as Mandy, list in hand, directed the patients towards us.

For a while there seemed to be a frantic jumble of to-ing and fro-ing as we examined our patients and reported to Mandy what we thought needed to be done. If she agreed she directed us to the larger end cubicle, where the items needed for treatment were stored, returning to assess our treatment before the patient departed. Staff Nurse Wilson kept a careful eye on everything.

There was no doubt in my mind that the lectures and practical exercises we had attended in our unit were a tremendous help now that we were at the sharp end of the job, and by the time Staff Nurse Wilson declared it was time for three of us to go for lunch at the staff canteen, to be followed by the other three on our return, I felt that I was beginning to get the hang of it and starting to feel it was all worthwhile.

For the next few days we persevered, learning a lot from Mandy and Staff Nurse Wilson, and eventually we did not need their advice all the time.

Some amusing incidents remain etched in my memory. The first occurred while Corporal Wallace, John and Alan were holding the fort and Arthur, Billy and I were having lunch in the canteen. As we returned we noticed that Corporal Wallace was extremely red and seemed quite distressed, while his two companions and Staff Nurse Wilson appeared to be hiding smiles – not very successfully. When I asked the corporal what was the matter he gave a gasp and shook his head and muttered, 'What an experience! I've never been so embarrassed in all my life!'

I grabbed his arm. 'Come on then – tell us all about it!' Somewhat reluctantly he told his tale.

A lady, plump, overdressed, reeking of expensive perfume, and probably in her late thirties, had complained to him about her painful knee, which Corporal Wallace, after carefully averting his eyes as she removed her stocking, diagnosed as a case of strained ligaments which needed a scotts dressing, and Staff Nurse Wilson confirmed the treatment. Having applied the dressing he averted his eyes again as she put her stocking back on. As he waited for her to depart, she turned to him and exclaimed, 'Oh, Doctor, I wish you would feel at my bust, please. I'm sure I've got some lumps.'

Corporal Wallace interrupted her. 'I'm not a . . .'

'I know you're busy, but please, please do check it for me.'

Corporal Wallace realised in alarm that the lady was unbuttoning her blouse, and began to panic. Fortunately for him, Staff Nurse Wilson had been keeping a watchful eye. She marched into the cubicle and said sharply, 'Now then, Mrs Appleby, I see you're up to your little games again. You really must stop embarrassing our young men like this!'

Mrs Appleby bridled haughtily, and exclaimed, 'Nothing of the sort. I only wanted the doctor to check my lumps.'

Staff Nurse Wilson laughed. 'He isn't a doctor, he's an NCO in the Royal Army Medical Corps – and what's more, you've tried this trick on every male trainee in this hospital. You know very well you haven't any lumps!' At this, Mrs Appleby stormed out in high dudgeon.

We could well understand Corporal Wallace's embarrassment, knowing he had been an only child, strictly brought up and never having much contact with girls, but as Staff Nurse Wilson pointed our, 'In our job you have to be prepared for people making a pass at you, and anyway, I was keeping a sharp eye on her, knowing her reputation!'

The second incident involved me personally. It again occurred during lunchtime. Arthur, Billy and I had eaten our lunch and relieved the other three, who went to eat theirs. For once the waiting room was empty, and we were enjoying a quiet sit down and a rest. Obviously it was not meant to be, as a sudden disturbance outside the door brought us hastily to our feet. The door burst open as a heftily built female ambulance attendant struggled into the room, literally dragging with her a short, tubby, middle-aged man. His hair and scalp were matted with blood, which had run in streaks down his face. He was staggering from side to side, and but for the ambulance attendant's firm grip would have ended up on the floor. As Arthur and I drew near the raw reek of whisky fumes was almost enough to overcome us, and as he was manoeuvred into a cubicle he warbled incoherent snatches of 'Blaydon Races' mingled with threats of 'A'll kill 'er, so ah will,' before subsiding into a maudlin fit of sobbing.

Staff Nurse Wilson hurried out of her office and asked, 'What happened to him?'

The ambulance attendant replied, 'He didn't go home all night, then he turned up in this state at lunchtime and started landing out at his wife when she tried to keep him out of the house. She picked up a bucket and gave him a clout on the head with it, which put him out like a light. She thought she might have done him some serious damage, so she sent for us. It's up to you now!'

Staff Nurse Wilson took one look at the man, turning up her nose at the reek of whisky and vomit, and said to me, 'Right, Nursing Orderly Hill, here's your chance for some real life experience. Check him out, decide how much damage has been done, make up your mind how we should treat him, then come back and tell me.'

By now the man was bawling a rendering of 'Whoa, me lads, yer should a' seen us gannin',' as Arthur, Billy and I gathered round. I said, 'Come on, better get started.' We washed our hands, and Arthur brought me a kidney-shaped dish of warm soapy water, and a newly opened packet of cotton wool with which I cleaned the area around the laceration. I was pleased to see a clean gash about two and half inches long. So I went to the staff nurse, who was writing up reports in her office, and announced, 'Lacerated scalp, not too deep, no sign of any damage to the skull. The area around it needs shaving, the immediate area cleansing with surgical spirit, then the edges of the cut need to be stitched together – two sutures, I would say.'

She walked across and had a look, nodded in approval, and said, 'All right then, I agree with you. Go ahead.'

I gaped at her in astonishment and panic. 'What, me?' I stuttered. 'I've done plenty of exercises on pretend injuries, but I've never ever stitched human flesh before!'

'Well, now's your chance to learn,' she replied briskly. 'Have you ever stitched leather?'

'Once at school I did some leather binders.'

'It's very much like that,' she answered, 'so go on, get on with it. I'll stay by your side and make sure you do nothing wrong.'

I realised she meant what she said and it was no use arguing, so I said to Arthur, 'Get the open razor and shave his scalp at least an inch on either side of the gash.' For a moment I thought Arthur was going to argue with me, but he went ahead, and began to shave the area as directed, bathing it with sterile cotton wool and clean water. While he was doing that Billy put his arms around the patient to prevent any movement and I washed my hands again, opened a packet of sterile rubber gloves and put them on, opened the steriliser with my elbow and took out a sterile kidney dish, needle forceps, a curved suture needle and some small scissors, and put them in a dish in some surgical spirit, dabbing the wound area with it.

Staff Nurse Wilson came and stood close beside me. 'From now on you touch nothing but sterilised things,' she murmured, opening a sterilised packet of catgut sutures and dropping the contents into the dish. 'Firstly pick up the needle with the forceps, cut off a length of catgut, and thread it through the eye of the needle, and, holding the forceps firmly, feed the needle at a point three-quarters of an inch from one end of the cut and a quarter of an inch to the outside and curve it through so that it comes out in the middle of the cut. Then reposition your forceps and pull the needle through, leaving at least two inches of thread sticking out.'

Steeling myself, I did as I was bid, and found it not as difficult as I had feared.

She exclaimed, 'That's the style. Now all you have to do is feed it through the other half, cut the catgut off leaving two inches, pull the sides together and tie it off.' Again I carried out her instructions, and as I finished tying the knot she exclaimed, 'Good work. Now do the same at the other end.' Dripping with perspiration, I continued as ordered until the task was completed. 'Now seal it with Collodion,' she instructed, holding out a small opened bottle of the sealant for me to dip in a cotton wool bud and smear over the closed gash.

During all this time the patient had not uttered a word of complaint, and now appeared to be completely sober. As for me, though, I was trembling like an aspen leaf. The staff nurse murmured, 'Come into my office – I'll make you a cup of tea. The first time's always the worst and you've done a good job there. I guess we'll make a decent nurse of you! Don't forget to take those gloves off and hand them to one of your mates for re-sterilising.'

Our patient returned, sober and sorry, to his wife, with instructions to beg her forgiveness for his behaviour.

The rest of our time in the casualty department did not present any further unexpected incidents, and with our final three weeks in the operating theatres completed we found ourselves back to the usual routine at the drill hall, expecting at any moment to be collared for guard duties or cookhouse fatigues. It was no great surprise, as we sat in the canteen one day enjoying a cuppa, to be approached by Sergeant Major Menham, who poked his head round the canteen door and exclaimed, 'Ha – there you are. I might have known you'd be dodging it in here!'

Billy glanced at me and whispered, 'Here we go again – back to the old routine.'

'The CO wants a word with you lot – in his office – right now,' barked the RSM. 'So come along, put a spurt on it – left, right, left, right.'

Inwardly quaking, we were marched into the CO's office, where he sat behind his desk, with Major Forsythe on one side and Captain Pomfret on the other, while Sergeant Ross and Corporal Wallace occupied two seats of a row against the rear wall. The RSM left us standing to attention in front of our lieutenant-colonel, and went out.

Our CO said, 'All right, at ease, men. Please sit on those chairs beside the sergeant and the corporal.' We did as instructed. 'Now that all of you who'll be involved in this latest venture are here, I'll explain the details.' I noticed Alan giving John a bit of an uneasy look, and our CO must have noticed it as well, because he continued, 'There's no need for you to be alarmed. First of all, let me congratulate you five nursing orderlies and Corporal Wallace, who have just finished your stint at the Infirmary. I've received some very favourable reports about your conduct there, and it's encouraged me to develop an idea that I've been mulling over for a while. It's abundantly obvious that we're overcrowded in our present quarters, with the extra RAMC men drafted in, and that'll be taken care of in the near future, but for the time being the long queues of men reporting sick are clogging up the proper use of our drill hall in the mornings. To this end I have obtained authority to open up our own treatment centre and sick bay hospital in quite a large house on the Cullercoats to Whitley Bay road, not quite a mile away from here. Captain Pomfret will be our main medical officer there, with any help as needed from our other officers. Sergeant Ross and Corporal Wallace will take charge of the premises, and with the expert help of you five will run it with the efficiency we can expect. As I said, it's a large house with plenty of room for you to move in, and also have plenty of space for treatment rooms and sick bay wards. There's a well-equipped kitchen, and Major Forsythe has been able to transfer one of the unit cooks down there.'

'That sounds very good in the short term, sir,' said Sergeant Ross, 'But what about the general overcrowding carry on?'

'Har – Humph – yes, well, I'm quite sure our deputy director of medical services will have an adequate answer to that problem in the not too distant future, Sergeant,' he said.

'You mean we'll be moving again soon, sir?' asked Sergeant Ross.

'Perhaps. Time alone will tell,' answered the CO urbanely.

Morning sick parade in our new quarters was almost over, with just a few stragglers hanging on for their treatments in the waiting room. I was syringing the ears of one of the new recruits, and Alan was busy wielding his forceps on the scabs of a severe impetigo infection that seemed to cover the whole of the patient's head; with each tug of the forceps he gave an anguished howl. Having finished with the forceps, Alan smothered the fellow's head with brilliant purple gentian violet, and sent him on his way looking a little sorry for himself.

Captain Pomfret who had been sick parade officer, leaned back in his chair, pushed his hat to the back of his head and remarked with a grin, 'I do believe you're a bit of a sadist, Wright. No gentle handling. You seem to be quite enjoying yourself!'

'Not enjoying myself, sir,' Alan replied. 'More a case of a firm hand causing less distress in the long run. Pussy-footing around would be a lot more painful!'

'But you could have said to him "This won't hurt too much" – it sounds a lot more sympathetic!'

I had finished swilling the detritus of hardened wax out of my patient's ears, and murmured to him in little more than a whisper, 'Can you hear me properly?'

The patient almost jumped out of his seat. 'There's no need to shout, mate,' he grumbled. 'I ain't deaf.'

'No, but if you think I'm shouting now you certainly were. I've moved a right load of old rubbish out of your ears!'

'What's happened to Private Hough?' asked Captain Pomfret. 'I sent him to the kitchen twenty minutes ago to get our mid-morning teas. Do you think he's slipped out to the local bookmakers to put a bet on a horse?'

'I heard that one, sir,' came Billy's voice as he entered bearing a tray full of steaming mugs of tea. 'You know as well as I do that there's no horse racing at the moment, thanks to Hitler. Anyway, whoever heard of a bookmaker's son gambling on horses?'

That raised a laugh – and, in truth, there wasn't an awful lot to laugh about. The daily news bulletin on the radio told us that Russian forces had overwhelmed the Finns, and there was an uneasy peace treaty. Mussolini, the Italian dictator, had finally decided to throw in his lot with Hitler and had declared war against Britain and France, and on 9 April German forces started an invasion of Denmark and Norway. Each day vague and conflicting reports were issued, and the only area that still appeared calm was the Maginot Line, a highly fortified series of constructions built by the French, which they insisted would be totally impenetrable by German invaders. All in all it was difficult to decide what was really going on.

We continued our daily sick parade routines, as well as tending longer term sick patients in our small bedroom wards, and a few days later, having completed all the treatments required, we were enjoying our mugs of tea, when Captain Pomfret remarked, 'You look a bit under the weather, Hill. Aren't you feeling too good?'

'To tell the truth, I've been feeling a bit woozy this morning, sir,' I answered. 'I didn't think it was worth making a fuss about it. I expect it's because it's so warm in here.' I wiped the perspiration from my brow.

'Whoa – you're wrong there: it's definitely not hot in here!' he exclaimed, reaching over and taking my wrist pulse. At the same time he pulled a thermometer from the metal case in his pocket, gave it a shake and stuck it under my tongue. Moments later he took it out, looked at it and shook his head, muttering '102 Fahrenheit, and your pulse is nearly twice what it should be. Let's have a look at your throat. Open wide!' He picked up a spatula, pressed down on my tongue and gazed down at my throat. 'Hmm. Bit red. Tonsils a bit puffy. Any aches and pains, headaches lately?'

'Not really, sir. Just a bit dizzy, that's all. If I have a bit of a rest I'm sure I'll be fine!'

'Oh yes, you'll be fine all right, because I'm admitting you as a patient to our own sick bay. Don't waste your breath arguing! Just think,' the captain added with a grin, 'You've presented us with a golden opportunity to get an expert opinion of the treatment we offer!'

I couldn't really argue; to tell the truth I was beginning to feel decidedly rough. A quarter of an hour later I had been installed in one of our sick bay beds, with my head pounding and my legs feeling like jelly. I yearned for nothing more than to close my eyes, and if possible fall asleep. My eyes closed, but the pounding persisted and when I opened them once more Billy was standing beside me. He was grinning like a Cheshire cat as he murmured, 'The lengths some people will go to to avoid a bit of hard work. Tell me how you managed it and I'll join you in the next bed! In the meantime, how do you feel about chips and corned beef for lunch?'

I groaned, and muttered, 'I can't stand the thought of food at all just now. Please go away and leave me to suffer in silence!'

He realised that I meant what I said, apologised for disturbing me and added, 'I'm on duty. I'll keep popping back to make sure you're all right.'

I have very little recollection of the next few days, just vague memories of waking up at times with a raging thirst and a blinding headache, and of someone holding my head and dribbling drops of water from a spouted cup into my mouth; of Captain Pomfret standing over me, and one or other of my companions shaking me and making me swallow tablets. Eventually, in the middle of the night, I found myself wide awake, burning like a fire and shaking so much that the bed was rattling. I realised that I was experiencing a rigor in which I would either overcome the fever or it would get the better of me, and I called out weakly for help.

Arthur answered my call, and the moment he saw my condition he said, 'Cold sponge down – that's what you need now!' I vaguely recalled this being mentioned in our lectures as the only effective treatment. He hurried back with an enamel basin filled with cool water, a sponge and a waterproof sheet which he slid under me, and he began sponging me. The coolness of the water felt absolutely wonderful and soon my shaking ceased, the raging heat subsided and my head began to ache less. I began to feel like a human being once more. Seeing the change in me, Arthur produced a thermometer, stuck it in my mouth, and when he removed it he exclaimed in relief, 'Thank goodness! Your temperature's down – we've beaten your rigor, and you should get better now.' Quickly he dried me, removed the waterproof sheet and replaced the bedding soaked with my sweat, and within moments I was fast asleep, sleeping soundly and properly, something that I had not done since falling ill. When I awakened the next morning to see the sunlight streaming through the windows I could tell that my temperature had remained normal, and although the thought of food held no attraction I was extremely glad to sit up in bed and drink the mug of hot sweet tea that Arthur brought me. Captain Pomfret called in before he started his morning sick parade, and was delighted to see the change in me. He felt my pulse, put his hand on my forehead, nodded approval and exclaimed, 'You certainly don't do things by halves, do you, Hill? We thought for a while that we were going to have to whisk you off to the Infirmary, but thanks to Private Copley's expert treatment last night you're now on your way to a full recovery.'

'When will I be able to get up, sir?'

'Whoa – steady on. Not for a few days yet. You've been quite poorly!'

I felt my eyelids closing, and I heard Captain Pomfret's voice, as if from a long distance. 'Don't disturb him. Let him sleep till he wakes up naturally, then you can offer him some food. He'll soon feel a bit better.' His voice drifted away as sleep overtook me.

During the next few days I grew stronger, finally able to enjoy the meals put before me, and one morning as Alan brought me my early morning tea he grinned and exclaimed, 'I don't know who's going to wait hand and foot on you tomorrow!'

'How do you mean?' I asked in some dismay. 'Come on, can't a chap spend a few days in bed without the whole system going haywire?'

'You know all those new RAMC recruits who joined us a while back? They've been formed into a new unit named the One Eight Eight Field Ambulance, and they're taking over this sick bay at six o'clock this evening!'

'How about us?' I asked.

'I don't know about you, seeing that you're a patient here, but the rest of us have to get our kit back to the Jesmond Road billet and move back there tonight. Captain Pomfret will have to decide about you.'

I reached out and grabbed Alan's arm. 'Are we moving? I mean us – the One Five One. Come on, what have you heard? You wouldn't leave me in the dark, would you?'

'There are loads of rumours flying about, George,' he answered. 'Off to France – somewhere else abroad – you know what it's like. But there's one fairly strong rumour that there might be some leave going for us One Five Oners, which means we're all desperately hanging around for Part One Orders to be put up.'

I ate my breakfast with a poor appetite, in view of the latest information, then got up, washed and shaved, dressed and sat in the chair beside my bed. At 9.30 precisely Captain Pomfret came into the ward. 'Good morning, Private Hill. I'm very pleased to see you up and about again. We don't know what laid you low, but it was probably one of those foreign flu bugs. Are you properly fit now?'

I could hold my patience no longer. 'Are we moving, sir?' I asked anxiously.

'You haven't answered my question, Hill, and before you do so let me inform you that I've just seen your name on a list of unit men who are eligible to go on a week's leave tomorrow morning, like your four comrades. Before you can go I need you to assure me that I can discharge you from sick bay today as fit for normal duties. What's your answer?'

With no hesitation whatever, I chuckled, 'Fit enough to walk all the way home to Bradford, sir, if there's a chance of some leave!'

'I imagine we can run to a railway warrant for you, Hill!' said the captain, his smile broadening. 'I was reasonably sure you'd want to stay with the One Five One and the rest of your friends. I expect you've heard that the new intake of men are breaking away from us and forming a new unit – the One Eight Eight Field Ambulance.'

'I did hear a whisper about it this morning, sir.'

'No surprise there – news travels faster than the speed of light in this unit,' observed Captain Pomfret drily. 'The thing is that anyone in our unit can request a transfer to the new one if they wish. Want to change your mind?'

'No way, sir! I want to carry on as part of my team, with all the friends I've made, and anyway I wouldn't fancy going through all that "Quick March, Left, Right, Left, Right," stuff again!'

'Glad to hear it!' he said. 'I'll write you up as being discharged from sick and back to normal duties as of this morning. Get your kit together, and when the ration wagon turns up here tell him I've said he's to run you and your kit back to Jesmond Dene Road. You can take it easy for the rest of the day. Along with the rest of the leave party you'll have an early breakfast tomorrow at the banqueting hall mess, then you'll pick up your leave documents and one of the trucks will run you down to the station.'

'Where are we moving to, sir?' I tried again.

'Persistent so and so, aren't you, Hill,' the captain replied with a grin. 'I don't know for certain – but I'm also sure that you don't need to get in a flat spin about it!'

As we ate our early breakfast in the mess next morning, Billy asked, 'Didn't he give you any clue at all? About moving, I mean.'

'Not a word – except to say that we needn't worry,' I replied. 'And anyway it can't be embarkation leave, or they'd have needed to say so on Part One Orders. Let's enjoy this leave while we can, and find out what's going on when we come back!'

I was panting as I struggled up the hill to the smart red-brick semi where Edna lived with her parents and younger brother. The combined weight of my greatcoat, webbing equipment and gas mask made me think that perhaps I wasn't as fully recovered as I had insisted. It was half-day closing at the Co-op, so I expected Edna would be at home. Then I saw her come out of the garden gate and turn to go up the hill, without looking in my direction. Once again I hadn't been able to let her know I was coming! I couldn't summon up enough breath to shout and keep walking at the same time, so somehow or other I put on an extra spurt, reached the house gate, dropped my heavy kit and gas mask on the garden path and hurried after her. I was almost level when she suddenly turned and wildly swung her large handbag at me. Fortunately it missed, as I gasped out, 'My – you take some catching!'

She stared at me in total amazement for a second, then almost sobbed, 'George – oh George, it really is you, isn't it? We've had a prowler around, dressed in Army uniform and bothering young women, and I thought that it was him following me. Why didn't you let me know you were coming? I'm so sorry I landed out at you – it's a good job I missed, isn't it?'

'I didn't find out about our leave myself until yesterday. I've been quite ill, as I told you in my letter last week, and it was only midday yesterday that I was declared fit to come home.'

'Why didn't you shout out after me?'

'I didn't have enough breath left in me after climbing that hill!'

'Oh, what am I thinking of?' Edna cried. 'Here you are, home on leave after being so poorly, and I'm keeping you out here in the cold. Come on, let's go inside.'

We turned back, rescued my kit and went into the house, with her arm linked tightly to mine.

We sat by the fire as her mother fussed around, making me a cup of hot cocoa and some potted meat sandwiches. 'I've been worried about you', said Edna, 'and I miss you so much. This leave isn't because they're sending you overseas, is it?'

'No, love, it's just ordinary leave, not the embarkation one. We're moving somewhere else – but it'll be in this country. I was just about to write when news of this leave came up, and I thought my presence would be better than a letter!'

Edna gave me a big smile, put her arms around me. 'Those are the truest words you've ever spoken. Things have been getting a bit grim lately, what with meat being rationed and almost everything in short supply. New clothes are hard to find, and everything that comes from abroad is pretty much unobtainable.' She stopped and smiled. 'Whatever am I grumbling about? Here you are with me and we've a whole week to spend with one another. We'll certainly make the most of it. I'm not going back to work while you're here, and if Mr Bingham doesn't like it he can jump in the mill dam. Come on, drink up – let's walk up to Headley Cottages and give your mother a big surprise!'

After a wonderful week's leave I stepped down onto the platform at Newcastle station, and almost bumped into Alan Wright as he alighted from the next compartment. 'Hello, George. Had a good leave?' I assured him that I had enjoyed every minute of it, and agreed that coming back was the worst part. We looked around to see if Arthur, John or Billy were about, but there was no sign of them on the platform so we set off to tramp up the hill in order to check in at the guard room before going on to our billet. We didn't hurry, as it was only 10.30p.m. and our passes did not expire until 11.30. As we walked in the darkness, slim pencils of light began to comb the skies from further down the coast, and Alan remarked that it looked as if they had unwanted visitors down there. To prove him right, flashes of anti-aircraft fire began pricking the sky. As we walked we chatted about the vague references on the radio bulletins to Russia, Finland, Denmark, Norway and all the rest of the complicated mess in Europe.

Soon we reached the big iron gate at the entrance to the guard room, and as we entered Sergeant Ross dashed out, muttering, 'Where the hell have you two been?' in an irate manner. 'Come on, put a spurt on: we've been waiting ages for you!'

'Why, Sarge, we aren't late – it's nowhere near 11.30 yet,' I said anxiously.

'I didn't say you were late! We're moving that's what,' grunted Sergeant Ross.

'You mean the whole unit, right now?' gasped an alarmed Alan.

'No! Captain Pomfret, myself and Corporal Wallace, together with you five nursing orderlies, are about to set up an advance dressing station close to the Scottish border and have it ready for action by mid-morning. That's why we're leaving now. And before you ask, no, I don't know whether this is an exercise or the real thing. So come on, get on that truck, at the corner of the drill hall yard there. Your kitbags and bedding are already aboard, and so are your mates – who are getting impatient!'

We hurried across to the vehicle that was waiting with its engine running, and scrambled into the rear to be greeted by the muted but ribald comments of our comrades, who were speculating on what we might have been up to all this time. Sergeant Ross climbed into the front to sit beside the driver, and we moved off, closely followed by Captain Pomfret in his staff car.

'Anybody know just what's going on?' asked Billy. 'I'm not used to setting off on a mystery tour at this time of night.'

'I don't know any more than you do!' exclaimed Corporal Wallace from the far corner of the truck interior. 'But as we can't do much about it I suggest we try to get some shut eye.'

This seemed like a very good idea, and we tried to follow suit. I shut my eyes and tried to recall some happy times from the leave that had just ended. The total darkness within the truck seemed to exaggerate every bump in the road and every swerve of the wheels, the sound of the engine was like a demonic drumming, and the way the equipment had been loaded ensured that whichever way I moved some sharp corner poked me. Sleep evaded me no matter how hard I tried. I was relieved when, after we had been bumping along for a very long time, the truck halted.

Everybody stirred, and Arthur called out 'Are we there?'

Captain Pomfret's replied, 'No – only half-way, but I thought you might all appreciate a stop.' We had pulled into a lay-by, and a small copse of trees was just at hand. 'I suggest we make use of them.'

We all agreed with his suggestion, and as we returned to the truck Sergeant Ross brought out one of the great big vacuum flasks used by our cookhouse. 'I managed to persuade the cooks to fill this with tea, and I've borrowed half a dozen mugs as well, so come on, let's get warmed up before we continue.'

The hot liquid was like wine from the gods to our parched mouths. As we finished drinking, and stretching our tired limbs, Corporal Wallace exclaimed, 'If you all suffered as uncomfortable a ride as I did, I suggest we move the equipment so we all have a comfortable surface to lean back on. Get rid of the sharp corners and put our bedding back last of all, so we can get to sleep.'

'Corporal Wallace, you're a genius!' said Captain Pomfret. 'Get cracking at once, so we can be on our way again.' Tired as we were, the possibility of getting some sleep seemed worth the effort, so we set about re-arranging the equipment and repositioning the bed rolls. In next to no time we were able to climb back on board and were on our way again.

As we moved swiftly along, I heard Billy, who was next to me, humming 'We'll meet again' and my eyelids grew heavier and heavier . . .

CHAPTER

7

Consciousness returned reluctantly. I stirred uneasily, trying to work out where on earth I was and how I came to be in this darkened enclosure with tiny rays of sunlight shining on me. For a brief moment I was back in my infant days, with dazzling sun shining through pinprick holes in the waterproof cover of my pram. Then reality struck. With a start I sat up, opened my eyes and recognised the interior of the truck.

I reached over and pulled aside the canvas flap that covered the vehicle's open rear, and gazed out, gulping the fresh morning air, which was like wine compared with the fetid atmosphere within. Corporal Wallace and my four other comrades were also beginning to stir themselves, with much stretching and yawning.

I sensed rather than heard the patter of an animal's footfalls, and a black and white sheepdog came into view, sniffing suspiciously at this great big metal monster. It caught sight of my face peeping out of the flap, and drew back, showing its teeth in a questioning snarl. I was not scared, as I was used to sheepdogs on a nearby farm in my childhood, so I smiled and said softly, 'Hello, dog!' The dog hesitated, uncertain. It must have decided that I was not unwelcome, stopped snarling and began wagging its tail as it stretched upwards on its hind legs towards me, barking, but not angrily, as if asking, 'What do you want?'

'Doon, Rabbie, doon. Heel, laddie,' exclaimed a voice in a lilting Scottish accent. The barking ceased immediately as the owner of the voice came into view. He was a short, thickset elderly man with grey hair who was attired in dark brown corduroy trousers and leather patched brown tweed jacket. He had the weather-beaten look of a man who spent most of his days in the open air, and the look of utmost trust that the dog bestowed upon him left no doubt that they were constant companions. Close behind the newcomer were Sergeant Ross and Captain Pomfret

The captain stepped forward, pulling the rear flap fully open, and exclaimed in feign dismay, 'The sight of you lot in crumpled uniforms, looking like death warmed up, would be enough to put the wind up Hitler's crack troops if they caught a glimpse of you! Come on, lads, rise and shine, get yourselves washed and shaved sharpish! We need to get our advance dressing station up and running by 10.30, and it's already seven!' He indicated the dog owner. 'Mr Kyle here will show you your quarters so you can stack your kit. Come on, let's get everything in place.' He turned away, adding, 'Incidentally, the lady who's cook at the big house just behind us has offered to prepare breakfast for us, so get out your rations and give them to her.'

We clambered down from the truck, together with our RASC driver Bert Bell. Captain Pomfret's driver/batman, Alf Brown, who stood behind his officer, stepped forward with Driver Bell to carry the rations for us. Mr Kyle turned to us and pointed to a long single-storey building alongside the truck, about thirty yards long by twelve yards wide, with four wooden doors equally spaced in the wall that faced us. 'This should do ye, lads!' he said. 'Oor estate workers used this once upon a time.' He threw the first door open to reveal a large room with two washbasins, a single tap over each, against the end wall, and in one corner a cubicle bearing the lettering 'WC'. Along the rear wall were two windows presenting a view of grassy fields. This would certainly be suitable as a treatment room. Doors led from one room to another, in addition to those that led outside. The next room was also large, again with two windows, and was completely empty. This would be suitable for casualties on stretchers awaiting treatment or further transport. The third room was similar, and would make ideal sleeping quarters for us nursing orderlies and Drivers Bell and Brown. The final room was even larger, divided into two sections by an inner wall. It had two windows in the larger portion, with access to the small walled area through a locked door.

Each of the large rooms had a light-bulb swinging from the ceiling and a switch on the wall. I reached out to put the light on, but nothing happened. 'Ye'll nae get a licht yet, laddie,' chuckled Mr Kyle. 'We have nae mains electric, just oor own. I'll show ye!' He produced keys and opened the further door to reveal a small paraffin-fuelled donkey engine connected to a generator by a flat leather belt. 'Paraffin's awfu' hard tae come by, so we only use it when it's dark.'

Captain Pomfret overheard the last remark, and promised that there would be enough paraffin to keep it going while we were there.

Having sorted everything out to his satisfaction, Mr Kyle called his dog, which had been waiting patiently beside the outer door, and left us to get on with washing and shaving ourselves at the cold water taps.

When Sergeant Ross poked his head round the door to tell us that breakfast was ready we were to follow him to the big house. We walked through a large kitchen to a smaller room that Meg, the middle-aged cook, told us had been used as servants' quarters in earlier, more affluent days. 'Nowadays, there's only me an' Elsie here to keep things goin'.' She indicated the young housemaid who was setting out plates of bacon, egg and baked beans on the large table, at which the two drivers were already seated.

Corporal Wallace asked, 'What's Captain Pomfret doing about his breakfast?'

Sergeant Ross laughed. 'He's got himself a real cushy number. They've fixed up a little room in the house here, fully furnished, washbasin and toilet "en suite" as they say, and he gets all his meals taken up there by Elsie.'

By the time our plates were empty Captain Pomfret had rejoined us. 'I can see from your satisfied expressions that you've no complaints about the food, so I'm sure you'll be pleased to learn that Meg has offered to prepare all our meals while we're here. All we have to do is give her all our ration supplies.'

'What about the lady and gentleman who own the house, sir?' asked Corporal Wallace. 'Won't they object?'

'You need have no worries on that score, Corporal,' the captain replied. 'They've gone to stay in another of their homes, way down in Cornwall, and they're pleased that we're making use of their property. They feel as though they're helping the war effort.' He turned to Sergeant Ross. 'Right. We've wasted enough time. We must do a quick survey of the place, and get cracking with setting up the advance dressing station.'

'Is this the real thing, sir?' asked Corporal Wallace. 'Are there going to be real casualties?'

'I don't know any more than you do, Corporal!' replied the captain.

'My orders were to do exactly what we've done – then wait for further information.'

There was the rumble of an approaching vehicle, and our pulses quickened as one of our unit ambulances trundled into the yard, halting with a squeal of brakes outside the treatment room door. We jumped to our feet to see Driver Smith and Ambulance Orderly Cliff Rigg step down from the front seats and amble unworriedly into our room. 'Where are your patients?' we asked anxiously.

'We've got no patients,' said Cliff. 'We've just come with the rest of the unit to Wooler, where they're setting up ready for action, and our CO ordered us to deliver this instruction to you straight away, sir.' He handed a sealed envelope to Captain Pomfret, who tore open the envelope and scanned the enclosed note.

The captain looked up with a puzzled frown as Sergeant Ross enquired, 'Trouble, sir?'

'No – not really. It seems that the situation's still pretty confused. We're ordered to stay here in a state of readiness until we receive orders to the contrary, so that's what we must do.'

Billy had been taking some more boxes of rations to the cook, and when he returned he said, 'Meg's brewed some tea in the kitchen, and says we're to get it while it's hot.' He stared at Driver Smith and Cliff Rigg. 'Trust you two to turn up the moment there's a brew going! Does your ambulance have a device alerting you to freshly brewed tea? How do you do it?'

'It's one of the principal qualifications of an ambulance crew,' chuckled Private Rigg, 'and we're sworn to secrecy about how we do it!'

We all crowded into the kitchen to drink the sweet and satisfying tea and to scoff some home-made cake. With a dreamy look in his eyes Billy remarked, 'I wish I could swap Meg for Corporal McCann . . .'

Cliff interrupted, 'You couldn't. He's just asked for a transfer to the One Eight Eight Unit, and has been accepted. He took over as corporal cook for their unit from first thing this morning.'

'They'll send him back!' exclaimed Billy.

'They can't do that because Jennings, who cooked for you lot when you went down to Ludford, has been promoted to new corporal cook!' said Cliff smugly.

With a wicked twinkle in his eye Captain Pomfret chuckled, 'You'll all miss his very special cooking abilities, won't you?' He turned to Sergeant Ross. 'The next thing we ought to do is prepare a roster, so that we always have someone on duty during the night. I'll leave that to you, Sergeant, while Corporal Wallace and I check our state of readiness.'

'We'd better not disturb Driver Bell or Alf Brown, sir,' said Corporal Wallace. 'They've just gone to sleep in our room after driving all night!'

It was early May and we had hung around uneasily for quite a few days without anything happening. We were able to listen to the radio in Meg's kitchen, and had learnt that further German advances had been made in Norway, despite a small British contingent being sent there. Most of our troops were grouped around the France/Belgium border, waiting for Hitler's next move. In the House of Commons Prime Minister Chamberlain made a statement about Norway and the general situation, followed by the usual vote. The number of votes by his party was not sufficient to support him against the opposition, so his resignation was now inevitable.

On 10 May we heard that German airborne troops had been parachuted into Holland, and German land forces had crossed the borders of Belgium, Holland and Luxembourg. The 'Phoney War' was over; the real one had begun. On the same day Chamberlain resigned and Winston Churchill took over, immediately forming a coalition government. British and French troops moved across the Belgian border to meet the enemy.

Also on the morning of the 10th an ambulance came tearing across from our main unit at Wooler, with an order from our CO to Captain Pomfret that we should pack up at once and join the rest of the unit, which was moving south immediately. It came as no surprise: we were accustomed to quick 'pack up and move on' situations. Our equipment and kit were back in the truck in next to no time, and we managed to join our main unit convoy as it headed south out of Wooler. I think some men hoped that we were heading back to Newcastle, but that hope was quashed as we continued down the Great North Road. Billy, grinning hugely, voiced the opinion that 'We're heading for Redcar racecourse, to be billeted in the Tote building, and tonight I'll buy you all a pint in my local.'

It seemed as if he possessed second sight when the CO's car came to a halt beside a large white gate. Alan, gazing over the tailboard, shouted, 'He must be right – it's a racecourse!'

Billy's face registered a mixture of incredulity and glee as he scrambled to see, before turning with a crestfallen grimace. 'Sorry, fellers – this ain't Redcar, it's Catterick!'

'Do we still get the pint, Billy?' asked Alan, hopefully.

'Oh no – you all buy me one instead!' chuckled Billy.

After all the trucks had been parked on the racecourse car park we were ordered to parade on the forecourt outside the Tote building, where our CO informed us that this was just a staging post, where we would halt for about a week until tented accommodation at Melbourne in East Yorkshire became available to us. There was no need to unload our trucks; just our bedding and small kit would suffice.

The weather further north had remained cloudy and cool, but now, as if to welcome us back to Yorkshire, the sun blazed down out of a cloudless sky. On the food serving table set up outside the Tote building sliced bread curled at the edges and butter ran into a sloppy yellow goo. RMS Menham informed us that 'shirt sleeve order' could be worn, except on the morning parade.

The week passed quickly, and we were soon on our way once more, this time with the front canvas covers of our trucks rolled back to allow fresh air to circulate as we travelled.

At Melbourne there were just a few uniformed men about as our trucks entered a gravelled square. Our RMS barked, 'Everybody out!' followed by 'Fall in three ranks!'

Stretching our limbs we obeyed, and our CO stepped forward to address us. 'Since we left our Newcastle headquarters we've done a lot of rapid moving up and down, and I must remind you that we're classified as a highly mobile rapid response unit – so we'll continue improving our technique in the rapid setting up and stripping down of our various sections while we're here. How long we'll stay here I don't know, but the accommodation is excellent and we should be quite comfortable. The rear party of the previous occupiers is moving away at this moment, and I call upon you, Sergeant Major, to organise the allocation of tents and so on.'

Our CO was correct about the tents, which were proper, strong bell tents, fitted with wooden floors to keep out the damp from the earth. The campsite was in attractive countryside, with a small river close by.

The news from Europe on our camp radio filled us with dismay. A tremendous evacuation of our troops was beginning on the beaches near Dunkirk. A German general named Rommel had succeeded in mounting a gigantic pincer attack, moving with lightning speed out of Belgium. He had bypassed and threatened to surround, cut off and capture our Expeditionary Force, which was forced back to the coast, after being ordered to leave behind heavy armament. It had been hoped that a further stand could be made there, but our troops were suffering unabated artillery shelling and constant machine gunning and bombing.

It was only, as we later learned, thanks to the bravery of the crews of our small naval vessels and hundreds of small civilian boats, which made countless perilous voyages to and from the Dunkirk beaches, that enabled the lives of many thousands of our troops to be saved. But with so much of our equipment abandoned in France, Britain was now exceedingly short of armour. We steeled ourselves against the threat that Hitler would follow up with an immediate invasion of Britain. Fortunately, though, he chose to increase the bombing raids upon our ports, factories, shipping and airfields, with the intention of bringing us to our knees before he invaded.

Luckily President Roosevelt in America helped us by sending huge amounts of heavy armour to replace the equipment we had been forced to abandon; while the use of radar aircraft detection equipment meant that our brave RAF pilots were able to shoot down many Luftwaffe bombers.

While all this activity was going on, our unit sections persevered with exercises to improve the speed and mobility of our work. It was now late August, and many more troops had been called up to be trained for active service. It was more than three months since we had been granted any home leave. The pessimists insisted that all leave would be cancelled, because Hitler was going to invade, but the optimists believed there was still a chance for leave. We were not sure which view was right, and were studying hard once more for our nursing orderly second class examination, which Captain Pomfret informed us would take place within a month. We had just finished one of our studying sessions when Cliff came bouncing into our tent. 'Just you listen to what I've just heard in the canteen tent!'

Mockingly, we called out, 'Go on Cliff, surprise us. Is the war over? Are we being demobbed tomorrow?'

'No, of course not, but it's good news for all that. The major's batman saw the orderly room lot typing up some leave lists – and the first lot go in four days' time!'

'I'll believe it when I see it,' said Arthur. 'You know that fancy tales sprout quicker than weeds in this mob.'

But it was the truth, and the lists went up on the board the next morning. We five were among the first party to go.

'I want to go home, please!' whispered Edna. We had gone to the Odeon in Manchester Road and the evening's programme still had about twenty minutes to run. 'Take me home, please!' she repeated. I could see that she was upset about something.

'Are you feeling poorly, love?'

'No, I'm all right – but I've got this funny feeling that something awful's about to happen. Please, please – let's go now!' Her voice had risen well above a whisper, and people sitting near us were beginning to stare and shush her. I knew there was no point in arguing, because on previous occasions when Edna had had these funny feelings something unexpected had followed.

We struggled past the people in our row, and made our way out of the cinema into the darkened street, hurrying to where the Thornton trolley-bus was waiting for the four mile journey home. The moment we scrambled aboard the conductor rang the bell and moved slowly away up the steep incline, with only the shaded lights of the bus to guide his way. We had been travelling for at least a quarter of an hour and had reached Bell Dean, half-way home, when suddenly the driver braked to a standstill. The conductor rushed to see what had happened, and immediately returned. 'Will all of you please get off the bus. I'm afraid you'll have to walk the rest of the way.' As we stepped down, we asked what had gone wrong. 'We've just been stopped by an air raid warden. Enemy aircraft have been detected heading our way, and the pulleys on the poles of our bus create a spark every time they pass a clamp in the overhead power lines.'

We trudged slowly and wearily up the hill to Thornton, stopping frequently to gaze back at the city we had just left. Searchlights were sweeping the skies, and there were flashes of exploding bombs on the ground and anti-aircraft fire in the sky. As we continued to watch, fires broke out on the ground – with flames reaching high up into the sky. It was like watching a macabre firework display.

We continued our journey, and Edna squeezed my hand. She didn't say 'I told you so', but I understood her implication.

As we reached the level ground where we could either turn right and call at Edna's home, or turn left to Headley, her brother Raymond appeared. 'Thank goodness I've seen you. Mother's been worried out of her mind not knowing if you were safe. I'll tell her while you go on up to George's house.'

We reached Headley, and as we reached the end cottage we saw my mother standing in the darkened doorway gazing anxiously towards the lane. She gave a little cry of relief. 'Isn't it terrible! I was so worried about you two. We should be all right here in the country – but down there . . .' She shuddered at the grim picture displayed before us. We watched for a long time, and there was no apparent let-up in the attacks. The sound of an aircraft passing close overhead had us staring anxiously into the dark. Moments later the whistling of descending bombs, followed by the crump of three explosions in a valley a couple of miles lower down, filled our ears. Fortunately they found no target, just missing two large gasometers filled with inflammable coal gas. If they had been struck what a mighty explosion there would have been!

Finally the hullabaloo died down, the anti-aircraft fire ceased and searchlight beams disappeared as the raiders returned home, leaving only the flickering flames of numerous fires burning in the city below us. Tired and hollow-eyed, we retired to get some sleep.

Looking out the next morning, still bleary-eyed, we saw a pall of smoke still drifting upwards from Bradford. We swallowed a hasty breakfast and hurried back to Edna's home, to discover her dad stretched out on the sofa. The previous night he had been conductor on one of the tramcar routes still operating, and in the first wave of bombings, with the tram empty in the middle of the town, he had been literally blown off the open rear platform by the blast from a nearby explosion. He had been very fortunate not to be injured, just bruised and shaken, but had been forced to spend the rest of the night in an air raid shelter on Tyrrel Street. Now, after walking all the way home, the thing he needed most was a bit of rest.

He told us that dozens of buildings had been damaged during the attack, including the Odeon – which had been virtually destroyed, luckily after all the audience had left. Lingards, a large drapery store, had been burnt to the ground, and countless other buildings had suffered. Hundreds of windows had been shattered, and many people had been injured, and some killed. The fortunate ones had managed to leave the city in time or had spent the night in an air raid shelter.

* * *

A couple of days later I returned to the calm and quiet of Melbourne, after one of the most nerve-shattering leaves I had ever experienced. The second batch of leave-takers departed and returned, and after another ten days the nursing orderly second class examinations were held, and we five, together with seven others, gathered in the orderly room tent, poring over questions that had been set by our CO and Major Forsythe. One of our new officers, Captain Gamblet, acted as referee.

I had a pleasant surprise the following Sunday. After lunch I was reading Edna's latest letter when Paul Sacco, who was on guard duty, approached our tent. 'George – George Hill – are you there? There's a young woman down at the gate asking for you.' I was sure he was joking, but my curiosity got the better of me and I followed him.

As I stared out of the gate I made out a female rear view that certainly reminded me of my fiancée, but I dismissed it as impossible. Then as I walked through the gate the girl turned to face me – and it was Edna! 'How on earth did you get here, love?' As soon as she got her breath back from my fierce hug, she explained that her mother and dad had come with her to York on the train, and she had come on by bus to Melbourne while they enjoyed an afternoon in York. The sun was shining, and we walked along the river bank arm in arm, totally absorbed in one another. It was only two hours before she had to catch the bus to rejoin her parents, but it was like being in a magic world of our own. It was one of the high spots of my time in Melbourne.

During August the Luftwaffe intensified its attacks on our military headquarters, airfields, armament factories, ports, naval vessels and merchant shipping, and these attacks continued day and night. It was only the tremendous courage of our fighter aircrews, up in the air day after day and night after night, that kept the enemy at bay. It was to these RAF men that Winston Churchill referred in his famous speech, 'Never in the field of human conflict was so much owed by so many to so few.'

Then something happened to alter the whole situation. On the night of 25 to 26 August some of our long range aircraft were sent on a long and hazardous flight to bomb Berlin, Hitler's beloved capital, and against all odds succeeded in wreaking havoc there. The idea that the '*Englischer Schweinhund*' had had the temerity to bomb his beautiful Berlin so enraged and infuriated Hitler that he immediately summoned his Luftwaffe commanders and ordered that their full force of bombers should concentrate on destroying British towns and cities and totally wipe out the civilian population.

What Hitler had not realised was that these swarms of high-flying aircraft could be more easily identified by our radar, and presented a much easier target for our fighter aircraft. The Luftwaffe losses proved to be so heavy that the bombing of our cities was called off and the invasion of Britain was postponed indefinitely.

Back in Melbourne, Billy summed up the situation thus: 'Colder weather, and open air ablutions, where we have to strip-wash and shave in the freezing air, using cold water taps that drizzle into wooden troughs. Not a recipe for our comfort or well being!'

The results of our second class orderly exams were published, and again we five passed, along with several others. Our rate of pay was increased again. Those who failed had to undergo further training before retaking the exam, and the men who had not passed any of the tests were employed in more manual tasks – like ablution cleaning, latrine digging, kitchen fatigues, as QM stores staff, on guard duty, as orderly office clerks and so on.

One morning Alan came racing back to the tent to impart the information he had just gleaned from Major Forsythe's batman. 'He swears we're moving to proper billets. You know, real buildings with fires, warm bedrooms, proper bathrooms with hot and cold water.'

Billy interrupted him. 'Are you sure the batman hasn't been at the major's gin bottle?'

'No, I don't think so. He also said we won't be staying there very long because our unit's going overseas.'

'Where to – and when?' our voices joined in anxious chorus.

'Oh, he didn't know that, but he was prepared to lay odds of five to one that before another week's out we'll be fixed up in proper accommodation.'

An icy hand gripped my heart at the prospect of finally leaving our homeland and being transported to some foreign country – with no way of knowing when we would return. However, more hospitable conditions certainly had their attractions. Speculation turned into certainty the next morning, when an advance party headed by Major Forsythe, QM Watkins, Sergeant Winter and ten of the original

Territorial men departed for a destination 'somewhere south'. During the following days the rest of us spent most of our days on route marches, or doing physical exercises or playing football – anything to keep us warm! We were all right for meals, because the cookhouse, with its ovens, boilers, preparation rooms and so on, was housed in a brick shelter.

During a particularly soggy afternoon spent slithering around a muddy football pitch, word was passed from player to player that tomorrow was 'The Day!' Later on the expected notice appeared, declaring that 'One Five One Unit, with the exception of a small Rear Party, will move to our new location tomorrow at Ten Hundred Hours. The convoy will proceed in the same order as on the journey from Catterick.'

Billy was adamant that we were immediately off to foreign lands – but, as Arthur pointed out, we had sent an advance party the week before, and we hadn't been given embarkation leave. As our convoy left Melbourne Camp next morning, we scanned the main road ahead for any clues to our destination.

At five minutes past five, in the fading light of the evening, our convoy pulled on to a tarmac square in the centre of a small town, where Private Watson, one of the advance party, was waiting to greet us. Alan Wright was the first to climb out of our truck, and he called out, 'Hello, Watson. Where's Sherlock Holmes?'

Private Watson, familiar with this kind of sarcastic banter, replied, 'He's out catching criminals – so I'd watch my step if I were you! Anyway – welcome to the town of Warsop in the shire of Nottingham!' He pointed to the open door of a building at the side of the square. 'That way, gentlemen, please. Your evening meal awaits you!'

We enjoyed a well-cooked and highly satisfying meal before one of the advance party came to conduct us and our truck the hundred yards from our new mess hall to a fairly large old house reminiscent of the vicarage at Malton. Again, there were several rooms fitted out as bedrooms, one of which was to house us five and Corporal Wallace, but the thing that had me staring wide eyed was the presence of six camp beds and a tiny coal fire flickering in the grate. There was also a washbasin in one corner of the room – with two taps! I couldn't believe my eyes, and exclaimed to our guide, 'Hey, Geordie, this must be the sergeant's quarters – these beds, this washbasin, this coal fire?'

'No, George. All the billets are as good as this. Proper home from home it is!'

'If I'm dreaming please don't wake me up till I've warmed myself by this fire,' crooned Billy, doing a twirl in front of it. We dumped our kit on the camp beds, and joined him.

As soon as we had thawed out we peeped along the landing to discover a door marked WC. There was a proper flushing toilet, somewhat ancient but in working order. As Arthur commented, 'After Melbourne's tents, this is like being in heaven!'

At the next morning's parade RSM Menham addressed us. 'As the houses in which you're billeted are somewhat scattered, I'm instructing you to make out a rota for each house, whereby one of you will be billet orderly each day in rotation, acting as a security measure when no one else is there.'

Paul Sacco, who was in the room opposite ours, volunteered to be our first billet orderly, and when we relieved him so he could go for lunch we could see that he was bursting to tell us some news. It seemed that a lady had turned up during the morning to ask how we liked our billet. Was it warm enough, was there anything we needed, and so on. Paul assured her that it was wonderful compared with the tents we had just left, and the only possible complaint was the meagre ration of coal, which was only sufficient to light the fires in the evenings. And, oh yes, the hot taps only ran cold water! She pulled a face, and said, 'We'll soon do something about that', and departed.

He thought no more about it until she reappeared a short time later, accompanied by our CO and the orderly officer of the day, who were both, Paul assured us, looking quite embarrassed. The lady said, 'Now look here, Colonel Swindler or whatever your name is, I'll not have our gallant boys suffering because of poor heating when there's an abundance of coal to spare in my collieries!' Our CO humphed and hawed and stuttered, 'Yes, your Grace' and 'No, your Grace' as she lectured him. 'It seems,' Paul continued, 'that the lady's the Duchess of somewhere and owns most of the collieries round here. She'll guarantee ample supplies of coal to keep us warm and heat the boiler that supplies the washbasin taps!'

★ ★ ★

At the end of our first week in Warsop, a notice was put up announcing that within the next ten days all those who had passed their nursing orderly second class examination would be able to sit for their first class, and would be excused guard duties and fatigues to allow them to study.

Nine days later we five, along with seven others, gathered in the dining room, under the eagle eye of Major Forsythe, and tried to answer the questions on the papers in front of us.

Five days later still, Billy came haring back to the billet at teatime in a state of great excitement. 'There you are!' he gasped, panting for breath. 'I told you it was too good to last!'

'Why, what is it this time?' we asked.

'Embarkation leave, that's what!' he spluttered. 'We should have guessed when Part One Orders were late going up.'

A sudden chill descended as I asked in a toneless voice, 'When, Billy, go on, tell us all about it!'

'It's all there in black and white,' he said, 'it's headed "Embarkation Leave" and it goes on to say that we're adequately equipped and trained for active service, so all ranks are being granted seven days' leave, to be taken in two consecutive parties, on the conclusion of which we'll be under forty-eight hours' notice to move.'

'Does it say when the leave starts?' asked John.

'Yes – first party 12 to 19 December, second party, the 20th to the 27th. Guess which we're in!'

'First one,' grunted Alan. 'That means we won't be home on Christmas Day.'

'Did the notice say anything about where we're going – abroad, I mean?' asked Arthur.

'No, just that after 1 January no further passes will be granted,' said Billy. 'But there's one crumb of comfort. We've all passed our exam. We have to hand in our paybooks tomorrow!'

A general air of despondency seemed to settle over us, until John stood up. 'Come on, fellers, it's not the end of the world. I'm going down to the social club – anyone coming with me?'

Billy took him up on his offer, but I declined, explaining that I was expecting a phone call from Edna. I had become friendly with a Mr and Mrs Hanson, a middle-aged couple who lived nearby, and when I explained my difficulty in speaking on the phone to my fiancée

(I had no phone, while she had to use a phone box a hundred yards from her house), they gave me their number and suggested that Edna could ring me at their home at a pre-arranged date and time. Today was the day.

I hurried across to the Hansons', where the telephone was ringing as I entered. Mrs Hanson glanced up and saw me, and said into the mouthpiece, 'Yes, my dear, he's just come in through the door.' With a smile she handed me the phone, before disappearing tactfully into the kitchen. I told Edna straight away about my Christmas leave, explaining that it was from the 12th to the 19th.

'Ooh – that means you won't be at home on Christmas Day!' she murmured, sounding disappointed.

'No, but what do you think about this?' I replied. 'Why don't we get married during my leave?'

'It's only two days to the 12th,' she said uncertainly, 'but what a fantastic idea. We'd need to get a special licence, and I'd have Dad and Mother's written permission, as I'm not twenty-one until next July. Anyway, what's the rush? It's not as if . . .' Her voice faded away.

'Yes, love, it's embarkation leave. It had to come sooner or later, and if we get married at least we'll be able to spend a little time together as man and wife. I'm afraid I'll have to leave most of the arrangements to you, but I'll see to the special licence when I get home. Can we manage it, do you think?'

'Oh, George!' Edna gasped, with a sob in her voice. 'Of course we can! I don't know whether to laugh or cry. I'm so thrilled, but so upset at you having to go away.'

'Do you think your dad will object?'

'Don't you worry about my dad,' she said with a little laugh. 'I'll talk him round all right. But, oh, what a rush we're going to have!'

I whispered a fond goodbye, and as I put the phone down Mrs Hanson peered around the partly open kitchen door. 'I'm afraid I eavesdropped a little,' she said with a smile. 'If your bride can manage the journey down here on Christmas Eve we'd be delighted for you both to stay here with us from then until the day after Boxing Day. We've got a spare bedroom – complete with double bed.'

I thanked her with all my heart, assuring her that I would tell Edna about this wonderful invitation the moment I reached home.

★ ★ ★

The truck carrying the first leave party drew up in the station forecourt, and we clambered out with light hearts. My train to Sheffield, where I would catch my connection to Bradford, was waiting, and with a cheery wave to my friends I got on board.

When I reached number forty-nine the door was open, with Edna standing there, her arms open wide to greet me. For a long minute we clung to one another, then went into the living room where her parents and younger brother were waiting to greet me. Her father looked at me in silence for a moment, and then said, in a rather choked voice, 'I hope you two know what you're doing!' but the tears in his eyes were of love not anger.

'Oh, Willie,' his wife said gently, 'stop worrying. They'll be fine – just you see.'

A smile spread across his face. 'Aye, I know they will.' He turned to me and grasped my hand in his. 'You look after her, lad, won't you?'

With a lump in my throat I assured him I would.

Edna said, 'Let's walk over to Headley now and let your mother know, and I'll tell you what I've arranged so far.' We walked arm in arm, oblivious to the cold night air. 'Tomorrow you have to go to the register office about the special licence. I've already got the form of agreement, signed by both of my parents, and I've seen the minister about the service in church. You might find it hard to believe, but I had another funny feeling earlier in the day I was ringing you at the Hansons', so what was the point of saying no? The service is just two days before you return to your unit, so we won't have time to get bored with one another, will we?' She went on to say that two of her cousins were going to be bridesmaids, her brother an usher, and Kenneth Rimmer, who was my best friend and was now in the RAF, had been contacted and had promised to be my best man.

Not to be outdone in spreading good news, I told her of the offer by Mr and Mrs Hanson to welcome us to their home.

'Of course I'll come – let anybody try to stop me!' she exclaimed.

At Headley my mother welcomed the news with delight. 'He needs an anchor,' she said, 'and I've always known you were the one. How about your wedding dress?'

Edna explained that she had managed to find a rather plain one at a shop in town, and it was being altered to fit by her aunt.

Mother produced a large piece of very old and fine lace. 'I can give you "something old". It was part of my wedding dress.'

* * *

Time passed in a whirl of activity, and before we knew it our wedding day dawned, and the special licence had to be collected. I rushed off on the trolley-bus to the register office, where a rather bored lady informed me that the registrar was late, and the licence had not yet been signed. I waited and waited, growing more frustrated with every passing minute, until the official came hurrying in, apologising. He quickly signed the piece of paper and I ran back to the bus stop.

'... and now I pronounce you man and wife,' intoned the Reverend Mr Dennison, concluding the service. The organ burst forth with the 'Wedding March' as we made our way to the vestry to sign the register and collect our wedding certificate.

'Well, Mrs Edna Hill, we made it,' I chortled as we let ourselves into 1 Headley Cottages, which my mother had made available to us for the two remaining days of my leave, so we could spend some joyful time in each other's company. She was staying at 49 Springhead Road until I returned to my unit.

Too soon the day of my return to Warsop was upon us, and we agreed that Edna should go back to work when I caught the bus to town, with no heart-wrenching goodbyes at the station. After all, she was coming to Warsop in a few days' time.

By seven o'clock in the evening on Christmas Eve I was waiting impatiently for Edna's bus to arrive. I stood by the bus stop for a further ten agonising minutes and finally heaved a sigh of relief as a bus hove into sight and squealed to a stop. Several passengers stepped down – but no Edna! In a fever of apprehension I climbed the step, and asked the conductor if a young lady with a suitcase had boarded the bus at Mansfield to come to Warsop. 'She'd have a job, mate,' he answered, 'because we come from Worksop. The Mansfield bus is pulling up behind us now.'

I looked back, and heaved a huge sigh of relief as I saw my new wife, suitcase in hand, alighting from the other bus. I grabbed her in my arms, hugging her tightly and kissing her with fervour. 'Steady on, love!' she gasped. 'I didn't realise you were missing me quite so much!' I explained about my mix-up with the buses, and with a roguish smile she said, 'Oh, so you weren't really missing me that much!'

Picking up her suitcase and linking arms, I murmured, 'Just you wait and see!'

Mrs Hanson was waiting for us at her door and took our hands in hers. 'Welcome, and a Merry Christmas to you both.' She led us into the lounge where a cheerful fire blazed and a tinsel-garlanded Christmas tree sparkled. 'Supper's nearly ready. Sit yourselves down and get warm!'

She disappeared into the kitchen, and we sat down. I took both Edna's hands in mine and said, 'Welcome to Warsop, and welcome to my heart!'

With a cough, Mr Hanson poked his head round the door and exclaimed, 'Glad to see you two looking so happy – but come on now into the dining room.' We followed him through, and found the table laid, and plates of fish and chips waiting for us.

Drinking cups of tea, after finishing our meal with mince pies and Christmas cake, we chatted about the war, and how it was affecting all our lives. We told funny stories about things that had happened in our earlier days, and soon we felt as though we had known each other all our lives.

Suddenly Mrs Hanson stood up. 'I'm forgetting myself. You two must be tired out. Come along and I'll show you your bedroom, and show you where the bathroom is.'

She was interrupted by her husband. 'Nay, Ma, it isn't that late, and I'm right enjoying . . .' He broke off as his wife silenced him with a look that said more clearly than any words, 'Have you forgotten what it's like to be a young married couple?'

Mrs Hanson led us upstairs to our room, which had a comfortable-looking double bed, a wardrobe, dressing table and two chairs. She indicated another light switch dangling behind the bed-head. 'You can operate the light from here – and don't worry, we're very sound sleepers,' she added, with a twinkle in her eye.

A gentle knock on the door awakened us on Christmas morning, and Mrs Hanson entered carrying a tray laden with plates of bacon and egg, toast and marmalade and two cups of tea. Sitting up, Edna exclaimed, 'You shouldn't have gone to all this trouble, using your rations in these scarce times – but thank you ever so much; it's just like being at home!'

'When you come to visit us,' Mrs Hanson replied, with a warm smile, 'that's how we want you to feel.'

We were walking in the countryside later that morning when Edna remarked, 'How is it that you don't have to go on parade this morning?'

'There isn't one on Christmas Day, just Christmas dinner in the mess hall, and Sergeant Ross, who's orderly sergeant today, assures me that his eyesight will be quite bad today and he won't miss me when he does his rounds. And Major Forsythe granted me a sleeping out pass for three nights, so we've got nothing to worry about!'

When we returned to the Hansons' a family party was in progress, in which they insisted we joined, and we spent the rest of the day listening to the King's speech, playing silly party games and singing songs while Mrs Hanson played the piano. The next day was much the same, and almost before we realised it the 27th came round. It was time to say our goodbyes, which we did with heavy hearts.

Just before Edna caught the early bus for Mansfield, Paul Sacco approached us with a large brown paper folder in his hand. With a shy smile, he handed it to us. 'It's a song that Driver Davis and I have composed, and we'd like to dedicate it to you two. It's called "Always in my heart you will remain". Please keep it, and when you sing it in the future think about your friends here.'

We stood there with a lump in our throats, finding it difficult to answer him; then Edna leaned forward and kissed him lightly on the cheek. 'We'll remember you, Paul!'

The bus came in sight, and with a final embrace she clambered aboard, waving as it moved away.

The few days left in December dragged on with feet of lead, and the only redeeming factor was that I was able to go down to the Hansons' home to receive phone calls from Edna.

Then it was 1 January 1941, and we were on forty-eight hours' notice of readiness to move. A few days later it was reduced to twenty-four hours, meaning that any day we could be ordered to move on the next. Our truck drivers had already gone, the trucks loaded with all the unit's equipment. Their unknown destination was assuredly a port of embarkation.

It was morning parade, and instead of dismissing us to spend another day hanging around, our RSM kept us standing to attention as our commanding officer stood in front of us. 'Stand them at ease, Sergeant Major,' he ordered. We realised that our officers and NCOs had joined the parade, so it was something important. 'Good morning, officers, NCOs and men of the One Five One Light Field Ambulance. It will come as a relief to you that our days of waiting are over, and our training's about to be put to practical use. When this parade is dismissed Part One Orders will have been published, setting out the time of our departure from here to a major port, where we will embark for active service in a foreign country. Your breakfast meal tomorrow will be provided by a detachment of the Military Police. You may, if you wish, spend some time in town in the early evening, but must return to your billets by 2200 hours. Anyone not obeying this order will be treated as a deserter and punished accordingly. Finally, as you are dismissed from this parade you must call at the quartermaster's stores where tropical kit is waiting for you. Sergeant Major, you may dismiss the parade.'

As soon as we left the parade ground we rushed to queue up at the QM's store to collect and try on our khaki drill light shirts, shorts and tunics, exchanging any that did not fit, then went over to the board outside the orderly office where the notice stated that reveille tomorrow was at 5.30a.m. and breakfast at 6.00a.m., while the unit would depart carrying full kit at 6.30a.m.

Fortunately I had arranged that Edna would ring me at 7.00p.m. She could tell from the tone of my voice that the news we had been expecting had arrived. 'Tomorrow morning, very early, sweetheart, I'll have started on the journey. However distant I am you'll never be out of my thoughts. I'll write to you and you to me.'

She interrupted. 'How can I write to you when I don't know where you are?'

'Don't upset yourself, love,' I said gently. 'As soon as I reach my destination I'll give you my official army address and then we can write to one another all the time.'

The telephone operator interrupted, with 'Caller, your time is up!' and we quickly exchanged tender goodbyes before the call was cut off. The Hansons had emerged from their kitchen, and I thanked them for their wonderful hospitality to me and to Edna, and wished them farewell. Choked with emotion, I left them and returned to my billet.

★ ★ ★

An unfamiliar voice bawling 'Wakey, Wakey' had me struggling back to consciousness after a night of fitful sleep and dreams of journeys in far-off lands. 'Come on, wash yer dirty necks, breakfast's at 6.00a.m,' the red-capped Military Policeman shouted as he left our billet. We quickly washed and shaved, got dressed, donned our full kit, picked up our kitbags, and staggered to the mess hall, where several more Military Police were dishing out an unappetising breakfast, first to our NCOs and then to the rest of us. Breakfast over, we were shepherded, NCOs first, into several single-decker buses that were parked on our parade ground. Our officers, who had obviously had other breakfast arrangements, were climbing into large staff cars. With a wave from a red-capped sergeant we were on our way.

We five managed to sit together. Billy grumbled, 'There ought to be a law against being disturbed at this time in the morning!'

It was quite a short journey, and we climbed out to find ourselves at a railway station, where a wheezing steam engine moved away the moment we were all aboard, gathering speed as it rattled through the darkness. Some of us dozed a little; no one had much to say. As the morning light began to show up our surroundings we caught glimpses of buildings and traffic on the roads. We were approaching a large town. Billy, who had been staring out of the window, exclaimed, 'I know where we are – it's Liverpool. Look, there's the Liver Building.'

Moments later the train came to a halt. On the other side of the platform there was a huge black shape. We were ordered out by the red-capped sergeant, and we realised this shape was the side of a ship. A long queue of troops, all similarly burdened with kit, were slowly disappearing up a gangway on to the ship's deck, and we were ordered to form a queue at another gangway close by.

The Military Police sergeant approached our officers, who had gathered a little distance away, and said to our CO, 'You and the other officers can go aboard now, sir.' Quickly they moved up the gangway and disappeared from view.

'I'm thirsty – I could drink a well dry,' muttered John, and as if in answer to his plea a lady wearing a cotton coat that bore the WVS insignia trundled into view and began to pass round mugs of tea. It tasted like nectar!

Eventually our queue began its slow trek to the deck, where we were directed by another red-capped policeman to go down the metal stairs to decks three and four. When we arrived we discovered that these decks were totally enclosed, with no portholes and only a whisper of cool air from the grilles at each side. There were long tables with equally long forms on either side. The red cap had followed us down, and Arthur asked, 'Where do we sleep?'

Pointing upwards to the network of slender girders spanning the roof he answered, 'Hammocks on the hooks, mate.' Gazing upwards, we could just about make out regularly spaced hooks attached to the girders. 'You'll have to collect your hammocks later,' he added.

The throbbing of the ship's engines began, and soon we felt gentle movement as our voyage began. I dumped my kit on one of the tables, and scrambled back to the open deck. I stood by the ship's rail gazing at the slowly receding docks and buildings, and murmured, 'I'll be back, Edna, some day.'

Suddenly I realised Captain Pomfret was standing beside me. 'Saying your farewells, Hill?' he asked quietly.

'Yes, sir,' I answered just as quietly, and for a moment we stood there watching the disappearing port. Then I turned to him. 'We answered a lot of your questions in the exams, sir, so can I ask you for two answers, please?' He nodded. 'That time we went tearing up to the Scottish border. Was it just an exercise or a real scare?'

The captain replied with a grin, 'Let me put it this way. Our radio eavesdropping centre intercepted and decoded an enemy signal that appeared to be an order for German paratroopers to be dropped on the Lowlands. However, later events indicated that the Lowlands referred to were in Holland and Belgium. What's your next question?'

'How is it that we five nursing orderlies, along with you, Sergeant Ross and Corporal Wallace, are always at the front of the queue when they want somebody to try out something new?'

Captain Pomfret thought for a moment before replying. 'Maybe we're the wrong people in the wrong place at the wrong time . . . or perhaps we're the right people in the right place at the right time – depends how you look at it!' With that he turned and climbed the wide staircase to the officers' quarters.

After a moment or two I went back to our deck in the bowels of the vessel.

CHAPTER

8

I awoke with a start, vaguely aware that something strange was happening. It took another moment or two to sort out exactly where I was, and why. The regular swinging and swaying of the hammocks during our two previous nights at sea, caused by the rise and fall of the vessel as it ploughed through the waves (a movement that had made me quite queasy) had been replaced by a much more violent and irregular bucking and rocking motion, which was causing me much discomfort. I listened for the rumbling and drumming of the ship's engines, but that regular background noise was not there any more – just the fierce slap of waves against the hull.

Mutterings from the nearby hammocks indicated that I was not the only one to have noticed the change. One by one we lowered ourselves down on to the deck – quite an acrobatic feat at the best of times, but now only achieved by gripping the overhead girders firmly with both hands and dropping until our feet met the metal deck. As I tried to stand upright the irregular pitching motion seemed more noticeable, and one or two men made a dash for the toilets at the far end.

Suddenly the lights were turned full on, and Sergeant Ross, fully dressed and wearing his life-jacket, came hurrying down the stairway.

'What the heck's going on, Sarge?' asked Billy. 'Are we being sunk?' 'Don't talk nonsense, Hough!' said Sergeant Ross sharply. 'Do you want me to put you on a fizzer for spreading alarm and despondency? No – our engines have developed a serious fault, and the crew's trying desperately hard to repair them. The rest of the convoy's gone on ahead, leaving just one small naval cruiser standing guard over us. The orders are that we're to get fully dressed and put on our life-jackets and stay like that, ready for any emergency, until further orders are issued. Is that understood? All this tossing about is because we've been caught by one of the regular storms here in the northern part of the Irish Sea, and it's made worse because we're not moving forward!'

'Is it all right to go up on deck if we need to, Sergeant?'

'By all means, Private Hill,' he replied, adding with a grin, 'If this storm goes on much longer there'll be quite a few of us hanging over the ship's rails!' He turned and disappeared up the stairway.

I looked at my watch. It was 4.30 in the morning. There would be no more sleep nor, indeed, the inclination. We climbed into our uniforms and tied the life-jackets that had been issued firmly in position – one pad in front and one pad behind, rather like two pillows. Then we sat down on the forms either side of the mess tables to await daybreak. Every now and then one of our comrades staggered up the stairway, to return looking pale and wan, greatcoat glistening with drops of spray from the waves crashing against our bows.

Finally it was daytime, and breakfast was announced over the tannoy, but few were in a hurry to collect it. So far I had managed to keep my sickly feelings in check, but the prospect of eating greasy fried bacon made me shudder with revulsion. Eventually Alan, Arthur, Billy, John and I managed to stagger along to the troops' galley, where we collected a couple of slices of bread each and a mug of tea, eating and drinking them there on the spot – for we would have spilled most of the tea had we tried to carry it back to our deck. Feeling fuller, if not better, we made our way back to the forms again.

The day continued, like some strange nightmare. We discovered that the best way to keep our tortured stomachs quiet was to sit stock still, moving only when we had to, until the atmosphere in our deck became so unpleasant that we had to crawl up the stairways and on to the open deck. The fresh air was like nectar, but the spray from the crashing waves soon drove us back down again. The men on our deck formed a constantly moving caterpillar of humanity.

Towards evening the storm seemed to be abating a little, and the uneven dipping and rolling motion grew less apparent. As if on cue the tannoy sprang to life with a loud click, and the ship's captain announced that a temporary repair had been completed, so we could limp slowly back to land. Fortunately this was not too far, as we had drifted landwards, and we were due to arrive some time the following day.

Until then we were to remain fully clothed and wearing our lifejackets, in case an enemy U-boat attacked us.

As the tannoy clicked off we were greatly relieved to feel a gentle throbbing throughout the vessel as the engines began to turn the propellers once more, and the more normal roll and sway returned. As the lights were dimmed we lay on the metal deck floor, the rear pad of our lifejackets making a reasonable pillow.

Then it was morning again, and we dragged ourselves up from the deck floor to sit and await further events. One or two of our unit's men had already gone up to the open deck, and they rushed back in excitement, exclaiming that land was in sight. To me it was like waking up from a weird dream. I felt the tension slipping away from my tired and aching body, and I was able to relax at last. I must have closed my eyes for a while, because the ceasing of the sound of the ship's engines, followed by the loud rattling and clanking of the anchor chain, brought me back to full consciousness. It was just as well, because RSM Menham had just come down the stairway, followed by Major Forsythe and Lieutenant-Colonel Swindale.

'Sit to attention, and pay heed to our commanding officer!' barked the RSM. We sat up as smartly as we could, hampered by our kit and lifejackets.

'Good morning, men,' our CO addressed us. 'We're now at anchor in Gourock Bay in western Scotland, thanks to the efforts of the SS *Northumberland*'s crew, who have worked without a pause to get us moving again and back to a safe anchorage where proper repairs can be carried out, which is likely to take several days. I've been in touch with the military authorities via the ship's radio concerning the state of the deck space where you've spent the last few days, a deck that would usually only be considered suitable to carry cargo, way down at the very lowest part of the vessel. As a result we're about to be ferried ashore, and will spend the time required for the repair in a drill hall a couple of miles further along the coast at Greenock. Needless to say it's fully equipped to accommodate us. Before the ferry arrives I advise you to get a good wash and shave, and then enjoy the breakfast that's being prepared in the troops' galley. I should warn you that although we're going ashore we're still under twenty-four hours' notice of departure, so you'll all be required to stay within close proximity of the drill hall. In addition, on our return to the SS *Northumberland* you'll find yourselves situated on a different deck, in more acceptable conditions. That's all. Dismiss them, Sergeant Major!' Our CO turned and climbed the stairs. RSM Menham saluted, and followed the CO and Major Forsythe.

This was good enough news to dispel the ache in our tired bodies, and we quickly hurried to the washroom, or 'heads' as it was termed aboard ship, to enjoy the feeling of clean water on our bodies and to shave.

'I'm beginning to feel human again!' declared Billy, as we carried the plates of breakfast food from the galley to our table.

'So who says the age of miracles is past?' chuckled Arthur. We sat down, and enjoyed that meal more than any other since leaving Liverpool.

'I never thought I'd be able to look a rasher of fried bacon in the eye again,' said Alan, 'but that breakfast beats the lot!'

No sooner had we carried our dirty plates back to the galley than Sergeant Ross came hurtling down to tell us to put on the rest of our uniform, pick up our kit and get ourselves on parade at the top of the ship's gangway, adding, 'The sooner ye make a move the sooner we can set foot on Bonny Scotland!'

We obeyed his instruction, and clambered up the three flights of stairs to the open deck, joining the line of men already waiting there. The ferry was alongside at the bottom of the gangway, which had been lowered. It looked quite small, the great bulk of our ship towering over it, but we didn't care: we would happily have accepted a lift in a rowing boat. Our RSM was there, calling us smartly to attention as our CO and the rest of the officers stepped down to the ferry, followed by our NCOs, though RSM Menham waited until he had marched us down and followed us on to the gently rocking boat. Having satisfied himself that we were all aboard, he waved to the sailor at the helm, who started the engine and pulled away towards the small wooden landing stage ahead.

It was only a matter of minutes before we were being manoeuvred to a standstill. Our CO and officers stepped off, followed by our NCOs and finally the rest of us, under the steely eye of the RSM who ordered us to form up in the usual three ranks as soon as we reached the patch of tarmac between the landing stage and a narrow road leading away from the sea.

Alan Wright exclaimed, 'Hey – this ground's moving up and down just like the ship!' I was experiencing a similar sensation, but thought I had better not mention it.

Sergeant Ross had overheard him, though, and with a grin said,

'My dad was a sailor, and he always said the sea came home with you if it had been a bit stormy – but don't worry, he said it didn't last long.'

We congregated in three ranks as our officers disappeared out of sight round a bend in the road. 'Pay attention, men!' barked RSM Menham. 'Our officers have gone ahead in two large staff cars to inspect our new temporary quarters. We're about to follow them, on foot.' A murmuring was heard from the ranks, and he continued. 'Yes, you heard me correctly. It's only two miles to Greenock Drill Hall. Left turn – by the left – quick march!'

We marched along the road that roughly followed the Clyde estuary, and there were one or two muttered grunts and groans – but as Arthur remarked, 'It's a lot better than being cooped up in that miserable bottom deck.' I totally agreed, happy to breathe the fresh air and stretch cramped limbs.

It took about half an hour of steady marching, during which some of our number struck up the popular ditty 'We're going to hang out our washing on the Siegfried Line' (which, to my surprise, RSM Menham made no attempt to silence), before we reached the small town of Greenock and began to climb a steep incline, with the drill hall plain to see fifty yards ahead. It was not as large as the one at Newcastle, but quite big enough to offer shelter and a place to sleep with no rocking and rolling.

By the time we passed through an open gateway to a concreted yard at the side of the building we were sweating profusely. 'Stand at ease, lower kitbags to the ground!'

Our officers were already there, and our CO stepped forward. RSM Menham was about to order us to attention again, but the CO said, 'Let them stay at ease, Sergeant Major.' He turned to us. 'I shan't keep you long, but before we go any further I want to explain the whys and wherefores of our present situation. First of all, the SS *Northumberland* is not a proper troopship. It's a New Zealand registered cargo vessel that normally transports frozen lamb carcasses from that country to our own, returning home with other merchandise. It was commandeered into use by the military authorities when one of our troopships was torpedoed and sunk as it returned to Britain. A rough and ready refit was carried out at very short notice. The reason the One Five One were placed in the very bottom hold was because we were the last to turn up, and that was the only space still available. When we return to the vessel we'll find that the space has been reorganised and our situation will be much more satisfactory. It seems that the storm, though it made us very uncomfortable, will be a blessing in disguise. I have to warn you, however, that though we're ashore we're still in effect continuing our journey. We're under twenty-four hours' notice to re-embark when the work is completed, and that period of notice may well be reduced to two hours if necessary. As regards this drill hall, there's a small QM stores where you will collect blankets for sleeping and a cookhouse where food is being prepared, both of which are being looked after by some retired Territorials. If things go according to plan we'll only be here for a few days. I must ask you not to discuss any details of our journey with the local people. Right, Sergeant Major – you may dismiss them!'

It was early evening. We had collected our blankets and picked a spot for them on the wooden floor, and piled our kitbags, webbing kit and greatcoats beside them. We had been to the cookhouse where we had been handed fish paste sandwiches and mugs of tea, which we ate at the tables and chairs at the far end of the drill hall. 'Wonder what our evening meal is going to be like,' murmured Alan, wiping the crumbs from his mouth. 'I never expected to enjoy fish paste sandwiches so much!'

'Beef stew and dumplings, I heard one of the cooks say,' replied Billy, 'and the smell of it made my mouth water.'

When the time came to collect our evening meal I was beginning to feel decidedly peckish, and although the food was quite plain we all ate it with gusto. Captain Pomfret came to ask if we had any complaints, adding, 'Before you answer, let me tell you that we're eating the same food as you in the officers' mess. Mind you, we do have the odd bottle or two of Scotch to soften the blow!'

'Whereabouts are our officers billeted, sir?' asked Billy with a cheeky grin. 'I haven't noticed any castles round about . . .'

'Just as well for you there aren't any, Private Hough,' replied Captain Pomfret, 'or I might be tempted to throw you into the dungeon for insubordination. As a matter of fact the Senior NCOs and officers are in two large old houses just beyond the drill hall.'

★ ★ ★

On our fourth morning at Greenock word went round that the twenty-four hour notice of re-embarkation had been reduced to two hours, and after breakfast we spent the rest of the morning doing physical exercises and playing five-a–side football, with several matches going on simultaneously on the field opposite the drill hall. All this activity was brought to an abrupt halt by the shrill blast of a whistle sounded by RSM Menham, who signalled us to join him. He said, 'In two hours from now we're ordered back aboard the SS *Northumberland*, so hand in your blankets, pack up your kit and be ready in full marching order in half an hour to start marching back to Gourock.'

We were fortunate that the weather had remained fine, so our trek to re-embark was not hindered, and a few local people stopped at the roadside and wished us a safe voyage. The gently rocking ferry boat manoeuvred into position beside the ship's gangway. As on the first occasion our officers were the first to go aboard, followed by the NCOs who signalled us to follow them. The Military Police who had shepherded us aboard the first time were conspicuous by their absence.

Sergeant Ross was standing at the top of the gangway as we reached the deck, pointing us forward this time, where a wide stairway led down. Just beyond the stairs a double doorway (with doors closed) had 'sick bay' printed above it. Signalling us to carry on down the stairs, Sergeant Ross said, 'First deck down the stairs – directly underneath the sick bay – that's where your new quarters are.'

We hurried down the steps, our boots making a harsh clattering noise on the metal – and halted in dismay. 'It's no different!' exclaimed Arthur, who was in front. 'Look – long tables and forms, just like we had on the bottom deck!' But when we took a closer look we realised the tables were set further apart, the roof was much higher and all along the hull, interspersed between storage lockers, were a series of air grilles; we could feel the fresh air blowing in. Hooks for hammocks were attached to the ends of flat metal bars, which when not in use could be swung up and out of the way. The five of us and Corporal Wallace dumped our kit to claim the first table from the bottom of the stairs and went on a trip of investigation. Beyond the main room a doorway led to larger ablution and toilet facilities than had been provided down below, and everywhere we could smell fresh paint. A corridor took us to a new troops' galley, and as we glanced in we saw cooks in white overalls busy preparing food.' We seem to have moved from steerage to first class,' exclaimed Alan. 'I hope I'm not dreaming this!'

We made our way back to our mess deck and started to stow our kit in the lockers provided. As we finished tidying away Captain Pomfret came down the steps. 'All right, no need to stand up,' he said as he came to our table. 'I just wondered what you make of this lot. Will it do? Any complaints, Corporal?'

'Not one, sir,' answered Corporal Wallace. 'We left a slave trader and came back to a cruise liner.'

'I don't think I'd go that far, Corporal,' chuckled the captain, 'but I think you'll have a much more comfortable voyage now.'

'Who's travelling in the bottom deck now, sir?' asked Alan.

'Why, would you like a transfer back there, Private Wright?' asked Captain Pomfret, with a huge grin.

'No, no, sir . . . I just . . .' stammered Alan.

'It's all right, there's no danger of that. It's just being used for storage. Quite a number of the troops originally aboard have been transferred to other vessels, to make up a convoy with our ship.' As the captain was speaking we heard the rumbling of the ship's engines and the clanking of the anchor being raised, and we immediately sensed forward motion accompanied by a gentle rise and fall. 'There you are: we're on our way at last. Oh, yes, if you have any last minute mail for home, let me have it within the next half-hour, so that the pilot who's guiding us out of the estuary to join the rest of the convoy can take it back with him. Incidentally, our troops' galley has been staffed with some Catering Corps men who are travelling with us, so I wouldn't be at all surprised if you find the food is much improved.' With a grin, Captain Pomfret departed.

We were three days into our voyage. We had carried out all the tasks that starting shipboard life again involved – collecting from the ship's stores items such as hammocks, blankets, lifejackets and eating utensils, including a set of large metal dishes with bucket-type handles for each of our tables, so that one man could collect cooked food for a whole table from the troops' galley. We had also noticed our improved sleep – thanks to the increased space between us in our hammocks and the roof, and also because of the fresh air.

We had attended our morning parade and lifeboat drill on the open deck and were now relaxing by the ship's rail, savouring the warmer breeze that was drifting towards us from the south. 'This is a bit more like it,' Arthur murmured, as the five of us and Corporal Wallace gazed out to sea, where the rest of our small convoy ploughed steadily forward in a diamond-shaped formation, with the ships' bows slicing through the big green and grey waves and leaving white frothy trails stretching out behind. The two naval cruisers continued their backward and forward patrols, like sheepdogs herding a flock of sheep.

'I wonder what all the flashing signal light messages are about,' muttered Corporal Wallace. 'Tthey seem to go on and on all the time!'

'Probably taking bets on how soon we'll reach our first port of call!' chuckled Billy.

Sergeant Ross, who had come up, exclaimed, 'Why? Do you fancy running a book on the odds, Private Hough?'

'No, Sarge,' replied Billy, with a wry grin. 'I don't fancy the odds!'

'I'm glad I managed to catch you lot together,' continued the sergeant. 'Captain Pomfret has come up with an idea. How'd you like to help out in the ship's sick bay?'

'What, all our unit?' asked Corporal Wallace.

'No, and I'm afraid I don't even mean you, Corporal,' replied Sergeant Ross. 'Two of the permanent sick bay orderlies were involved in an accident ashore at the last moment and had to be left behind, so at the moment there are only two RAMC orderlies and Medical Officer Captain Hardiman, and they're rushed off their feet. You five could make life a lot easier for them – and before you say no, you might like to consider the perks enjoyed by sick bay personnel.'

'Such as what, Sarge?' asked Billy with a suspicious frown. 'The RSM once had us lugging a whacking great heavy piano for him with a promise of "perks".'

'You're a suspicious lot, aren't you?' exclaimed Sergeant Ross. 'Look, if you don't want to spend your time doing something useful and helpful forget it. I'll tell the captain you don't want to know.'

I decided it was time I said something. 'Hold on – we aren't saying we won't do it. But what's the catch?'

'Well, you'd have to be prepared to take orders from Captain Hardiman and the two regular orderlies, but so long as you don't want to start running the show according to your own ideas you might find that you quite enjoy it. And it should help you from getting bored to tears. As to the perks,' Sergeant Ross added, 'we'll soon be in tropical regions, and as the sick bay has port holes that can be opened and whacking great cooling fans suspended from the ceiling, so it's going to be the most comfortable spot on the ship. Not only that – the food for the patients is collected from the officers' kitchen, with extra rations of tea, coffee, beef tea and Horlicks, as well as cool drinks from the refrigerator as and when required – and there's always enough to spare for the medical team.'

'Say no more,' exclaimed Alan with a beaming smile. 'When do we start?'

'How about right away? You'll be excused all morning parades and lifeboat drills, so I suggest you report to Captain Hardiman at the sick bay as quickly as you can!'

We hurried down to our mess deck to check that we were tidy and that our boots were polished, and then made our way back up the steps and along the deck to the sick bay, where a long queue wound its way from the closed door along the deck. There were mutterings of disapproval from the waiting men as we went straight to the door and knocked smartly.

'Who do you think you five blokes are, coming and pushing in at the front like that?' demanded a red-haired infantryman at the head of the queue. 'Get to the back and take your turn like everybody else!'

I pointed to the RAMC insignia on our uniform epaulettes and said, 'If we do go to the back of the queue and wait, you'll all have to wait a lot longer than if we go in right away, because we're here to help with you lot!'

At that moment the door opened, and a short, dark-haired, thick-set man aged about thirty, with RAMC badges on his uniform, looked out with a frown on his face. 'We're no' ready yet, so . . .' he started to say, but broke off with a smile as he spotted our RAMC badges. 'Ah tek it ye're the One Five One Laddies?' He waved us in, shutting the door firmly behind us. 'Hoo monny are ye?'

'Just us five,' I said. 'We were told to report to Captain Hardiman.'

'He's no here yet. Look, ma name is Angus Mcbride, senior orderly here, an' these twa others, Alex an' Edmund,' he pointed to two others, 'are second class nursing orderlies – the only staff we can call on since oor other twa had an accident in Gourock an' had to be admitted to hospital there, one o' them wi' a fractured femur, t'other a fractured skull. Left us varry short staffed that has!'

'We'd better tell you who we are,' I said, and made necessary introductions. 'We're all first class nursing orderlies, but don't worry we shan't try to take over: we just want to help in any way we can.'

'Right ye are,' replied Angus. 'Now we know who's who, what aboot a brew o' tea? The kettle's a'most on the boil.' He pointed to a small kettle simmering on a spirit stove. 'Ye show the laddies around,' he said to the taller of his helpers. 'Ah'll call ye back when the brew's ready!'

We followed Alex out of the door at the opposite end of the treatment room, which led into a large airy ward with portholes open to the fresh air along one wall. There were thirteen beds along the inner wall and eleven along the outer one, with a long table half-way along. At the opposite end of the ward swing doors gave on to a short corridor, with two four-bedded rooms down one side and a bathroom with toilets, a sluice and a storeroom down the other. Fourteen of the beds in the large ward had patients in them, some sitting up and others lying down. Four patients in pyjamas sat at a table playing a game that looked like Monopoly.

'Two bronchitis, one tonsilitis, a grumbling appendix, and the rest are pyrexia of unknown origin, PUOs for short, plus two scalded feet and three burns to arms, the latter down to carelessness in the troops Galley,' said Alex as he led us around, adding, to the patients who were eyeing us with curiosity, 'Just you wait till you get these highly qualified medical men looking after you. They won't pamper you like we do!' And he shook his head in mock-sadness as he led us through the swing doors at the far end and into the first room on the corridor, announcing 'officers' wards!' Three of the beds in the room were occupied, one by a portly, red-faced man in his late thirties. He was wearing silk pyjamas beneath an elegant dressing gown that sported an elaborate monogram on the upper pocket.

'Hah – there you are, Orderly!' he exclaimed curtly. 'Will you bring my hot shaving water immediately? I've already requested it twice. Now come along, chop-chop!'

'All in good time, sir,' replied Alex, unruffled. 'It's taking a little time to warm up. It'll be along shortly.' The other two officers smiled sympathetically at Alex as he shepherded us out and into the next room, where an older officer sat in bed reading a book. 'Are you all right, sir?' Alex asked him.

'Yes thank you, Orderly', he replied with a smile.

Alex led us back to the treatment room. 'Now there you have the difference. The last officer's a full colonel, but he treats us with courtesy, no snobbery, and there's never any trouble. He suffers recurring bouts of malaria, which make life unpleasant for him, but he doesn't take it out on us.'

When we reached the treatment room Angus was pouring tea into mugs. As if on cue the outer door opened, and a tall, well-built, ruddy-complexioned RAMC officer, hair receding, rounded features wreathed in a cheerful smile, bounded in. 'What did ah tell ye? Ah'm sure Sir can smell a brew a' tea a' the way fra' his cabin!' chuckled Angus.

'If you got on with the job instead of drinking untold mugs of tea we might get through a bit sooner!' the officer barked, though his broad grin belied his words. 'Anyway, where's mine?'

Angus produced the officer's mug from the cupboard under the table, and commented innocently, 'Ah thought ye might not want tae waste time drinkin' it, sir.'

The MO took one sip and roared, 'Has the enemy sunk the sugar boat again? You know I like my tea sweet – properly sweet!'

'Twa spoonfu' gone into it a'ready, sir,' said Angus, completely unmoved. 'Ye ken that ower-sweetenin' is nae guid for yer. But it's yer ain funeral – help yersel'!' Saying which, Angus passed the sugar basin to the MO, who ladled in two more piled-up spoons and drank the mixture with obvious relish.

Having satisfied his thirst, he turned to us newcomers. 'You must be the chaps from One Five One,' he exclaimed. 'Your Captain Pomfret has been singing your praises to me. Welcome to our team. We can certainly do with your help.'

'Glad to be of some use, sir,' I said. 'It tends to get a bit boring, gazing at the waves sloshing by all day!'

'Huh! You certainly won't have time to get bored in here,' said the MO. 'How about introducing yourselves?' We told him our names, and he turned to Angus. 'Have you decided how we can make the best use of them?'

Angus explained that Arthur and I would be in the treatment room with him and Alex, while Billy, John and Alan would work alongside Edmund in the sick bay wards. 'We can aye change roond if need be,' he added.

'Fine – so let's get cracking. Who have we got on the list this morning from the sick, the lame and the halt?' asked Captain Hardiman, as Edmund led his three henchmen through to the sick bay wards.

'Twenty-five new names an' twelve repeat treatments, sir,' said Angus, handing the MO a copy of the list.

'Right, let battle commence,' exclaimed Captain Hardiman. 'Wheel the first one in, Private Hill.'

For the next few hours we were kept hard at it, syringing blocked-up ears, applying hot fomentations to angry boils, preparing gargles for sore throats and putting antiseptic dressings on various cuts and grazes as directed by the MO. After the last patient had limped out, Captain Hardiman leaned back in his chair, loosened his collar and exclaimed, 'The treatment I recommend right now, for all of us, is another dose of hot sweet tea before we start our ward rounds!'

'Nigh on ready, sir,' said Angus, who was used to the captain's ways and had already put the kettle on the stove.

'That was a good morning's work, thanks to you One Five One chaps,' observed the captain. 'Without you we'd have been struggling on for at least another hour.'

Although I ached a bit from all the activity I felt a sense of satisfaction that our training was being put to useful purpose.

'Don't our lads in the sick bay get any tea?' I asked Angus as he filled the mugs.

'Dinna worry aboot them,' he chuckled. 'They'll hae supped theirs ages ago – fra' the officers' kitchen when they get it for the patients. They used tae bring us some, but it went stone cold afore we could drink it so now we brew oor own.'

Putting our mugs down, we accepted the captain's invitation to accompany him round the sick bay: 'Gives you an idea of what it's like looking after patients while we're at sea,' he said.

As the days went by we settled easily into the routines of the treatment centre and the sick bay, following the good-humoured instructions of Angus under the benevolent and eccentric Captain Hardiman, who quickly realised that we were all capable of dealing with whatever situation arose; and Alex and Edmund took over regular night duty on the sick bay.

I was carrying out treatments in the sick bay one afternoon when I caught a glimpse of one of our naval cruisers passing close by. I moved to the porthole to see that both our escorts, which had kept a close eye on us since we left Gourock, were moving away, with their crew lining the deck and waving to us as they went by. I called out to Angus, who was in the next room. He looked out and called back, 'Och, mon, it's the changin' o' the guard. Yon escorts are awa' back hame!'

Billy followed him into the ward. 'Lucky devils,' he muttered enviously, 'going back home.'

'Maybe lucky, maybe not,' grunted Angus. 'One o' their lot got torpedoed an' sunk goin' back last time, along wi oor own ship, the SS *Lancaster*. We managed to get awa' in a lifeboat an' to be picked up by another ship. I guess that's how we came tae be on this revamped New Zealand meat boat.'

A shiver ran down my spine as Angus's words brought home the grim reality of the war at sea. Until then I had not let my mind dwell too much on the dangers posed by the roving German U-boats. 'Were Captain Hardiman, Alex, Edmund and the other two lads with you when that happened?' I asked

'Aye, they were. We've been on several runs together before this one.'

Billy interrupted our sombre discussion. 'Look – over there. I'm sure those are our two new escort vessels.' Straining my eyes, I caught a glimpse of two long grey ships, winking their signal lamps in greeting as they joined our convoy.

'Where did you say we're heading, Angus?' I asked.

'Freetown – a port on the west coast of Africa. "White man's grave" it's called.'

'How long before we reach it?'

'Och, nay long. Twa days mair. Ye'll notice it getting a lot warmer, an' maybe the day after that we'll drop anchor in Freetown harbour.'

Arthur had joined us. 'Any chance of going ashore there, Angus?'

'Oh aye, aboot as much chance as a snowball in hell,' he exclaimed. 'It's not called "White man's grave" for nothing. It's fu' to the brim wi' tropical diseases, foreign spies an' mosquitoes as big as magpies. Ye'd come back wi' dysentery, malaria an' mebbe a lot o' even worse things.'

'I take it you don't think much of Freetown' I said.

'Och man, it's fine seen frae a guid mile oot tae sea!' Angus grinned.

As Angus had forecast, it got considerably warmer over the next few days. Having eaten our lunch in the treatment room one day we popped out on to the deck in the hope that we might see land. It was Alan who spotted not land but seagulls, three of them, wheeling and dipping and calling, over our heads. 'We can't be far off land now,' he exclaimed. 'Let's go as far forward as we can and stare straight ahead.' He must have possessed sharper eyesight than the rest of us because he soon called out triumphantly, 'There, that's it, straight ahead! I'm sure that's land!'

We followed his pointing finger and picked out a grey smudge on the horizon. We were joined by more of the troops, who were equally excited, before Sergeant Ross approached. 'I'm glad I've managed to locate you five. Our CO has issued an order that the unit must start wearing tropical uniform from tomorrow morning. You'll have to go and collect your kitbags from the ship's stores, get out your khaki drill uniform and stow your battledress uniform in the kitbags instead. The unit has to parade on deck in their khaki drill tomorrow morning.'

'Do we have to parade as well, Sarge?' asked John.

'No, I guess you five will manage to dodge off as usual,' replied the sergeant, 'but you must still change your uniforms like the rest of us.'

Next morning, after climbing out of our hammocks, the mess deck descended into total uproar as everybody put on the voluminous shorts that reached below our knees, with long, cuff-like turn-ups buttoned up but sagging between the buttons like the pockets on a cobbler's apron. With the Boer War-style pith helmets jammed on our heads we looked, as Billy put it, 'like something out of *Beau Geste* as played by the Three Stooges'. Hesitantly we made our way to the sick bay to start our day's work, to be greeted by howls of laughter from Angus, Alex and Edmund, who had not yet retired to their sleeping quarters. All three were very smartly attired in immaculately pressed khaki drill shirts and full-length slacks.

'Ye canna come workin' in here dressed like that!' hooted Angus. 'Awa' wi' ye an' bring yer KD slacks for me to press, an' yer spare KD shirt, an' while ye're aboot it please dump them rubbishy tropical helmets well oot o' sight somewhere.'

We rushed back to our mess deck, collected our slacks and spare shirts and whisked them over to Angus, who had plugged in his travelling iron and rapidly improved the appearance of our tropical attire. Soon we looked as well turned out as Angus, who commented, 'Ah never did ken why they still issue them rubbishy helmets an' passion killer shorts. Nobody wears 'em on active service.'

As we started our daily round of treatments Captain Hardiman commented on our smart appearance, and Angus gave us a conspiratorial wink.

By the next morning we were grateful that we had changed into our lighter clothing, with the heat increasing as the day wore on. Even the big fans in the sick bay offered little cooling. When we came out of the treatment room before starting the sick bay round, Billy pointed and gaped in astonishment. 'Will you just look at that!' We had skirted a headland and entered a large bay, where the water was covered by a mass of ships of all shapes and sizes, dotted around at anchor. A sleek naval vessel was nosing out to greet us, signal lights flashing.

'There ye are. What did ah tell ye?' exclaimed Angus, who had come up quietly behind us. 'That's oor convoy –the one that left us behind!'

It was certainly an impressive sight. Large three-funnelled vessels floated majestically at anchor, next to single-funnelled steamers like the SS *Northumberland*, and across the harbour some low, flat-decked ships were laden with military trucks and vehicles securely roped in position, others with bulky tarpaulin-draped items and massive wooden crates carrying all the multitudinous paraphernalia of war. All about us small motor vessels were phut-phutting around the harbour, negotiating their way through the maze of shipping. Here and there we caught glimpses of naval uniforms.

Something else caught Billy's eye. 'Hey, Angus. What's that lot coming out here?' He pointed at a small armada of native canoe-style boats rapidly advancing towards us, manned by black semi-naked lads, standing upright as they paddled their craft with powerful strokes.

'Bumboats,' said Angus, with a scowl.

'What boats?' asked Corporal Wallace, who had just joined us.

'Bumboats,' repeated Angus. 'That's what they call 'em. They're loaded up with fresh fruit, which these native boys are desperate to flog tae unsuspectin' innocents like ye!'

'Oh, that's great,' said Corporal Wallace enthusiastically. 'I love fresh fruit. Do you think they'll take English money?'

'Oh aye – yon fellers will tak onybody's money,' growled Angus, 'but ye'll no be buyin' anythin' frae them if ah can stop ye!'

'Why, what's wrong with it?' asked Billy, frowning.

'May the guid lord save us!' Angus exclaimed. 'Hev ye not minded anythin' at all from all yer lectures on tropical diseases? Yon fruit constitutes a sure-fire route tae dysentery. typhoid an' cholera! It's not like the carefully picked stuff that's taken straight from the trees and bushes to dealers, who soak it, wash it and thoroughly clean it before selling it. That lot fell on the ground and has been nibbled at and deposited upon by countless animals, reptiles and insects before bein' shovelled into buckets.'

The Africans in the boats look healthy enough,' remarked Alan.

'Aye, well, they're born an' bred here, so they get immune to it,' said Angus. 'An' anyway, they don't want to eat it – they want tae sell it tae us. Let's get back to the sick bay to do some work, not to become patients.'

Captain Hardiman was waiting for us. 'Impressive sight, eh, fellers? I hope Angus has warned you off buying that stuff. There's going to be a tannoy message shortly.' Even as he spoke the tannoy boomed out, warning everyone to avoid the fruit on offer, and also stating that after taking on more coal and drinking water our ship would be leaving the following day – as part of a great convoy.

'Drinking water!' exclaimed a horrified Arthur. 'After all we've been hearing about tropical diseases!'

'Och, dinna fash yersel',' grinned Angus. 'It'll be chlorinated an' sterilised in the dockside treatment room afore we tak it on board.'

'Yes,' agreed Captain Hardiman, 'that's one thing you can rely on. The drinking water's completely safe.'

As darkness descended, after coal and water had been taken on-board, the whole of Freetown became a blaze of light, every road picked out by the star like street lamps and every window illuminated like a picture, while each moving vehicle joined the ever-changing pattern of red and white lights.

'Beautiful, isn't it?' murmured Arthur, as we stood by the ship's rail savouring this extravaganza of light. 'Not like the blackouts and air raids at home!'

'I guess they won't bomb us here,' I said. 'They'd never make it back home.'

'I'd almost forgotten what street lamps looked like,' said John, shaking his head.

Eventually we retired to our hammocks, aware that tomorrow we were about to start another stage on our long journey to goodness knows where.

CHAPTER

9

We were now a couple of days out from port and the whole convoy was moving steadily, maintaining position, signal lights flashing, escort vessels patrolling back and forth like farm dogs guiding a herd of sheep. It was good to be out at sea once more, away from the smell of rotting vegetation that hovered around us during our halt at Freetown.

Sergeant Ross came bounding down to our mess deck just as we were about to make our way to the sick bay. 'Hang on a minute! Captain Pomfret wants a word with everybody before you disappear.' He brought us smartly to attention as our captain followed him down the stairway.

'All right – at ease, men,' he said. 'I want to tell you that as it gets hotter we all need extra Vitamin C to prevent us getting scurvy and other horrible things. We have a good supply of concentrated lime juice on board, and this is now going to be issued – two pints a day to each table. You have to mix it with your drinking water. Make sure you drink plenty!'

'That's great news, sir,' said Corporal Wallace. 'I'm very partial to fruit drinks.'

'You might not be all that keen, Corporal, as it's a bit strong and acidic, but you do need it. Just make sure you collect your ration along with your morning meal.'

The captain was certainly right about it getting hotter. Each day was warmer than the last, and when we were on the mess deck perspiration poured from us every time we moved. He was also right about the concentrated lime juice, which tasted more like varnish than fruit, but as our drinking water now tasted of the chlorine with which it had been treated, the fruit juice was the lesser of two evils.

We found some relief from the heat in the sick bay, where open port holes and the ceiling fans created some movement of air. The waves were now little more than ripples, and it was difficult to believe that we were sailing onward, though the creamy foam trail behind the vessels confirmed our progress.

We were making our way towards the sick bay one morning when we spotted several members of the crew putting up a wooden frame and stretching a tarpaulin over it, making a kind of pool structure. As soon as we reached the sick bay I said to Angus, 'What's this tarpaulin thing they're messing about with?'

'Och, it's all tae dae wi' crossing "the line". Tomorrer we cross the equator from the northern intae the southern hemisphere.'

'Yes, but what about the pool thing?' asked John, 'are we going to get a chance to swim in it?'

'If ye've no crossed the line before, ye'll hae tae wait an' see,' chuckled Angus, 'an' that's all ah'm goin' tae tell ye!' and he totally refused to explain any further.

During the afternoon the ship's tannoy boomed out that on the following day at eleven o' clock an important ceremony would take place and that all who could, particularly any who were new to the sea, ought to attend. The heat made sleeping uncomfortable, so we were glad to be out of our hammocks, washed and dressed early, and agog to discover what this important ceremony was all about. We worked at breakneck speed as ordered by Captain Hardiman, who also encouraged us to attend the ceremony but refused to tell us anything more about it. We dealt with the last of our patients by ten to eleven and hurried along to the makeshift pool, now filled with sea water. We noticed that a chair draped in green and gold fabric had been secured at one end, over the water.

As the rest of the troop passengers crowded round, the sound of a clanging bell was heard, and the ship's captain, splendidly dressed in his white tropical uniform, sat down in one of several large chairs beside the pool. He drew a microphone towards him and announced that King Neptune, 'keeper of the vast oceans', had expressed his displeasure upon noting that a number of landlubbers had strayed upon his royal territory, and that certain punishments had to be made. As he spoke a tall bearded figure, swathed in a flowing green and gold robe, wearing a gilded crown on his head and carrying a trident in his right hand, came striding along from the direction of the prow, his face and hands coloured green. Following close behind him were two smaller figures, also with green-daubed faces and hands but with shorter green robes.

Neptune clambered into the chair above the pool and bellowed in a deep voice to the captain, 'Have you provided a hostage upon whom our punishment may be meted?'

'Yes, Your Majesty,' replied the captain, pushing forward an RASC lieutenant, who was clad only in a swimming costume. 'Here's your hostage!'

With a snap of his fingers Neptune summoned his two assistants, who grabbed the lieutenant and thrust him into the water, holding him under for several seconds. This was repeated twice more, until Neptune roared, 'That is sufficient! He has paid the price!' upon which the two assistants released the hostage, allowing him to stagger, red-faced and panting, away from the pool. Then Neptune stood up and said, 'All is now well – you may proceed across my territory!' – and he and his assistants marched away towards the prow.

There was a round of applause, and the audience started to drift back to their various mess decks. At the sick bay Angus was waiting for us. 'Did ye watch it?' he asked.

'We certainly did!' said Billy, 'but what I'd like to know is, who's the big joker who played the part of Neptune?'

'Hush, mon, hush!' exclaimed Angus with a fierce frown. 'For guidness sake dinna let the king o' the oceans hear ye speakin' disrespectfully, after a' that effort tae calm him doon.' As he turned away I thought I detected a twinkle in his eye.

Shortly afterwards Captain Hardiman returned to the sick bay to start his afternoon round, and I could have sworn that he had one or two smears of green on the back of his hands. I pointed these out to him, and he snatched a quick glance before muttering, 'Oh yes, so I have. I must have splashed them. It's my hobby, you see. I spend my spare time doing watercolour paintings!' I realised that was the only answer I was likely to get.

A week had gone by since we crossed the equator, and the scorching stifling air was at last becoming fresher and cooler, and the sun's rays a little less fiery. Our daily routines in the treatment centre and sick bay kept us busy during the daytime, and in the evenings we were happy to relax on the open deck. 'I never thought I would complain about too much sunshine,' said Alan as we strolled along the deck in the cooler evening air, 'but you can have too much of a good thing . . .'

Since Freetown the water in our showers and ablutions had come from tanks filled with seawater, and I was finding it increasingly difficult to raise a lather from the toilet soap I had brought on board. I mentioned this to Angus, who grinned and said, 'Leave that tae me – ah can help ye wi' that!' He disappeared in the direction of the cabin he and the permanent sick bay staff used, to reappear with several yellowish tablets of what looked like ordinary washing soap. 'Try that,' he said, handing one to me. I took it into the sick bay ablutions, turned on one of the basin taps and started to wash my hands. To my amazement, within seconds they were fully lathered. 'Salt water soap!' exclaimed Angus. 'As ye can see it really works!'

'Can we get this stuff on board?' asked Billy, 'I haven't seen any in the canteen!'

'Normally ye can but it's aye run oot,' said Angus, 'but ah mek certain ah have plenty. When the troops leave the ship ah go roond all the ablutions an' collect all the tablets left behind!'

A few days later, as we carried out our duties in the sick bay, Billy cried out to me and Alan, 'Hey, just look out here!' We dashed over to the porthole. 'Down there,' he said. We crowded round the circular open window and caught a glimpse of flapping wings, and heard the raucous cries of three or four seagulls wheeling and diving into the water for the titbits that had been thrown from the deck above.

'We can't be far off land!' exclaimed Alan.

Arthur, who had been forward on the open deck, came dashing in. 'Land straight ahead of us! It's only a tiny speck at the moment, but the seagulls are a sure sign.'

The patients who could get out of bed came and stared out with us, then Angus poked his head around the door of the treatment room to see what all the fuss was about. 'Och aye, that's South Africa. Come mornin' an' we should be nigh on Cape Toon. Watch oot for a mountain wi' a lang flat top – Table Mountain.'

As the day progressed the speck grew to a narrow grey strip, then a defining land mass as we steamed nearer. We were disappointed that no lights were visible, but we were certain that by morning we would see our first glimpse of Cape Town.

We did not need a morning call to wake us. We scrambled out of our hammocks and dashed up on deck in the early morning light, throwing on our KD shirts and slacks as we went. We were not prepared for the sight that met our eyes. Gone was the open sea and the narrow strip of coastline. The huge land mass on our port side was filled with tall warehouses, business premises, office blocks and all the paraphernalia of a busy seaport. In the early light arc lamps brilliantly illuminated the quayside, making everything as bright as day. Dominating the skyline, just a short way inland, a mountain so long and flat that it might have been formed with a straight edge made a perfect backdrop for the scene below. The port was crammed with ships of all shapes and sizes, and some of the vessels in our convoy were already heading in. A large cargo vessel, deck spaces crammed with army trucks, crossed our bow, heading to land. But we went straight on, along with two more large ships and two escort vessels.

'Looks as though we aren't going in to Cape Town,' said Arthur.

'It does look a bit crowded,' I replied. 'When we start our morning routine we'll see what Angus has to say about it.'

The red and gold rays of the rising sun touched the scene with a hint of magic, making us loath to go down to breakfast, but from the way our ship was ploughing steadily onward there could be no doubt that Cape Town was not our stopping place.

We swallowed our breakfast of porridge, followed by bacon and beans, as quickly as we could, and hurried to the sick bay treatment room to ask Angus if he could throw any light on the situation. 'It looks like we are goin' on tae East London – or mebbe even Durban!' he answered, as we bombarded him with questions. 'It aye happens that way when part o' the convoy has tae wait a wee while.'

'What a stunning sight Cape Town was in the early morning light!' observed John. 'That massive town, the beautiful green background, and the great flat-topped mountain towering over it all!'

'Aye, there's not monny tae match it,' said Angus, 'especially when ye come frae blacked oot Britain!'

We continued with our duties in the sick bay as our little convoy journeyed on in close formation, hugging the coastline close enough for us to make out tiny white buildings here and there amid the lush greenery. When darkness descended, tiny pinpricks of light caught our eye, occasionally a cluster of them. A day or two more passed, and tall buildings and cranes stood out on our port horizon, but still we carried on.

'So it's no East London!' exclaimed Angus. 'It has tae be Durban – an' that means ye'll be stoppin' there a while.'

'Any chance we might go ashore?' asked Arthur. 'I've always fancied visiting South Africa.'

'Ah wouldna' be at all surprised – if ye are waitin' any length o' time, that is.'

The sticky, overbearing heat of the tropics had gone, leaving the weather fine and warm with a cooling breeze wafting across from starboard, making conditions on our mess deck much more comfortable. Our only problem was that fresh drinking water was running low, and could only be collected in the mornings or evenings; a refill would soon be an urgent necessity.

'Why do we always seem to reach our stopping places first thing in the morning?' exclaimed Alan, as we woke a couple of days later. The throb of the ship's engines was reduced almost to a murmur, and it was hard to tell whether we were moving or not. We threw on our uniforms and dashed on deck to discover that our little convoy was gently nosing in towards a medium-sized port, where a few cranes and seaport buildings clustered around a quay, with the rest of the town spread out behind in a green and pleasant background.

A voice behind us made us jump. 'Hey, listen you five,' called out Corporal Wallace. 'Our unit has to be on our mess deck immediately after breakfast, because Captain Pomfret has some important instructions – so get washed, eat your breakfast and hang on down there.'

Filled with curiosity about the news, we made a hurried trip to the ablutions and back to the mess deck, where everyone was buzzing with excitement and guessing what would happen next. We ate a hurried breakfast and waited impatiently. A late arrival informed us that two tugboats had manoeuvred our ship gently into position alongside the quay.

Then Sergeant Ross came down the stairway, quickly followed by RSM Menham, who snapped out, 'Squad, Attention!' We all scrambled to our feet and stood as smartly as we could between the tables.

'It's all right, Sergeant Major, let them sit down now,' came the voice of Captain Pomfret.

'Squad, sit!' barked the RSM.

Captain Pomfret gazed round the packed deck from his vantage point on the stairs. 'I know you're all anxious to know what's going to happen next, and how it will affect us. First of all, let me tell you that quite a lot of things have been going on in the Egyptian/Libyan desert area of North Africa while we've been on the high seas. The Italians, who'd colonised a large part of Cyrenaica, a northern part of Libya, in recent months sent their Armoured troops to cross the border into Egypt, only lightly guarded by Egyptian troops, and managed to penetrate to Mersa Matruh, over a hundred miles away. To cut a long story short, the British Seventh Armoured Division, stationed in Cairo, has counter-attacked and taken hundreds of Italian prisoners, who in their retreat left most of their armour behind, and now Major General O'Connor, who's commanding our troops up there, has cleared the Italians out of Cyrenaica and is chasing them back to their base further west, in Tripolitania.

'There's a rumour that Hitler's rushing reinforcements out to help the Italians, so the situation's quite tricky. New Zealand has made a contingent of their troops available to us in the Middle East, and this ship is going back there to pick them up – which means, of course, that we all have to disembark. Most of us will transfer to one of the other ships in the convoy, but the One Five One Light Field Ambulance will go ashore here in Durban and travel approximately thirty miles inland, where we'll be billeted in a brand new rest camp for a short time, until one of the four diesel-driven ferry-type vessels doing the run between Durban and the Nile Delta has room to take us. The disembarkation will start today, but our turn won't come until tomorrow.

'Our CO and Major Forsythe are going ashore any time now to get the final details for our departure, so in the meantime I'll leave RSM Menham to sort out your programme of preparation, which should keep you well occupied.'

Our RSM brought us to our feet once more, and saluted as Captain Pomfret turned and disappeared up the steps. 'Right, men, you all heard what the captain said. We're going to collect our kitbags, then spend the rest of the day checking the condition of our uniforms, polishing our boots and cap badges, scrubbing our webbing equipment and so on, so that we look like properly trained and drilled soldiers when we disembark.'

'What about us who've been working in the sick bay, sir?' asked Billy. 'Ought we to carry on there today till the sick bay's been cleared?'

'That's exactly what I was going to tell you next,' barked the RSM. 'You five will report to Captain Hardiman as soon as I dismiss you and give him any help he requires in dealing with the transfer of his patients.

I'll expect you to be as smart as the rest of our unit when we disembark, so bear that in mind!' With a fierce grin he called, 'Parade, dismiss!' and we hurried to the sick bay.

'Sorry we're late, sir,' I started to explain, but Captain Hardiman waved us in with a smile. 'It's all right. I heard Captain Pomfret was giving you a pep talk this morning. I'm trying to get through our sick parade as quickly as possible, so we can spend more time getting the sick bay patients ready for the ambulances which will collect them.'

Angus was starting to put out the mugs for our mid-morning tea, but the captain called out, 'No tea yet, Angus. We've got to clear the sick bay first – decide who can walk to the ambulances and who'll need to go on a stretcher.' He pushed open the door of the sick bay, where the patients were animatedly discussing their imminent transfer to the British sector of the local military hospital.

Angus exclaimed, 'Ye lucky laddies will soon be under the tender care o' real feminine nurses – an' then there's the fantastic grub . . .'

As the morning wore on we saw companies of troops marching down the gangway on to the quay and away out of sight. In the mid-distance smoke from railway engines puffed into the air, and their mournful hooting could be heard.

Captain Hardiman started with the patients who could walk, completing the records of their ailments and treatments, and we carried out any final treatment he called for. Then we assisted them down the gangway with their kit, which had been collected from the ship's stores by Alex and Edmund. The stretcher patients were the next to go. The ambulance orderlies brought a stretcher in for each patient, lifted him on to it and carried him down to the ambulance. For a while it was all hustle and bustle, but by lunchtime the sick bay wards were empty and the beds had been stripped.

'That's a job well done,' exclaimed the captain. 'Let's go and have lunch and then finish packing up the medical equipment.'

With a wave he strode out of the sick bay. Angus, who had been absent for the last few minutes, appeared with a tray bearing our lunch.

Alan said anxiously, 'We'll have to start scrubbing our webbing equipment soon if we want to get it smart enough for our RSM. I brought our kit up earlier on.'

Angus snorted. 'Did ah hear ye say the word 'scrubbin'?' he asked. 'Look, let's hae oor lunch, an' then ah'll show ye Field Ambulance laddies how tae deal wi' this webbin', an' ah dinna mean scrubbin'!' He wouldn't tell us any more until we had eaten, so we sat down and enjoyed the superbly cooked haddock and new potatoes, finishing off with cheese and biscuits. As soon as we had finished eating he said, 'Come on. If ye have tae set a perfect example tae yer mates, we'd better get crackin' wi' yon webbin' stuff.' He produced a glass bottle labelled hydrogen peroxide and several rolls of cotton wool, then turned to me. 'Come on then, George. Might as well start on your stuff, seein' as how ah hae tae prove ma' words.' He put on a pair of rubber gloves and held his hands out. Feeling slightly uneasy, I tipped the contents out of my backpack and sidepack and passed them over, along with the straps and belt, and Angus set to work soaking a large pad of cotton wool in the hydrogen peroxide and rubbing it thoroughly into the surface of my equipment. It started to remove the smudges of dirt and grime and grew paler by the second. After a few moments Angus said, 'There, that should dae it. Noo ah gi' it ten minutes i' the food warmin' oven, an' ye'll aye see the difference.' I was quaking in my shoes in case it all went wrong, but when he brought the equipment out again after ten minutes it was as white as snow. The brass buckle and clasp were a bit cloudy, so he picked up a cloth, gave them a sharp rub, and quickly had them shining like gold. 'There ye are – what did ah tell ye?' Angus exclaimed triumphantly. 'Now let's get crackin' wi' the rest o' it!' He passed round pairs of rubber gloves and we all set to with a will. In no time at all the whole lot was finished and looking as good as mine.

Arthur was totally fascinated. 'To think we used to spend hours scrubbing the wretched stuff when we were in training!' he muttered.

'Aye, well, ye learn a trick or twa' when ye sail around a' the time,' said Angus, 'an' ah hae somethin' else tae tell ye. Captain Hardiman is on his way doon again, tae say farewell. We need tae clear this treatment table because he's fixed it wi' the officers' kitchen to make up a few sandwiches, an' he's also donated a bottle o' scotch whisky: a sort o' farewell party, ye ken.'

We cleared the treatment table just as Alex and Edmund came in with two large plates of sandwiches, triangles of white bread filled with thinly sliced corned beef and garnished with onion and tomato. Angus reached into the medicine cupboard and brought out the unopened bottle of whisky – just as Captain Hardiman bustled in, a beaming smile on his face.

'Ah, I'm glad to see you're all here and the feast is prepared!' he exclaimed. 'I asked Angus to arrange this little effort to thank you Field Ambulance chaps for the first-class help you've given during the voyage. I'm going ashore in half an hour. But first of all let's fill our glasses and drink to the confusion of our enemies – and a speedy and safe return home for all of us.'

Angus poured the whisky and we all raised our glasses and drank, each solemnly echoing in his heart the sentiments the captain had expressed.

'Are you staying with this vessel on the voyage to New Zealand,' asked Billy, 'or are going back to Britain on another ship?'

'Don't know yet, laddie,' boomed Captain Hardiman. 'That's one of the reasons why I need to dash off so quickly – to find out what they propose to do with me and my assistants; that and to see if our patients are settled all right at the military hospital. If we're staying with the SS *Northumberland* we'll probably be on our way by tomorrow afternoon. But if the military bigwigs decide otherwise we'll probably manage two or three days' leave here. Anyway, all the best to you fellows. Perhaps we'll meet again some day!' And with a cheery wave he left.

'So there ye hae it, ma friends,' said Angus with a wry smile. 'We canna tell ye which what way! Either we hae twa or three days here, or we're off tae New Zealand in the mornin' after ye lot have disembarked an' gone tae the rest camp. So let's eat up oor sandwiches, an' finish up this whisky, an' then ye can show yer sergeant major how ye've been slavin' awa, scrubbin' yer webbin'!'

We chatted for a while, and soon the sandwiches were gone and the whisky bottle was empty; it was time to say cheerio to Angus, Alex and Edmund. 'We've enjoyed working with you, Angus,' I said as we wrapped our pristine webbing in some paper towelling and got up to go. 'Thanks for looking after us so well.'

'Awa' wi' ye, man. It's aye us should be thankin' ye lot for helpin' us oot in oor time o' need. If we stay in Durban for a day or so we'll be in the United Services Club of an evening. If ye laddies are allowed tae come in tae visit then come an' look us up. We can share another bottle an' a bite tae eat!'

We shook hands all round and departed to our mess deck. Corporal Wallace was sitting at our mess table. 'Where the hell have you lot been?' he demanded crossly. 'You know very well you've got to get your webbing scrubbed!'

I interrupted him. 'We think it's clean enough, Corporal. Just have a look.' We removed the paper wrappings, and he gaped in amazement.

'I thought you lot went to help with the patients, not to do your fatigues,' he stammered.

'We cleared up early and got a bit of help,' said Alan, with a sly wink at me.

'You rotten so and so's. Why didn't you tell me instead of letting me go on about it?' spluttered the corporal, quite red in the face.

'You looked so worked up, sitting there with steam coming out of your ears, that we couldn't resist confirming your worst fears!' grinned Billy.

'Come on, look lively,' barked RSM Menham from the head of the gangway. 'No need to go mincing down like a troupe of ballet dancers. Get yourselves into three ranks as soon as you reach the quay.'

We had retired to our hammocks early the previous evening, having been informed that we would have to go to the galley for breakfast at 7.30, hand in our hammocks, collect our kitbags, put on our webbing kit and be ready to march off by 8.30.

When we were assembled on the quayside our officers, led by our CO, appeared on deck, and as our RSM barked 'Squad, shun' they joined us. Our CO stepped to the front. 'We're staying for a short while in a newly opened rest camp at a race course called Clarewood, which is thirty miles inland. The train's waiting for us at the station, just a short march away. Right, Sergeant Major, follow me!'

★ ★ ★

The train was speeding through the open South African countryside. It was just three coaches, smart and clean in silver and green. Seats and tables were on either side of a central aisle, and sitting on the soft leather seats we gazed at the rapidly passing scenery. Durban itself and the area around it had been lush, but I noted that the grass was now a dingier shade than in the English countryside, and the soil had a yellowish sandy appearance. Though it was early March – equivalent to autumn north of the equator – a heat haze arose from the land, creating ripples in the air that distorted the view. Corporal Wallace, who was sitting across the aisle from us, pulled a face. 'It's not like the films of Africa we used to see – no lions and elephants roaming around.'

'I think we're in the wrong area for lions and suchlike,' said Alan, 'but just look out of this window: that's a sight you won't see at home.' He pointed to another train passing us, going in the opposite direction. It had two rickety old coaches at the rear crammed with dark-skinned South Africans, and an open platform at the rear, with standing passengers hanging on by the skin of their teeth.

The countryside now seemed greener, with farmsteads nestling among clumps of trees and neat vineyards stretching away as far as the eye could see, while wayside stations with huddles of patiently waiting Africans flashed past. We seemed to have been travelled for ages before we finally stopped at a small station decorated lavishly with hanging baskets of flowers and greenery.

'Everybody out,' thundered RSM Menham. 'Come on – into three ranks on the platform!' We gathered up our kit and stepped down, to immediately feel the heat of the sun on us and our perspiration beginning to trickle. Our RSM cast a practised eye over us. 'I don't know what you lot are getting yourselves all hot and bothered about!' he barked, with a ghost of a grin on his face. 'We'll probably end up in hotter places than this, so you might as well get used to it!' He turned to the CO who, with the rest of the officers, was standing in the shade of the station awning. 'Ready to march off now, sir,' he said.

Lieutenant-Colonel Swindale led the way down a narrow path, with the rest of the officers following behind, while our RSM led the rest of the NCOs and our three ranks brought up the rear. Billy, who was marching next to me, gasped, 'If we've much further to go with all this kit I think I'll melt by the time we get to this flaming rest camp.' Fortunately after a short distance along a tarmac road we soon caught sight of lines of large white tents on a low hillside reflecting the morning sunshine, no more than a couple of hundred yards ahead. There was an audible sigh of relief as our CO turned in through a wide gateway and came to a standstill outside a corrugated iron reception office. A large notice-board beside the office read 'Clarewood Rest Camp – South African Army'.

A sergeant, dressed in khaki drill uniform that bore South African Army Service Corps flashes, saluted and spoke to our CO, who motioned our RSM to join them. After a short discussion RSM Menham turned back to our parade and growled, 'Parade, dismiss. Take your kit over to the grass opposite and await further instructions. Our CO thinks you may be hot and tired after our pleasant stroll up from the station.'

We sat down on the hillside with relief, and tried to find a sensation of coolness from the breeze that was blowing so softly that it barely stirred the grass. 'I'm so thirsty I could even enjoy a mug of that horrid lime juice!' croaked John.

The CO came across. 'You're to stay where you are and wait for some camp orderlies, who'll escort you in groups of six to the tents, after which showers are available in the block opposite. Lunch will be in the dining room behind the shower block. I want you back here for pay parade, clean and smart in your KD uniforms at two o'clock prompt.'

When the orderlies arrived Corporal Wallace tagged along with us five. Our tent was even better than we had expected – a roomy rectangular structure of strong white canvas, fitted with an inner blue sheet to cut down the sun's glare and allow air circulation. We gazed at the six camp beds, positioned three each side, with plenty of space between them, and we dropped our kit on the wooden floor. 'Bliss!' exclaimed Arthur, sinking down upon his bed with a contented sigh.

'What are the blankets for?' I asked, pointing to the three blankets and a pillow at the bottom of each bed, 'I mean, it's pretty hot.'

'Night time, Soldier,' replied the orderly. 'We still have cold nights.'

'Is there much bull – you know, fatigues, route marches, parades and so on?'

'Not in this camp. This is our rest camp, and you're our first visitors. We want you to enjoy your stay here!'

'Are the officers and Senior NCOs staying here as well?' enquired Corporal Wallace, 'because they might have other ideas about what we should do.'

The orderly laughed. 'Senior NCOs are a couple of miles and the officers are two and half miles away, so I don't think they'll bother you much.' As he left he pointed out the shower block and the dining room behind it.

'I'm going for a shower!' exclaimed Alan. 'I feel as if I've been doing a shift as a stoker in the ship's furnaces. Anybody else coming?'

That sounded like a first-class idea, so we grabbed our towels and headed for the shower block.

Half an hour later, less smelly and much refreshed, a booming gong called us to the dining room, a structure of brick and corrugated iron. We stepped inside and stared in amazement. Twenty large tables, with six chairs around each one, had a large wicker basket in the centre of each one, literally piled high with fresh fruit of every description, and Billy cried out, 'Take me no further – this is my idea of heaven! Just look at those whacking great peaches!'

'What about some real food?' grumbled Corporal Wallace.

'Well, there are two tins on each table,' said John, reaching over and picking two up. 'Tomato jam and passion fruit jam,' he read, with a sly wink to the rest of us.

'Jam be . . .' Corporal Wallace's aggrieved outburst faded as he noticed a queue forming at a large serving table bearing tureens of steaming food at the end of the room. 'You've done it again, haven't you?' he exclaimed, with a sheepish grin. 'You fellers try to wind me up every chance you get. I'll get my own back on you, just you wait and see!'

Chuckling, we joined the queue, and were handed plates of hot roast chicken, new potatoes and green peas, with an iced raspberry sorbet to follow, and, of course, the soldier's delight – a mug of sweet tea.

At two o' clock, smartly turned out, we joined the rest of the unit outside the camp reception office and were addressed by our CO. 'I ask you all to remember that we are guests in this country, ambassadors for Great Britain. We're obliged to abide by the laws of this country and in particular the laws of segregation. We're at liberty to visit the seaport of Durban from lunch time to 2300 hours each day via the railway. When you're dismissed from this parade you will each collect a pass from the office, as well as your pay in South African money. The fare for troops is reasonable, but you must remember to travel in the first-class carriages – like the ones that brought us here. In town some places are marked

'Whites Only' and some 'Out of Bounds'. If the Military Police ask for your pass, show it to them. We're on twenty-four hours' notice to depart so our stay is on a day to day basis, dependent on the availability of small transit boats up to the ports in Egypt, and the military situation in that area. We've been told that German troops have moved into Tripolitania, but so far have made no moves towards our small forward division in Libya.

'You'll find plenty of entertainment in Durban. Service clubs provide meals, writing rooms and games rooms, and there are several cinemas as well. You'll receive a great welcome here.

'I've heard on the radio news that German troops are massing on the Greek borders, and because our country is committed to helping the Greeks anything could happen. Keep your kit ready for immediate departure, and enjoy your stay here, however long or short it may be. That is all. You may dismiss them now, Sergeant Major!'

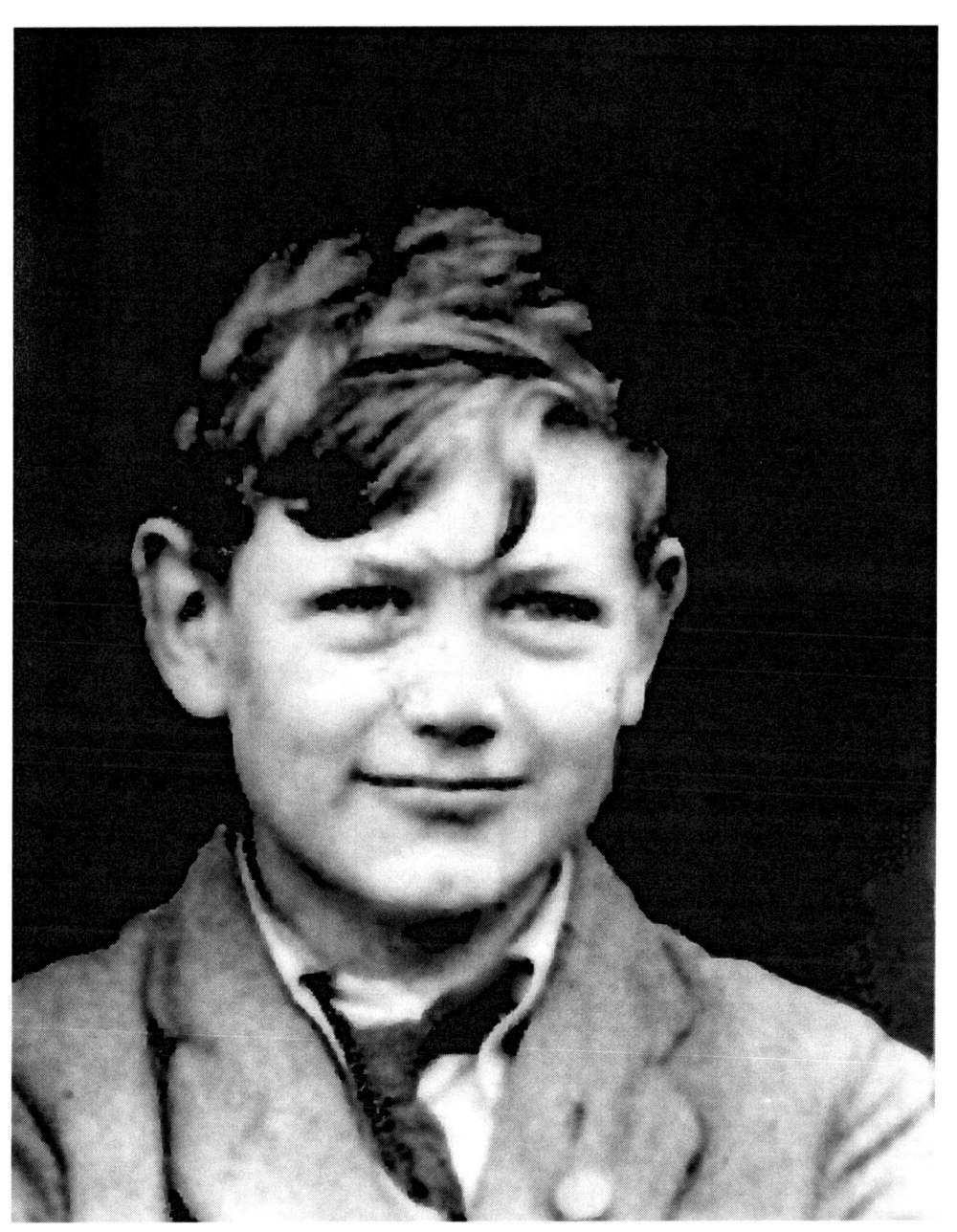

George as a schoolboy.

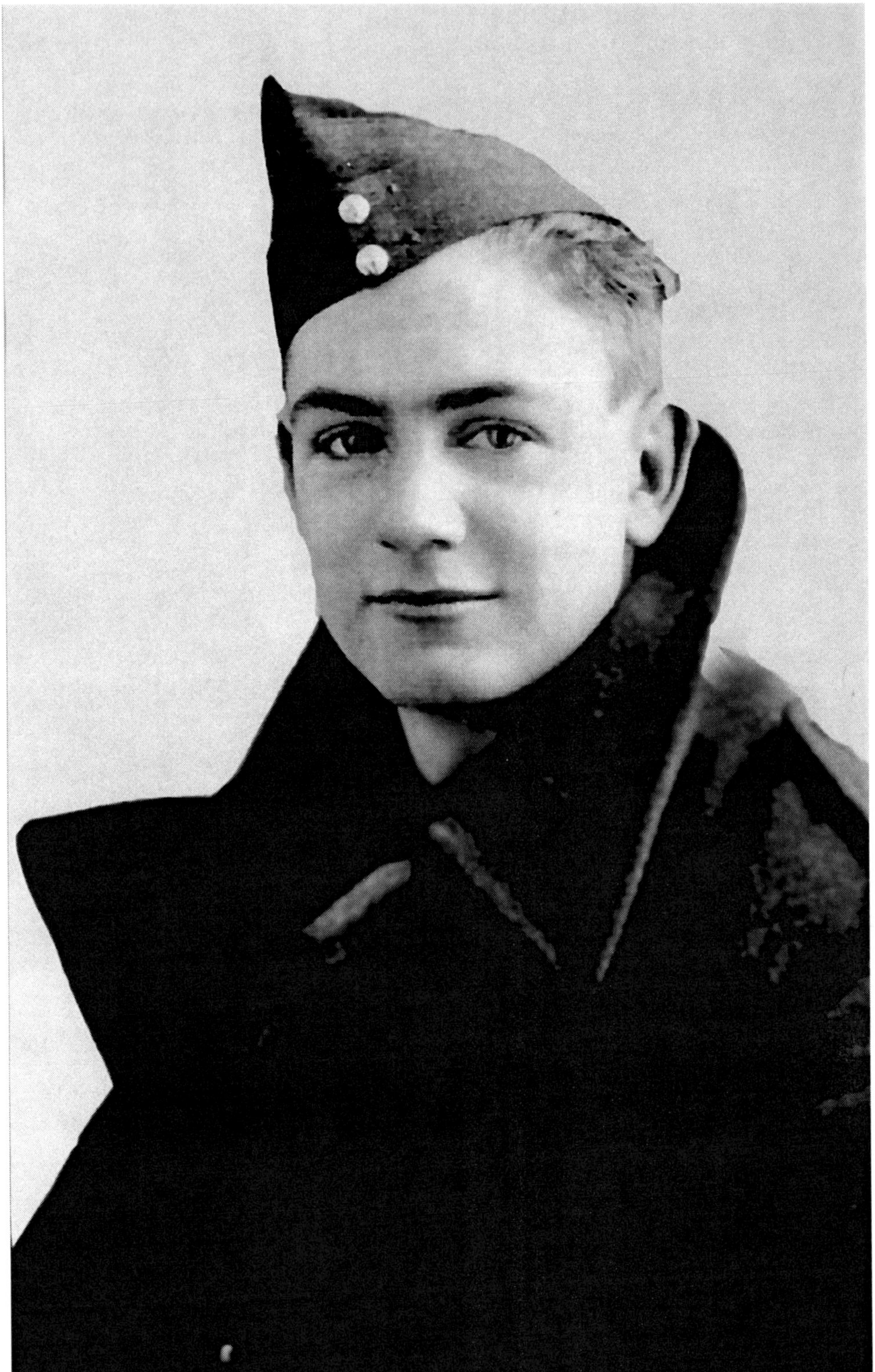

(above) **An off-duty moment with army pals.**

(facing page) **George in uniform in 1938.**

(right) **An official army portrait.**

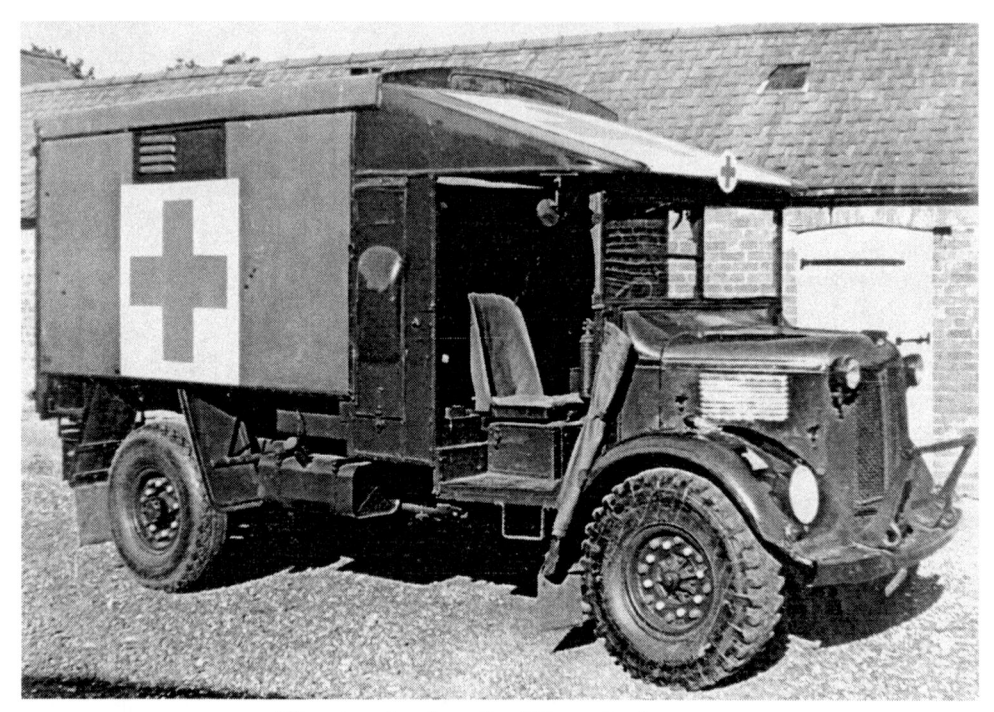

The trusty Austin K2 ambulance.

The *Toscana*—the Italian hospital ship, as photographed by Sister Maria Luisa Bernardi.

A casualty is loaded into an ambulance by members of the Medical Corps.

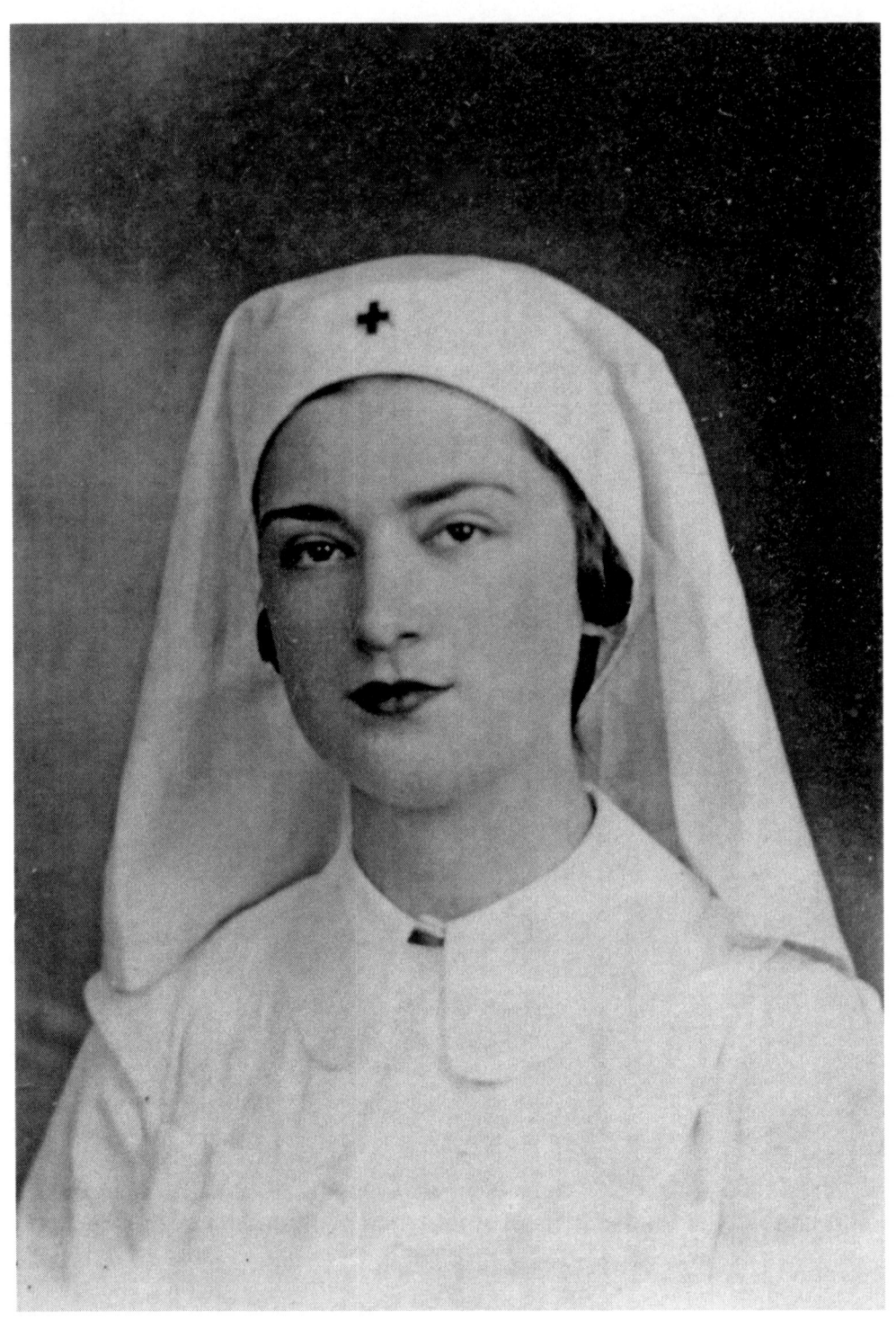

Sister Maria Luisa Bernardi.

George in desert uniform.

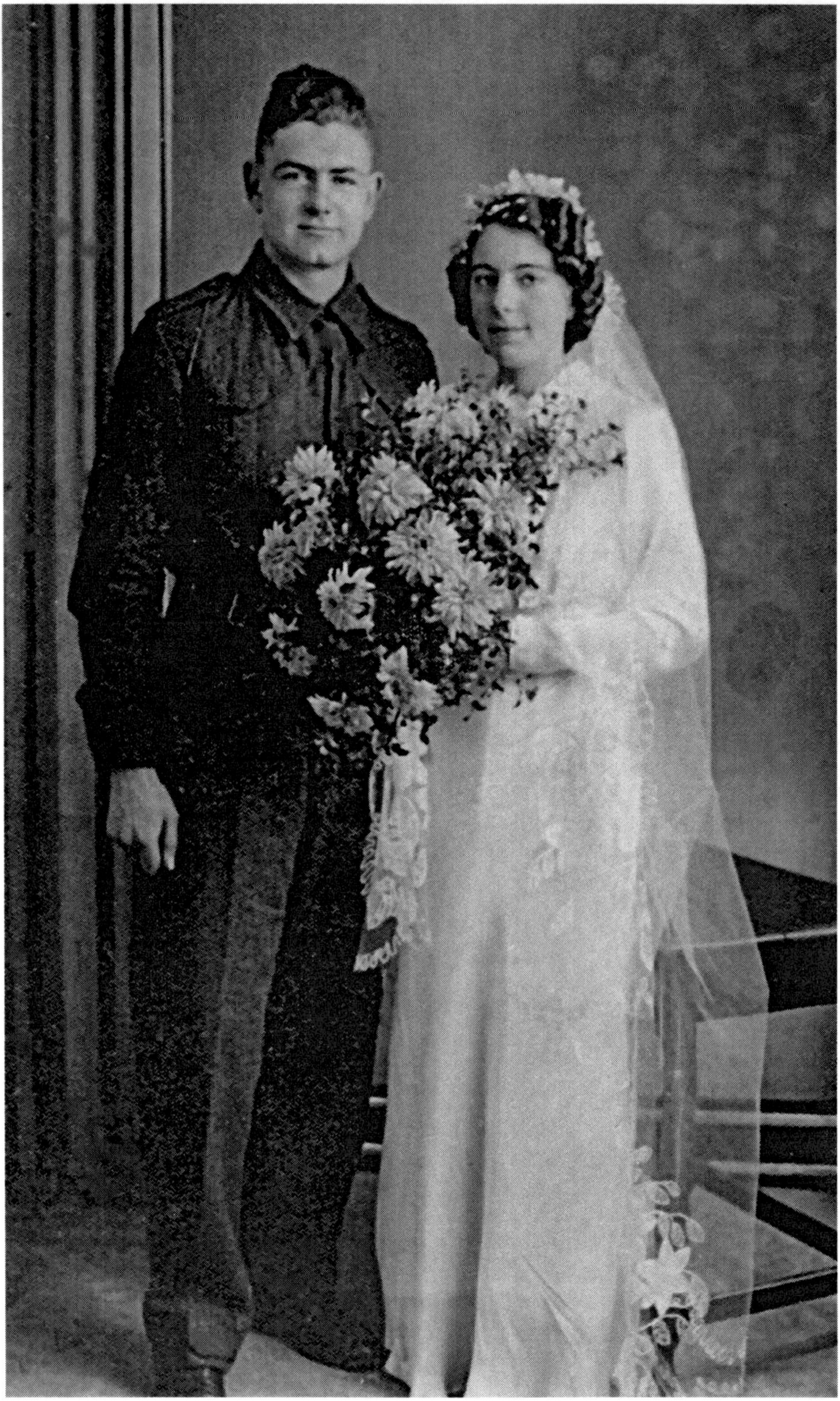

George and Edna on their wedding day, and together in 1945.

George today.

CHAPTER

10

Half-way between sleep and wakefulness, I sensed rather than felt that unmistakable rocking motion of a vessel at sea. For a long moment I lay there with my eyes shut, thinking I was still aboard the SS *Northumberland*, and that all those images of the wonderful rest camp and daily trips into Durban, where we had been welcomed with open arms, must have been a dream. If it was a dream I was keen for it to carry on a bit longer.

A heavily accented foreign voice penetrated my sleep, chanting 'Wakey, wakey – washy decky.' As my eyes opened I realised I was lying, wrapped in my blankets with my life-jacket as a pillow, on the deck of a ship. I sat up and looked round to see my four friends, Corporal Wallace and several others stirring as a group of Lascar deckhands approached, carrying long-handled scrubbing brushes and hoses. As their obvious intention was to scrub the area where we had been sleeping, we grabbed our blankets and lifejackets and made for the wide stairway leading below. As we reached it I glanced back to see one unfortunate sleeper who had not heard the calls being sprayed with the cold seawater; I guessed he would not be so hard of hearing in future!

We had come aboard this low diesel-powered vessel, the *City of Canterbury*, on the previous day. Our break at Clarewood was marvellous, and we had spent happy hours in Durban, thanks to the hospitality of the residents. Our CO had warned us we were on twenty-four hour notice of departure so, although we were a bit sad to say farewell, our departure had come as no surprise.

After a quick wash and shave we collected our breakfast from the galley, which was only a few yards astern. As we finished eating, Sergeant

Ross came down the stairway to our table, and said, 'Captain Pomfret wants a word with you. He's by the ship's rail in the officers' quarters.'

As we went to find out what particular task we were about to be lumbered with, Billy, grinning hugely, said, 'Hey, Corp, who was that fancy piece we saw you dancing with at the church hall the other night?'

Corporal Wallace frowned at him. 'I'll have you know that she was no "fancy piece", as you so rudely put it. She's a thoroughly well-brought-up young lady who works in a public library in Durban. She invited me to go and visit her parent's home next weekend – but we've moved!' By now we had reached the officers' quarters. Captain Pomfret turned as we approached and acknowledged Corporal Wallace's salute. 'You wanted us, sir,' our corporal said.

'All right – no need to get alarmed!' said the captain, grinning at our faintly anxious expressions. 'The ship's captain has asked that we should look after any sick parades and treatment during this voyage as we're a medical corps unit. It shouldn't take too long. The previous RAMC crew got collared for another vessel in Durban, which left this one without. And anyway, you lot are first-class nursing orderlies, so is it any wonder we've been chosen?'

'Right place right time again, sir?' I asked, with a wry smile.

'Hit the nail on the head first time, Private Hill. We might as well get cracking and show them what we're made of!'

Captain Pomfret led the way to the sick bay, which was quite small compared with the one on our previous ship, just a small treatment and examination room, and one further room with a couple of beds in it. 'We shall manage all right with this,' he said. 'Considering the speed at which we're travelling, our fellow travellers won't have a lot of time to get poorly!'

We checked the equipment and dealt with a couple of sunburn cases, and sat and waited. 'By the way,' remarked our MO, 'I was talking to the ship's radio officer this morning, and he told me that this German general called Rommel who's taken command of the enemy troops in North Africa made a counter-attack at El Agheila on the Tripolitania-Libya border, and chased our chaps back into Libya, where we're managing to hold them. The situation's quite tricky because a large portion of our armour has been transferred to Greece, so we're very light on the ground. I imagine that's why the fighting troops in our convoy have been rushed northward ahead of us, to get organised and in battle order before he starts anything else.'

* * *

We settled into the routine aboard this smaller, newer, faster vessel, and several days later we had crossed the equator once more, heading north across the Indian Ocean, keeping the African coast in sight on our port bow all the time. Although the daytime heat had increased our vessel's speed created some movement of air, and sleeping on deck made conditions much easier. This time 'crossing the line' was not marked by any fancy celebration: it was obvious that the aim was to get us to our final destination as quickly as possible, so the ship could be away to pick up another lot.

As the days went by we felt the heat easing As we stood by the ship's rail, gazing at the coastline, Arthur produced a diary. 'Found it in my backpack. I'd forgotten I had it. There's a map of Africa, and I thought we might be able to work out how far we've travelled, and how much longer it'll be before we reach North Africa.' We stared at the tiny map, trying to match it with the indistinct shape of the nearby coast, hazy in the heat of the day.

We were not having much success, and were about to give up when Captain Pomfret came along from the officers' quarters. 'Loafing around as usual eh? No customers in the sick bay?'

'It's very quiet this morning, sir,' I said. 'We were trying to work out how soon we'll reach our destination.' I handed him the tiny map, and he studied it for a moment before shaking his head. 'I can't tell you, but the radio officer will know. I'll go and ask.'

Clutching the diary the captain went back to the officers' quarters. He was back in a few moments with the young radio officer, who said, 'I wouldn't like to be relying on this map! Later today we'll steer west as we enter the Gulf of Aden – there, look, it's like a dragon's open mouth.' He pointed to an inlet that separated the African coast from the eastward-leading coastline of the Arabian countries. 'The only way you'll be able to tell we're going west is that the setting sun will be directly forward instead of on our port bow. At the far end of this Gulf is a narrow neck, Bab-el-Mandab, which leads into the Red Sea and stretches northward again.'

'How long before we disembark in Egypt, sir?' asked Billy.

'Just a few more days, depending on the traffic in the Suez Canal. If there are no big vessels coming south we should make good progress.'

Anything fresh in the desert situation, sir?' asked Alan.

'There certainly is! Rommel's troops have made a breakthrough again, and our lot were so depleted that we had to fall back into Egypt. Some of our latest armour – part of your big convoy – managed to move up in time to stop the Germans just inside the Egyptian border, where the coast road descends a corkscrew route down a kind of cliff-face from Libya into Egypt. It's named Halfayah Pass, but our desert troops call it Hellfire Pass.' The officer handed Alan's diary back, and with a wave returned to the radio office.

As predicted, the land began to close in on us from both sides; Bab-el-Mandab, the gateway to the Red Sea, lay directly ahead. We were passing within a hundred yards of a rocky outcrop when John suddenly exclaimed 'Ugh!' in disgust, flapping his hand wildly at his face. 'Get away from me, you filthy beasts!' We were suddenly aware of swarms of flies, buzzing and settling around our eyes and mouths and everywhere else where there was an inch of exposed flesh, searching out every drop of moisture. As we looked around we saw that everyone was being troubled in the same way, as flailing arms attempted to deter the flying pests. Fortunately the narrow neck was quite short, and as soon as we were back in the open sea the flies disappeared as rapidly as they had arrived.

'Hell's bells!' exclaimed Billy. 'Talk about the plagues of Egypt – they were just about eating us alive!'

The radio officer happened to be passing. 'You didn't expect anything like that, did you? Well, I've got news for you. They're going to be your constant companions as long as you remain in this quarter of the Middle East, but don't worry: you'll learn to tolerate them.'

'Are you really going to be plagued by them all the time?' asked Arthur, aghast.

'Well, not all the time,' grinned the officer, 'only in the hours of daylight .'

'There won't be any out in the desert,' I said. 'I mean, it's all bare sand and rock – there's no life about at all.'

'Don't you believe it, laddie. I was talking to a Tank Corps officer from the Seventh Armoured Division a week or two ago in a bar in Port Said, and he told me that you keep running across patches of desert scrub – cactus-style greenery, teeming with crawling things like lizards, scorpions, snakes – and flies, of course. He said the moment you pull up anywhere the flies are back. Nobody knows where they hide but there they are, on your face, your hands and anywhere else they can get. And don't forget the sandflies. A bite from them can give you sandfly fever. Don't worry, you'll get immune to it eventually!'

'He's kidding us . . . you are kidding us, aren't you ?' asked Billy anxiously.

'All right, lads, have it your own way,' chuckled the radio officer, 'but if you think I'm kidding you could have a few surprises in store. Don't say I didn't warn you!'

If the Indian Ocean had seemed calm, the Red Sea was like a duck pond. Although we were now a considerable distance above the Tropics the sun beat down upon us with a brassy yellow glare, and what breeze there was seemed to be hot, searching and very dry. Thankfully, when the sun had set we could cool off nicely on the open deck.

After four days land came in sight once more. After consulting our little map we decided that it must be the coast of Egypt near the entrance to the Gulf of Suez. An occasional clump of palm trees in a patch of greenery relieved the dry, flat, sandy landscape, with a few white, flat-topped buildings bordering black ribbons, which could only be tarmac roads winding their way into the sandy interior. The wind had now changed direction, coming down from the Nile Delta in the north, and it wafted a cooler breeze, carrying with it a hint of strange and unusual odours.

On the morning after we had entered the Gulf of Suez, we were sitting at our tables on the mess deck along with the rest of our unit, having enjoyed a well-cooked breakfast, when Sergeant Ross came down the stairway. 'Stay where you are, all of you!' he said. 'Our CO's going to address everybody.' As he finished speaking the rest of our Senior NCOs entered, followed by RSM Menham, who barked 'Attention'.

As we scrambled to our feet, Lieutenant-Colonel Swindale and the other officers entered. 'Sit down,' he said. 'As you'll have realised, we're now close to Egypt, and very shortly will be entering the Suez Canal. This means we'll be within the range of enemy aircraft, now that German Armour has occupied all Libya. We've had a comparatively quiet and uneventful journey so far, but now I'm ordering you, as requested by our ship's captain, to carry your steel helmets, as well as your gas masks, with you at all times. If you hear continuous short blasts on the ship's siren an attack by enemy aircraft is imminent, so you will put on your steel helmets and take what cover you can. Captain Pomfret, Corporal Wallace and the five sick bay orderlies will remain on duty to give aid to any injured personnel. I hope none of this will be necessary, but at least we'll be prepared. Dismiss them, Sergeant Major.'

We collected our steel helmets and gas masks as ordered, and followed Captain Pomfret to the sick bay. We had no patients in the beds, and the morning queue for treatments had been growing smaller every day. That particular morning there were half a dozen with red and inflamed backs through sunbathing during the hottest part of the day without their shirts on, a couple with cut fingers after using the potato peeling knives in the galley carelessly, and one man who had missed his footing on the stairway and twisted his ankle. As we finished our morning stint Captain Pomfret said, 'I'll put a stop to this sunbathing lark – they don't realise just how much harm they could be doing to their skin. I'll ask our CO to issue an order that any man not wearing his shirt on deck will be put on a charge. That'll stop it.' He turned to go, then looked back with a grin. 'That applies to you lot as well!'

We tidied up the treatment room and wandered back to our usual spot on deck, with our steel helmets looped over our right shoulders and gas masks slung from our right shoulders across to our left sides and feeling a bit encumbered – but as Corporal Wallace remarked, 'Better safe than sorry!'

As we approached the ship's rail Billy, who was leading the way, pointed straight ahead and exclaimed in amazement, 'Hey, just look there! Buildings and cranes floating up in the air!'

Corporal Wallace stared, and snorted crossly. 'Don't talk such rubbish, Hough. How can buildings float in the air? Have you got a bottle of brandy stashed away somewhere?'

Alan, who was directly behind them, joined in. 'No, he's not talking rubbish. Just look ahead towards the horizon. The sea's a straight line, and then there's a gap of clear blue sky between the sea and the base of some tall buildings and cranes!'

We clustered behind them and stared. Billy and Alan were right. There could be no argument about the strip of blue sky that seemed to hover between the base of some buildings and the sea on the horizon. I saw the radio officer further along the deck. 'Can you come and explain this, sir?' I explained about the floating buildings, and he burst out laughing.

'What a bunch of landlubbers you are! It's plain you've not been in hot climates before,' he spluttered, scarcely able to contain his mirth.' What you're seeing is Port Suez, which is out of normal sight beyond the horizon, and the heat in the air is bending the rays of light – like a sort of lens. In about an hour Port Suez will appear on the horizon, joined up all good and proper. I mustn't waste any more time: I've gopt to make radio contact with the port authorities. We're carrying some equipment that needs to be offloaded there.' With a wave and a chuckle he turned and left us.

The radio officer was proved correct. Within an hour the floating buildings had disappeared; then they grew gradually out of the sea; at last the coastal strip on which they stood was plain for all to see, larger every minute. Before another hour had passed we were manoeuvring alongside the quay of the large port. A gangway was lowered, and the detachment of Royal Signals marched down laden with their full kit, under the watchful eye of a captain and staff sergeant. Further along, one of the huge cranes swung out over our ship and began lifting ashore light trucks and various crates of equipment that had been roped to the deck with steel hawsers. At the same time a line of veiled Arab women clothed in flowing black robes and each carrying a large bundle on her head trotted up our gangway, to disappear down the stairway in the direction of the ship's store, returning moments later to line up at the top of the gangway. Then they went down to the quay once more, where a swarthy Arab man sitting on a wooden chair directed them to another pile of bundles. The process was repeated until all bundles were aboard.

'We'll be on our way in no time now,' came a voice from behind us. It was our friend the radio officer again. 'Our sister ship, which is travelling south towards us, is about to enter the long lake.'

'What's the long lake?' asked Corporal Wallace.

'The Suez Canal's in two stretches with a long lake in the middle, and larger northbound and southbound ships travelling in opposite directions have to pass each other in that lake. It's very tricky for them to pass in the actual canal – especially the northern part, as you'll see when we reach it. That's why we have to use a Suez Canal Company pilot to steer us through – and if I'm not mistaken that's his car pulling up at the foot of our gangway. See you later, chaps.'

We looked down and as the car halted we saw a swarthy-featured Egyptian officer, resplendent in a pale blue uniform and wearing a peaked hat with gold letters proclaiming 'Suez Canal Company Pilot', step out. The ship's captain and his first officer greeted him with much handshaking before accompanying him to the bridge.

Moments later our ship was on its way, edging slowly and carefully past numerous ships at anchor and heading for a narrow inlet, not much wider than a river mouth, where Arab sailing dhows leaned at drunken angles against the mudflats of either bank. As the land closed in so the flies returned, not in such vast swarms as before but still enough of a nuisance to have us constantly brushing them away.

We soon left the big European-style buildings of the main port. Now there were only the rough, flat-roofed hovels of the Fellaheen huddled together along the bank sides, with dogs and chickens scratching among the dirt and rubble. The jumble of mean hovels thinned out then disappeared altogether, leaving only the tarmac road disappearing into infinity, bordered by tall telegraph poles. The bare and sandy landscape was relieved only by the odd clump of palm trees and patches of spiky cactus scrub. Occasionally the desolate emptiness gave way to an oasis of parched greenery with a few flat-roofed buildings scattered around it.

'Did you see how quickly darkness fell?' asked John as we sat on the mess deck that same evening. 'It went from daylight to pitch dark in about a quarter of an hour. Come on, let's take our blankets up on deck, and get some sleep.'

With the now-familiar cries of 'Washee deckee' stirring us to wakefulness, we hastily grabbed our blankets and hurried out of the range of the spraying hosepipes. Before we disappeared below we looked around in the morning light to see that although the bank on our port side was still as close as it had been the far bank was beginning to fall away quite rapidly. We had entered the Long Lake.

Later that day, with our usual sick bay routine completed and lunch digested, we were discussing our recent stop at Port Suez, and I remembered to ask if anyone knew what was in the bundles that the Egyptian women had brought on board on their heads.

Corporal Wallace laughed. 'I mentioned them to Captain Pomfret this morning, and he said he'd watched them being emptied in the stores. They were fresh vegetables, enough to last until we reach Port Said.'

A single hoot on the ship's siren had us grabbing our steel helmets and gas masks, ready to dash to the sick bay if necessary, although, as Billy reminded us, it was supposed to be continuous hooting for an air raid warning. When we went up on deck we realised that the single hoot was a salute to our sister ship, which was about fifty yards away. We made out the figures of a few men lining the deck, some appearing to be heavily bandaged – seriously wounded casualties from the battle zone being transferred for more treatment. We waved at them, but it was difficult to tell if they could see us and soon the ship was out of sight.

The next morning we realised that our ship was moving very slowly and that both banks had closed in upon us. The ship's tannoy suddenly crackled into life. 'This is your captain speaking. We're now entering the narrowest section of the canal, which means that we're well within the range of enemy aircraft operating from airfields just over the Egyptian border. If we're attacked I'll make a warning call on this tannoy in addition to continuous hoots on the siren. May I remind you to wear your steel helmets while on deck and, unless you're required in other sections of the vessel, to stay on your mess deck until the "all clear" is announced.'

I felt a shiver run down my spine as I realised that we were finally in the combat zone, and had to be prepared for anything.

Later that morning we had finished our sick bay treatments in record time. As we relaxed Captain Pomfret said, 'Remember, if there's a raid we have to get along here as fast as we can.'

'Something like our call up to the Scottish border, last year, sir?' asked Corporal Wallace.

'Yes, something like that, only it won't be an exercise this time,' replied the captain drily.

When we finished our lunch Alan said, 'Let's go up on deck and have a proper look at this Suez Canal – now we've got to the narrow part. They reckon it's quite something to see.' Making sure our tin hats were strapped to our shoulders, we trooped up the stairs to our usual vantage spot, and stared in amazement.

Our vessel was moving at a surprisingly fast pace along a waterway not much wider than a minor road, with the massive stone slabs that formed the banking whizzing by hardly more than a few yards away. Billy rolled his eyes in mock-horror. 'I hope this pilot chap is good at steering, or else we shall have an almighty pile-up!'

At intervals on alternate sides, sandbag-reinforced machine gun emplacements were dug into the bank tops, gun barrels pointing skyward, and at longer intervals there were larger enclosures housing Bofors anti-aircraft guns. All of them were manned by Allied soldiers who were tanned to a deep coppery brown – a legacy of long service in a sunny region. As we passed close by we were hailed by cries of 'Get yer knees brown!' and 'Get some service in', while one young gunner shouted, in a thick Scottish accent, 'Are ye doon-hearted?'

We all chorused back a loud 'NO!'

'Ye ruddy soon will be!' his retort wafted back faintly on the wind.

Our progress continued uneventfully, and we had started to relax when the 'bom-bom-bom' of a Bofors gun suddenly started blazing away as we passed. For one heart-stopping moment we stared desperately skyward, expecting to see a hostile aircraft swooping down, but as none of the other guns joined in it dawned upon us that it must have been a practice firing, no doubt timed with Machiavellian glee to coincide with our passing, to keep us 'rookies' on our toes.

By early afternoon the canal banks had begun to widen out once more, and as we watched some small grey spots appeared in the sky ahead, just above the horizon. John saw them first. 'Hey – look over yonder. Is it anti-aircraft fire, do you think?'

We stared hard for a few minutes, then Billy exclaimed, 'It can't be the smoke from anti-aircraft fire, because smoke drifts away and they're staying where they are.'

A chord of memory must have struck in Arthur's mind. 'Barrage balloons!' he exclaimed in triumph. 'I knew I'd seen something like that before. I used to notice them over the harbour at Newcastle. I bet that's Port Said.'

Fascinated, we continued to watch as vague outlines formed on the skyline, and grew until we could clearly distinguish dockside installations. As our ship moved out of the widening mouth of the canal into the harbour, we saw that the whole waterfront was covered with ships at anchor. All around, slender cables climbed skywards to the familiar grey blimps which were riding proudly over the crowded harbour.

It required some careful and complicated manoeuvring for our vessel to thread its way through the maze of ships, many of which greeted us with a loud hooting of their sirens, to end up alongside a bare wharf with a single railway track running the length of it. The ship's tannoy crackled into life. 'This is your ship's captain. All personnel of the RAMC One Five One Unit will assemble on the foredeck with full kit in one hour's time, to disembark and travel by train to one of the large military transit camps here in Egypt. Goodbye – and the best of luck to you all!'

'We'd better get cracking, lads,' murmured Corporal Wallace, 'before our RSM starts to get steam coming out of his ears!'

CHAPTER

11

I stirred in my blankets as I heard the familiar sound of the Lascar deck cleaners making their morning round. But there was something different about it. I pulled the blanket away from my ear as the call came again. 'Shai – Naafi-Shai.' Suddenly I came fully awake, and sat up to find myself in a large canvas tent with ten wickerwork bed frames facing inwards towards the tent poles. As the occupants of the other beds sat up they revealed themselves to be my four friends, Corporal Wallace and four others. Full remembrance came flooding back. We were in El-Tahag Transit Camp in Egypt. Yesterday's horrendous journey in decrepit railway carriages from Port Said returned vividly, thanks to the aches and pains in my back and legs. As Arthur had grunted when we finally marched the short distance to the barbed wire enclosure in which our camp was enclosed, 'That train didn't have square wheels – it had oblong ones!'

Reaching the open gateway in the fence, we followed our CO and the rest of our officers and halted outside a large hut marked 'Reception Office'. At last RSM Menham explained that we were being put into the tents on section twelve. Each tent had ten beds, and camp orderlies would take us in groups to our tents, nine men and a junior NCO in each. We (Corporal Wallace, my four friends, four others and I) joined the first orderly and were led some distance up the hill to a tent at the end of a line. He threw back the flap and ushered us in, indicating the small paraffin hurricane lamp. He also pointed out the dining mess for our section, the toilets and ablutions, and also, some distance away, a large NAAFI building. He said that in the early mornings Egyptian staff would bring large cans of hot sweet tea that had been brewed in the NAAFI kitchens, and insisted that we should pay no more than one piastre per mug, although the Egyptians would try to haggle.

As all these memories came back to me I climbed out from under my blankets and reached into my backpack for my enamel drinking mug. As if on cue the tent flap was pulled aside and a dark-skinned Egyptian young man repeated the call 'Shai'. He held forward a large metal container still more than half-full of hot, sweet and milky tea, which he proceeded to ladle into our mugs as we held them out. 'How much?' we asked him.

'One shillin',' he asked, a hopeful gleam in his eye. We shook our heads.

'Two piastre.' We shook our heads again, took out some small English change and offered him two pennies each, which he grabbed with a glare. Gratefully we drank.

Billy put his empty mug down with a sigh of contentment. 'Wonders will never cease! That's the first time someone has brought me an early morning cup of tea since we were called up!'

Corporal Wallace pulled a face. 'Don't get carried away,' he said dryly. 'We'd better get washed, then across to the men's dining mess for breakfast. We've got to be on parade at nine o'clock outside that orderly room tent, and you know what a stickler for discipline our RSM is. If we don't turn up spick and span, dead on time, he'll have us polishing the tent pegs or something equally daft.' We couldn't argue, so, grabbing our toothbrushes, toothpaste, soap, shaving tackle and towels we headed for the ablutions – pleased to note that in the early morning coolness the hordes of flies had not yet descended upon us.

Breakfast eaten, clean and smartly attired in our khaki drill uniforms, cap badges gleaming brightly as gold, we presented ourselves for the nine o'clock parade.

'We'll be here for several days,' said our CO, 'during which the RASC drivers, who travelled along with their vehicles on a different vessel to us, will rejoin us together with all our stores and equipment, and, I'm informed, newer, larger trucks. While we wait perhaps we'll become more acclimatised to conditions out here – even our over-friendly flies. To keep us mentally alert, our officers will refresh our memories by repeating some of the lectures they gave during our earlier training. You'll also be pleased to know that a pay parade will take place in the orderly office tent, in piastres – the local currency. You may dismiss the parade now, Sergeant Major.'

It turned out to be a fairly boring day, as we listened again to some of the lectures we had sat through during our training. When Captain Pomfret's turn came round, though, we knew we would have a good laugh, because he always enlivened his talks with a few anecdotes about his days as a junior doctor back at the Royal Victoria Infirmary.

That evening we persuaded Corporal Wallace to go to the NAAFI with us. As we drew near we saw that although it was quite a large building it was also a primitive affair, constructed with a cane framework with a thick coating of plaster of paris skimmed over it. The atmosphere inside was warm and smoky, swirling around the bright electric lamps like fog. Somewhere outside the chuff-chuffing of a donkey engine driving a generator could be heard. A counter stretched across one end, behind which several men in white coats served a line of uniformed men with anything from a bottle of beer to a cup of tea, from a block of chocolate to a plate of fried egg and chips. Having missed the evening meal in the dining hall we decided to risk the egg and chips. Billy and John chose to try a bottle of locally brewed beer, while the rest of us opted for a mug of tea. We paid with the ten piastre notes we had been issued with that morning, and received as change a handful of coins with a hole in the middle and squiggly Arabic characters on them. 'Looks like a right load of old iron,' muttered John as he threw the coins down beside his plate. 'Our CO said we were being paid in piastres, but this lad in front of me in the queue was calling them "ackers". It's all very confusing,' he said grumpily.

'I don't care what they call it as long as it buys this stuff,' chortled Billy, taking a swig from his beer bottle. 'To your very good health, gentlemen!' he said, raising his bottle in salute before taking another thirst-quenching gulp.

Although the place was very busy, we had managed to find an empty table large enough to accommodate the six of us, and as we sat down Alan nodded to the four Royal Artillery gunners at the next table. They were obviously not newcomers, with faces tanned to a deep bronze and hair bleached to blond, a sure sign of many days spent in the desert sun. 'Seen the film showing down at "Shafto's Shuftis"?' one of them asked. 'It's one of George Formby's early ones.'

'Film? Shafto's Shuftis?' exclaimed Corporal Wallace. 'Are you telling us there's a cinema with a fancy name out here in the desert?'

The second gunner laughed. 'This Egyptian bloke called Shafto has fitted up a series of open air cinemas in the Allied military transit camps.

"Shufti" is Egyptian Arabic for looking, seeing or showing. They're just a rectangle of desert fenced around with a tall cane and plaster fence, plain wood seats, a big screen at one end and a projector at the other. It costs twenty-five ackers to get in. The films go back to the early 1930s. They're all scratched and the sound's tinny. They break down regularly too. At least it reminds you of life at home.'

'How long have you lot been out here?' enquired the third gunner.

'Well . . . to be honest, this is our first full day ashore,' murmured Corporal Wallace, with a sheepish grin.

'No need to apologise. I could see your skins were a bit pale. Anyway, it's time we had some fresh faces out here.'

We sat chatting as we finished our eggs and chips, and learned that the gunners' unit, part of the original Western Desert Force, had come back for a rest and refit after falling back, greatly out-numbered and out-gunned but fighting a rearguard action all the way, against Rommel's Afrika Korps. It was only the 'wire' – the massive barbed wire fence with minefields on either side, which separated Egypt and Libya – and the fact that the Germans needed fresh supplies which had enabled our weary desert troops to escape capture.

'We were among the first lot sent in to chase the Italians back across the border when they invaded Egyptian territory. We chased them all the way back through Western Egypt, all the way through Libya, as far as El-Agheila on the borders of Tripolitania. You should have seen the Italian prisoners, thousands of them, all waving their white flags and waiting to be picked up. If only we'd had the fuel, ammunition and supplies to keep going we could have made it all the way to Tripoli before Rommel and his Afrika Korps came out here. Fuel, ammunition, supplies over vast distances: those are the big problems,' said the fourth gunner, shaking his head sadly. 'We lost a lot of good mates out there, particularly at Halfaya Pass where the only proper road comes down into Egypt from Libya. Some of the Jerrys got through as far as Sollum, but fortunately for us some of the troops who came out in your big convoy managed to make it up there with their tanks and guns, and that's where they've held him.'

'What's it like in the desert?' I asked the first gunner.

'Like it is in this camp, mate. Sand and more sand – only up there you get firm stuff you can drive on as well as soft stuff you get bogged down in. Often there are rocky patches, steep hills and deep valleys – we call them wadis. Then you get big patches of desert scrub – a cactus kind of greenery, and you need to keep well away from them. That's where the desert life flourishes – scorpions, black ones and green ones, snakes, spiders, lizards and flies of course, thousands of them, ready and waiting every time you halt. Don't worry: you'll soon get used to them. There's only one proper tarmac road, and that hugs the coastline all the way up from Egypt, Libya, Cyrenaica and through Tripolitania to Tunisia. There are no front lines or trenches, so apart from the odd minefields like the ones at the Egyptian border wire, and around Tobruk, a port on the Libyan coast where the Ninth Australian Division troops managed to establish a strongpoint during our withdrawal eastwards, it's all a great big open space where each side can nip around the enemy and duff them up – until you run out of fuel or ammo.'

The second gunner spoke up. 'What mob are you in, lads?'

'RAMC,' replied Corporal Wallace. 'Light Field Ambulance. We'll be setting up mobile advance dressing stations and main dressing stations as close to battle as we can get, to give proper emergency treatment to casualties as quickly as possible and move them out of danger. I guess you lads think we might be in the way, with all this to-ing and fro-ing.'

'No way, Corp!' exclaimed the third gunner. 'Emergency treatment's what we need. Just one word of advice. Organise your setup so that you can always make a quick move if something brews up. Then you'll be able to carry on with your job as soon as the skirmish dies down, instead of having your trucks shot up and being taken prisoner of war.'

The fourth gunner laughed and stood up. 'Come on, you three. It's a mile back to our lines, so we'd better be on our way now we've managed to put the wind up these newcomers. Maybe we'll meet you again some day – though not in your official capacity, I hope!' With cheerful waves, they walked away.

'Do you think they really were trying to put the wind up us?' asked John.

'Maybe just a bit,' I said, 'but it makes sense when you think about it. After a quick move you're out of danger and still able to give assistance where it's most needed – a bit like those rapid moves up and down we did during our training exercises. We used to moan and call it a waste of time and energy, but it looks as if we'll soon be doing quite a bit of dashing up and down.'

★ ★ ★

A few days later the boring calm of our days in El-Tahag were interrupted by the sudden return of our RASC drivers and personnel, bringing with them all the trucks, lighter vehicles and officers' staff cars. As they drove into the campsite, and quickly dispersed on to a large empty space just beyond the next block of tents to ours, we realised that our one ton trucks had been replaced by larger three tonners, loaded with stores and equipment. There were also quite a few fifteen hundredweight vehicles. All had been painted a dull yellow-brownish colour, instead of the light and dark brown and green camouflage used in our home country. We noticed that every vehicle had a small emblem painted on its front mudguard.

We had just finished our breakfast and were waiting for the morning parade, when Captain Pomfret, accompanied by Sergeant Ross, approached, and Corporal Wallace immediately saluted. Captain Pomfret acknowledged him with a smile. 'Don't get worked up – I'm not grabbing you for fatigue duties. I just want to let you know that we're about to embark on a further stage of training.'

'All the unit, sir?' we asked.

'No, they need a bit more time yet, but Corporal Walter, you five, Sergeant Ross and myself, after our extra work together as a small team, are about to be sent "up the blue" – which is how the seasoned troops refer to the desert – as a first experimental advance dressing station.'

'You mean we're actually going into action, sir?' asked Corporal Walter, a trifle anxiously. 'Up among the tanks and guns?'

'No, not quite so far yet, Corporal. We'll be going about ninety miles, about half-way to the present forward position, where we seem to have reached stalemate. You've just seen our vehicles arrive after a very early morning start from the docks, so after our driver has finished his breakfast we'll join him at our new three ton truck, to check out the equipment on board, collect any further stuff we need and re-pack it if necessary for comfort in travelling. You're excused from attending the morning parade, so until our driver turns up I suggest you pay a visit to the NAAFI and stock up on personal necessities like razor blades, shaving cream, soap, toothpaste and so on. There's no telling when we'll get another chance.'

'What's that funny little emblem on the mudguard of our vehicles, sir?' asked Billy.

'That funny little emblem, as you call it, is the Jerboa or desert rat, the insignia of the recently depleted Seventh Armoured Brigade who took such a bashing from Rommel. They've now been re-formed, rearmed with newer, heavier armour, and consolidated into the Seventh Armoured Division, all displaying the Jerboa emblem, and we're part of it. "Desert Rats", that's what we are. Now make yourselves scarce, before RSM Menham decides you ought to join the morning parade. We'll be moving out immediately after lunch.' Our captain left us and, taking heed of his advice, we disappeared to the NAAFI to purchase most of our requirements and then enjoy a mug of tea and a scone while the morning parade was completed.

As we walked back to the new trucks we caught sight of new ambulances sweeping in through the gateway. They too were sandy coloured now, with giant red crosses on white circles adorning the sides and roof. Billy chuckled, 'Not much camouflage there!'

Reaching the trucks we caught sight of Bert Bell, the RASC driver who had been with us during our previous training. He stood at the back of one of the three-tonners, gazing anxiously around. As soon as he saw us he waved and beckoned. 'I was waiting for you lot to come off parade, but you weren't there. I've just been told I'll be transporting you and Sergeant Ross in the wake of Captain Pomfret's staff car and one or two other vehicles way up the open desert to goodness knows where. Come on, climb aboard, and I'll run you down to the QM stores tent so you can check the tackle I'm carrying, pick up anything more we need and stack everything properly. The captain and Sergeant Ross are waiting for us down there.'

When Bert pulled up at the stores tent a small petrol-burning cooking stove was being loaded aboard a fifteen hundredweight truck, to stand amid crates and boxes of rations already in place. Jim Miller, one of the cooks who had been with us down in Ludford, was supervising the operation. He saw us and called out, 'A bit like Ludford and the Scottish borders, only more so, eh?'

After a couple of hours' hard labour in the heat of the sun, we had checked everything, collected several more items such as half a dozen metal water carriers shaped a bit like petrol cans, which we filled with water from the taps outside the cookhouse, added the stack of medical equipment, medicines, dressings and bandages that our captain and sergeant had selected from the QM's store, and reloaded the whole lot with care. We were left with a huge folded square of heavy canvas sheeting.

'Where on earth are we going to put that?' asked Corporal Wallace, frowning. 'It's going to clutter up the space where we sit!'

'It's very important,' said Captain Pomfret. 'It's our new treatment tent – a single canvas sheet we fasten to the truck's front superstructure, and peg out behind, giving cover and shade to a lot more casualties on stretchers than the original side shelters. If you look you'll see ropes attached to it. You haul it up on top of the truck body and tie it on firmly. Then when we set up to do our job we spread the sheet out, pinning it down with those big steel tent pegs you've loaded aboard.'

It was a bit of a struggle to haul the sheet up on top of the truck, but it was soon secured firmly.

We were on our way, our little convoy led by Captain Pomfret's staff car driver/batman. As we boarded our truck after eating our lunch and collecting our kit and bedding from the tent, waving cheerio to a group of our comrades, we noticed that another two vehicles had joined our line-up. One was an ambulance, with Cliff Rigg as orderly and driven by Driver Smith, the other a strange boxy looking fifteen hundredweight. Before we set out Billy, inquisitive as ever, questioned little Jack Turner, the driver, about it.

'Only the most important truck in our unit from now on,' was his reply. 'I'm the water cart man. Once we're out in the desert every drop of water we use will come from this special tanker. I've been on a course to learn how to test and purify the water we'll be collecting regularly from the oasis wells scattered about. There ain't no water mains and taps there, you know!'

We travelled for quite a time on the tarmac road heading west before turning off. A small cairn of stones marked the beginning of a hard, rocky, sandy track leading toward the bare landscape, and our staff car halted with a swirl of dust. Captain Pomfret stepped out, signalling us to join him. 'Before we go any further I think it's as well to talk about what we're aiming to do on this final training exercise, before we find ourselves in the thick of the desert conflict. From this point we'll be out in the open desert with no tarmac roads and no road signs. As the leader of this convoy I have to find our way, using map references and compass readings, to a point close to Bir Habiba, which I've highlighted in red on my map. We're fortunate that this rocky track continues for most of the distance, with only the final stage through bare desert. Even so, I must stress that we will now keep one another in sight all the time.

I expect you noticed that as soon as we started driving on this track we raised quite a cloud of dust, getting worse as each vehicle stirs up more, so each of you must watch the one before you and make sure the one behind is still in sight. Can you understand the logic in that?' We all nodded agreement. 'We'll move off in the following order: my car first, then the water truck, the cook's truck, the ADS truck and, bringing up the rear, the ambulance. Right – everybody back on board and off we go.'

After we had travelled for some time along the track it became clear that our progress was not going to be comfortable. For some reason the dust clouds raised by the vehicles in front swirled into the open rear of our truck, covering our sweating faces and arms, getting into our noses, eyes and throats and making us cough and splutter. We took some lint dressings from one of the panniers and held them over our faces, which brought some relief.

When our staff car drew up beside another cairn of stones and the captain signalled us to join him once more, we staggered down, hair, faces (apart from a small area where we had held the lint) and clothing covered in a film of fine yellow dust. Captain Pomfret stared in amazement. 'Who are you strange desert creatures?' he exclaimed, a broad grin lighting up his face. 'And what have you done to the fine medical treatment team who set out from El-Tahag with me?' After a lot of flapping, shaking and wiping we began to look human, and Captain Pomfret was serious again. 'We need to make some changes. I'm all right at the front, but each vehicle is throwing up such a dust cloud in its wake that I think we need to travel in an arrow formation rather than a straight line. We'll still be close enough to see one another, but we'll each have a clear space in front of us. As for you "sandmen" in the ADS truck, by travelling with the truck front canvas closed you created a vacuum, which sucked in the sand. Try opening it and tying it back. In our new formation you'll have a virtually dust-free breeze blowing through – it'll make it cooler for you as well. Come along then – just a mile or two more.'

Of course he was right. Though a narrow slipstream of sandy dust stretched out behind each vehicle, our 'arrow-head' formation kept everyone clear of too much dust, while out open front canvas cooled us. The rest of our journey, if not idyllic, was at least bearable.

After a couple more miles we crested the brow of a low hill to see that we were approaching a flat plain, with another low hill half a mile further on. The surface of this level stretch seemed to be quite firm, and was dotted here and there with small clumps of dull green cactuses.

The staff car halted, and our captain waved us all to join him. 'Well, this is it!' he exclaimed. 'It tallies with our map reference and mileage reading – and I was told to look out for a firm plain between two hills. We won't put the shelter up today because it gets dark quite early out here, so Sergeant Ross, if you will supervise the parking of our section truck thirty yards further in with its front facing this way, and have your men pitch their bivouacs a little further on – avoiding any desert scrub, I would advise. Cookhouse truck, thirty yards to our left: set up the cooking stove and get our evening meal cracking sharpish. Water truck, next to the cookhouse. My driver will put up my tent and his bivouac in the middle, with the ambulance close by.

For a while it was bedlam as we carried out the captain's orders, but soon the whooshing sound of the petrol-fired cookhouse stove could be clearly heard, followed shortly afterward by the bonging sound of spoon on pan as our cook Jim Miller yelled out, 'Come an' get it!' Grabbing our little-used rectangular mess tins and our enamel mugs from among our kit, we hurried over to see what was on the menu.

'Help yourselves to bread and marge,' said Jim, indicating some large metal plates on the truck tailboard. There's two big pilchards each, and you can take a spoonful of jam to finish off with. Make the most of the bread while it's still fresh – I managed to cadge it from the camp cooks. When that's done it'll be plain dry biscuits – with marge, of course, along with pilchards or bully beef for our evening meal. Mind you, I've got oats to make porridge with for breakfast, and tins of meat and veg for dinner. The tea's in the dixie there, just dip your mugs in, and there's sugar in a bakelite box and tinned milk if you want it.'

We were about to walk back to our truck with our food when we heard music coming from the cookhouse truck. We turned back to ask Jim about it. 'Oh, it's that radio we used to have in the canteen truck back in England. It got shoved in with the stores that were brought out here. I spotted it this morning in the QM tent and managed to bung it in the truck along with our rations. I connected it up to the truck battery, and then I just switched it on and twiddled the knobs.'

We listened for a moment, then the music ceased and there was the unbelievable but quite unmistakable sound of Big Ben chiming, followed by the mellow, modulated tones of a BBC newsreader faintly but quite clearly saying, 'This is London calling.' We stood transfixed as the voice recounted the latest news. There had been a heavy air raid on London the previous night with a large number of fires. Rommel's Afrika Korps had made another attempt to penetrate Allied positions within the Egyptian border, but thanks to heavy and accurate fire by our artillery the attack had been beaten off and the Germans had been forced to retire without gaining any ground. The news concluded with the statement that fresh Allied troops and Armour had recently arrived in the Middle East, greatly strengthening General Wavell's Western Desert Force.

'That must be our convoy,' I said to Alan.

'It's not quite the radio miracle you imagine,' said Captain Pomfret, who had come up behind us with his batman. 'What you're hearing is Radio Cairo. They've agreed to relay the BBC six o'clock evening news for the sake of our troops in Egypt.' He turned to Jack Turner, who had collected his meal and was about to go back to the water truck. 'I'm glad I caught you. Tomorrow morning, after you've filled up everybody's water bottle, the cookhouse and any other containers, I want you to go to the nearest oasis desert well to test, purify and refill your water container. It's only a mile the other side of the hill that's facing us, and I've asked Sergeant Ross to accompany you on this first visit. He'll take my compass and you'll travel on a compass bearing there and back. It'll be a good exercise for both of you!

'Once you've all eaten your meal, and before the daylight's disappeared entirely, pass the word round that I want you all to be outside my tent so I can tell you what we must and mustn't do out here in the desert.'

A little later, as instructed, we gathered outside the captain's tent. 'Firstly, no lights to show after dark – as they tempt enemy aircraft,' he said. 'Next, we need a night guard: three men, four hours each, 8.00p.m. to 8.00a.m. for safety's sake for tonight, then we'll work out a rota later. What about you three tonight – Hill, Wright and Copley?'

The transition from twilight to darkness had happened very rapidly, but now a bright moon gave an eerie glow. I, as the first guard, had been on duty for two hours, pacing around rather nervously, when I heard a rustle behind me. Spinning round, I saw it was Captain Pomfret. 'We're so cut off and on our own out here, sir,' I stammered.

'No, you're wrong. Just over the hill a small detachment of Royal Signals is in daily radio contact with Tahag Camp. Our CO and I could communicate at any time.'

Much relieved, I finished my duty.

CHAPTER 12

'Fifteen minutes to put it up, ten to take it down!' exclaimed Sergeant Ross, consulting his watch. 'Better, but still not good enough!'

'Not good enough!' muttered Billy, wiping the sweat from his brow and brushing the flies away from his eyes. 'He's turning out to be a proper slave driver!'

'I heard that, Hough,' grinned Sergeant Ross. 'One of these days you might thank me for pushing you to the limit!'

It was now almost three weeks since we had left El-Tahag, and each morning Captain Pomfret went over the nearby hill with his driver to contact our CO via the radio link. This was now made easier by the arrival in our main unit of a radio van complete with operator, a vital and permanent addition.

During our short time up the blue we had begun to adapt to the new routine imposed by life in the desert, one of the hardest being fluid intake. Our daily ration was limited to one full waterbottle a day and three mugs of tea, one at each of our three meals. This presented a problem with our early morning wash and shave until we noticed that every morning, because of the cold nights, the outside of our bivouac roofs were covered in drops of dew. If we wiped it on to our facecloths before the burning sun could evaporate it we had enough moisture to sponge ourselves and to shave. This also solved for me the mystery of how the clumps of cactus, with their population of flies, insects and reptiles, managed to survive in this dried-up desert area.

Most mornings we persevered with our 'put up, pull down' exercises, leaving the canvas erected in the afternoon. In its shade Captain

Pomfret discussed with us the problems we would have to face during any forthcoming battles. 'I'm convinced that after carrying out the first examination and treatment, such as cleaning up wounds, stopping haemorrhages, and applying sterile dressings and so on, we ought to move them out of the forward area as rapidly as we can. We may need more than one ambulance – one for stretcher cases and one for walking wounded.'

One morning we had managed to get our shelter erected and ready for use in the record time of ten minutes, and, feeling quite proud of our achievement, were about to start the 'pulling down' process, when Captain Pomfret's car swished to a halt in a cloud of dust beside us. With a word to his driver to park the car he stepped out and waved us to join him. 'Leave that canvas up. Our services are needed!'

'Why? What's happened, sir?' asked Sergeant Ross, an excited gleam in his eye. 'Has Rommel made a break-through?'

'No, nothing like that, although something could brew up at any time, I'm sure. A small REME section's moved up, close to the Royal Signals, and one or two of their men have gone down with sand fly fever. They need bedding down and a bit of nursing care for a few days. Some of the others have scraped their hands, and the abrasions are turning into desert sores. Both lots would like us to do sick parades for them. Our CO said to go ahead. Oh yes, and another thing. Our unit's setting out to join us later today.'

'Here, in this narrow plain, sir?' asked Billy. 'It's going to be a bit crowded, isn't it?'

'No, not just here. They'll be about half a mile over the hill there while they get acclimatised to conditions out here – water rationing, tinned or hard tack food, burning sun during the day, chilly during the night. Just the sorts of things we desert-hardened veterans have got used to!'

'So we stay here and do sick parades, that's the idea, is it, sir? How long do you think we'll stay here?'

'Hard to say, Sergeant. There are quite a few units moving up into this area at the moment, quietly and without a lot of fuss, so my guess is that something's brewing. I think it's a case of which side starts first. Anyway, I understand that our CO and RSM Menham intend to drop in on us, so I suggest you put out a few stretchers and blankets, lay out treatment and dressing trays on the tailboard, and make a bit of a show for 'em. Oh yes, put your boots on, all nicely polished. Let's give the RSM nothing to moan about – you know his obsession with boots!' he chuckled.

★ ★ ★

'Ha – very impressive set-up, Pomfret,' murmured Lieutenant-Colonel Swindale. 'Most impressive. You obviously haven't been wasting your time out here. Don't you agree, Sar'nt Major?' He turned to the diminutive warrant officer for confirmation.

'Erm, not too bad, sir,' muttered RSM Menham reluctantly. 'One or two of the stretchers not quite straight, blankets a bit out of line, but not too bad. Glad to see you've kept your boots in good nick. I'll expect to see you fellows back on parade in the morning!' he added, frowning fiercely.

'No, I think not, Sar'nt Major,' said our CO. 'I've authorised them to do sick parades and sick bay facilities, both for us and several other nearby units, so they'll have to miss your parades, I'm afraid.'

'They could come over in two lots – half one day and half the next,' said the RSM, with a hopeful gleam in his eye.

'No, leave them be. They have the experience,' said the CO in a voice that brooked no argument.

For the next couple of weeks we were kept busy treating the desert sores that the REME mechanics developed whenever they grazed their hands or arms on the equipment they were servicing. The slightest break in the skin quickly deteriorated into an ulcerated sore, unless the afflicted patients had the affected area washed and re-dressed three times daily. The really stubborn cases were treated with powdered sulphanilamide – a new drug. As John remarked, the voracious foraging flies were on to a cut or scratch the moment it occurred. 'Must be one of the ancient plagues of Egypt. I bet they don't have to put up with them up in Libya!'

'Don't you kid yourself, mate,' exclaimed a REME corporal who was waiting for treatment. 'We got up as far as Benghazi in the last push, an' they were still there waiting to pounce every morning when the sun came up.'

Next morning, having dished out breakfast to the three recovering sandfly fever patients in our sick bay, as well as their final treatment dose, we went off to the cook's truck to collect our morning meal. As we returned we noticed a familiar-looking staff car pull up outside Captain Pomfret's tent. We watched as Major Forsythe jumped out and hurried into the tent.

'There's something happening – you mark my words!' exclaimed Arthur, and as if to prove it both the major and our captain came striding over.

'Sorry to disturb your breakfasts, chaps,' said Major Forsythe, 'but the CO insisted that I should pop over right away and give you ample warning.'

'Warning?' asked Sergeant Ross. 'Is there going to be some action at last?'

'You could say that, Sergeant. You need to send your remaining sick bay patients back to their units if they're well enough or further down the line if they aren't. I'll leave Captain Pomfret to fill you in with the rest of the details. See you all shortly!' Saying which, he jumped back into his staff car, and his driver drove him away.

'You'd better all come over to my tent for a few minutes so I can put you in the picture,' said Captain Pomfret, 'all of you, drivers, cook, ambulance orderly.' We quickly swallowed our food, drank our tea and hurried across. 'Right. We don't want any of this discussed in the presence of the patients, so be wary. Later on today we'll be moving to rejoin our main unit, and at first light tomorrow we're joining up with a mobile column – part of the Seventh Armoured Division, I believe – who'll do a rapid move south, then west, then up behind Rommel's lot, who got through the Egyptian border as far as the escarpment at Sollum and have been impossible to dislodge up to now. We'll nip up behind them and catch them unawares, with any luck.'

'A bit like Rommel did to our lot – I like the sound of that!' exclaimed Arthur.

'Yes. So it's back to the shelter, discharge our patients who were due to go back to their units, deal with the sick parade, then pack up and rejoin our unit. It looks as if we'll see some action at last.'

It was first light the following morning. The guard on duty had awakened us in the first dim half-light as dawn broke, reminding us that we had rejoined our main unit the evening before. 'Not too early,' as Sergeant Ross had warned with a grin, 'or our RSM will jump at the chance of making up for the times you've missed guard duty!' We had timed it very nicely, just in time for the evening meal but after the night guard had been appointed. We had emptied our water bottle dregs into a tin that we had stowed in our truck for a quick wash and shave, before refilling the bottles at the water truck, then queueing at the cookhouse truck for our ration of porridge, made from dry biscuits and tinned milk, followed by tinned beans and sausage, and, of course, a mug of tea.

We sat waiting in anxious silence for the order to move away. Our RASC officer, Lieutenant Landon, had instructed our drivers concerning the order in which we would travel, and now we were parked in that order, taking into account the lessons we had learned during our section's first desert move. In the silence I wondered if I could cope with the injured, comfort the dying and stay calm, as I had been taught.

The CO's staff car was at the point of the arrow, with Major Forsythe to the right and behind, the radio truck to the left and behind, with the rest of the vehicles fanned out in V formation behind. We were part-way down on the left-hand side. The upper front of our truck was open, and Billy was perched on the front of the framework, so that he could alert us of any hostile aircraft. When he saw the radio truck driver wave a green flag out of his window – the signal to move off – with the revving of many engines the convoy began to travel south, working on the compass settings and mileage readings given to our leading vehicle.

We had travelled for several hours when a red flag was waved from the radio truck window and the CO's car halted, followed by the rest of us. Major Forsythe hurried forward to the leading car, waving the rest of the officers to follow him, and a short discussion took place, at the end of which the officers drove round the convoy to pass on further instructions. Captain Pomfret went to the cookhouse truck first, then over to us. 'This is our southern limit. We halt here until our radio operator gets our westward compass and mileage settings. You're to go from each truck in turn to collect the bully and biscuits and tea that was prepared this morning. If you need to answer the call of nature don't stray too far: we could be moving off again at any time.'

'I haven't seen anything of the armoured column we're supposed to be with, sir,' said Billy, with a puzzled frown.

'No, you won't – they're a good ten miles west of us, and we'll maintain that gap until we reach our stopping point. Now off you go and collect your delightful three course lunch!'

We had just finished eating when the green flag appeared again at the radio truck window. The sounding of our CO's car horn had us scrambling aboard once more, this time heading west. I said to Billy, 'You've done a long spell on lookout. I'll take over so you can have a break' He settled into the niche I had occupied during the first part of our journey while I clambered up on top. The sun beat down relentlessly, and it was only the breeze from our forward motion that saved me from getting overheated. We were now in an area well away from any proper desert tracks, its surface fluctuating between rocky hardness and soft sand, and divided by shallow wadis and banks, so it was impossible even in my lofty position to see very far ahead. I once saw a moving speck in the sky which looked like an aeroplane, but it never approached us so I didn't know whether it was ours or theirs. During the afternoon the red flag appeared again, and the CO's car stopped as the radio operator ran to him with a slip of paper. We wondered whether we should dismount, but our lieutenant-colonel signalled us to stay put, pointing in a north/north-westerly direction. We were changing direction again, following our armoured column towards the rear of the enemy.

We started off once more and continued until the sun was sinking in the west, when the red flag was hoisted. Captain Pomfret told us that we were stopping for the night and would move off again the following morning to our destination point. We were to sleep in our trucks or wrapped in our blankets on the sand. Night guards had been notified and would keep watch over us as we slept. Our cookhouse was going to heat up tins of 'Machonachies' meat and veg on the portable stove, and the gong would sound when it was ready. We all started climbing out of the vehicles, stretching and yawning and staring north, as if expecting hostile activity to erupt at any moment.

The next morning the guard on final shift bawled 'Wakey, wakey' in the half-light of early dawn. We had opted to sleep in the truck because, as Corporal Wallace reminded us, 'There's no telling if any of our insect or reptile friends are waiting down there in that rough patch to greet us.'

After a quick sponge with a damp facecloth, and a hurried breakfast of 'biscuit burghoo', as our desert porridge was nicknamed, our convoy moved forward once more. After about three-quarters of an hour, at a further signal from the radio truck, we came to a sudden halt. As the racket of our travelling ceased another, more disturbing, sound fell on our ears: the solid 'whump' of artillery fire, intermingled with the staccato rattle of machine gunning, had the hairs on the backs of our necks rising and our hearts beating faster.

'What's going on out there?' asked Corporal Wallace of John, who was on lookout above.

'Don't know – I can't see anything. It seems to be coming from somewhere ahead, beyond a range of low hills. But Captain Pomfret's car's on its way towards us.'

'Park the section truck a hundred yards over there and get your shelter up,' called our captain grimly. 'We're in business.'

Bert moved the truck to the position indicated, and we whipped the canvas into place, pegging it securely, and laid out the stretchers on the floor and equipment on the tailboard, the thumps and rattles rising and falling in intensity ahead of us, becoming a background chorus.

Captain Pomfret, who had gone to join the CO at the radio truck, returned. 'We've sent a couple of the ambulances to a spot four miles further north to pick up some casualties, where our armoured column's come up against fierce resistance. We may need to send more if we have many wounded troops. So this is it – this is what it's all about, chaps.'

We stood there, Sergeant Ross, Corporal Wallace, Alan, Arthur, Billy, John and me, tight lipped and in grim silence now the time of testing was upon us. Our nerves jangled with the new experience.

Captain Pomfret took one look at us, and his face split into a huge grin. 'What miserable-looking sods you are! I wish you could see yourselves in a mirror. The last thing a wounded bloke needs to see when he comes in for treatment is nursing orderlies pulling faces like a bunch of funeral directors. Come on, lads, lighten up. After all, this is what I spent hours lecturing you about, isn't it?' His grin was infectious and we relaxed a little, recognising the truth in what he said.

We had not long to wait before the first ambulance growled to a standstill outside our shelter. Cliff Rigg came in with four walking wounded and said, 'I've got four stretcher cases as well. Can you help us bring them in, please?'

Now we had something positive to do the adrenalin started to flow, and John, Arthur and Alan went out to assist. As the first walking patient, wearing the badges of an infantry regiment and the rank of sergeant major, staggered in, I stepped forward, and felt my stomach constrict into a tight knot at the sight that confronted me. All of one side of his face was a mass of raw bleeding flesh, with bits of his jawbone missing. I swallowed hard, took a firm grip on myself and started to direct him towards one of the stretchers, but he shook off my hand and growled, 'I'm all right. See to yon other lads on stretchers first.' He steadfastly refused to sit down, much less receive attention, until all the other casualties had been seen by Captain Pomfret and we had carried out the treatments ordered. Sergeant Ross documented number, rank, name and details of injuries and treatment on a special card and envelope, and handed them to each patient as he departed.

'A brave man, that,' murmured our captain, when the casualties were back in the ambulance ready to continue their journey down to the casualty clearing station.

No sooner had the ambulance departed than two more drew up. Soon, as they came and went, we became so immersed in carrying out the treatments that our apprehension lifted. We had put on rubber gloves in order to avoid spreading infection in the wounds, but smears of blood were beginning to appear on our khaki shirts and even on our faces. We were so busy that we hardly noticed when our CO accompanied by Major Forsythe strode into the shelter and held a muttered conversation with our captain, and it was only when there was a lull in the constant stream of ambulances that we realised our CO and the major had departed.

Sergeant Ross, thankful that a breathing space had arisen, stepped outside to make sure that we really had caught up with the flow of ambulances. He dashed back in, exclaiming, 'We're on our own, sir – the rest of the unit's disappeared!'

Captain Pomfret looked up with a tired grin. 'That's right, Sergeant. They've been ordered back east fifteen miles, to set up their main dressing station as a staging post.. Apparently our Armour's come up against some quite formidable opposition, and it could go either way. We're staying here as the advance dressing station until this lot gets sorted out. It won't be too long before our lot breaks through and starts moving again, I hope. When that happens Captain Gemmel's section will leapfrog us and be forward ADS – unless, of course, we make a major breakthrough, in which case we'll all move up.'

Even as our captain spoke two more ambulances rolled up, and we were working once again.

'What's happening up there?' Alan enquired of an infantryman with a flesh wound in his arm.

'It's sheer hell, mate! Jerry was waiting for us on three sides, and we didn't stand a chance!'

His companion on the next stretcher butted in. 'I saw some of our tanks going in as we came away. They'll soon sort Jerry out!'

When the next lull came, Billy said, 'My mouth's like the inside of an old brick kiln. Let's put the dixie on the primus stove and have a brew!'

'We'll need to be quick about it,' muttered Corporal Wallace. 'We no sooner get rid of one lot than another turns up.'

'I'll do it,' said Arthur, rooting in the back of the truck for the soot-encrusted aluminium container, and pouring some water into it. Above the noise of the lighted stove the background noises continued to rise and fall in intensity. Bubbles were just beginning to rise in the dixie when the arrival of another ambulance brought an anguished groan of frustration from Billy. All thoughts of quenching our thirst had to be put on one side, as every hand was needed to cope with the fresh influx. I helped Cliff bring in a stretcher carrying a badly burned tank driver. 'What do you make of things up there?' I asked. 'Are we making any headway?'

'Hard to say,' he answered. 'You see, there's this escarpment that's changed hands four times already today. At the moment Jerry's got it again.'

'Trouble is, we keep getting our tanks knocked out before we get our guns in range of theirs.' grunted another tank man whom Alan was attending. 'A lot of their tank guns have got nearly twice the range of ours, so unless we can dash in and get them at close range they pick us off, one after another!'

'Doesn't sound too good,' said Billy.

'Never mind about that – where's that mug of tea you were on about?' asked Captain Pomfret, running a tired hand through his hair.

'Sorry, sir,' murmured Arthur apologetically. 'I'm afraid that last influx of patients put the kybosh on it!'

'Oh no it didn't,' came a voice from the front of the truck. Bert stepped into the shelter. 'It's ready. I could see that you'd no chance, the way the casualties were turning up, so I carried the primus and the dixie round to the front of the truck and kept the water on a low light till I saw you were getting clear.'

'Thanks, Bert', said Sergeant Ross. 'I reckon you've just about saved our lives. I couldn't have gone on much longer without a drink!'

'It's the least I could do,' replied Bert, handing out the wonderful steaming hot tea. 'I feel so useless standing around while you lot are up to your eyeballs in blood and bandages. I've opened a tin of corned beef as well, and fished out some packets of those dry biscuits – anybody want any?'

'Bert – you're our guardian angel!' said Captain Pomfret. 'You do a fantastic job driving and caring for our section truck and we'd be completely lost without you, so no more talk about being useless if you please!'

We had hardly time to gulp our tea and snatch a bite of 'bully and biscuits' before the next ambulances were outside. They kept on arriving, sometimes singly, sometimes in twos or even threes, with very little respite, until daylight faded and was replaced by brilliant moonlight.

Now we could see, over the northern horizon, flares, flashes and other disquieting evidence of the continuation of hostilities. Billy muttered, 'I've got an uneasy suspicion that our breakthrough isn't happening yet!' I must admit that I was thinking much the same myself.

The ambulances continued to arrive and depart, though not as frequently as before. We worked on steadily in the dim light of a paraffin hurricane lantern, which one or other of us held close by as our captain examined each patient and we carried out the treatment he ordered.

It was well on the way to midnight when Cliff and his driver pulled up outside, and when I climbed into the ambulance to see what he had brought I was a bit taken aback to find five wounded Italian carabinieri. 'This is the last lot I picked up at the collection point,' said Cliff. 'It's getting too dangerous to do any more moving around tonight, so they will have to stay here overnight and we'll take 'em further down in the morning. They're our POWs, of course.'

Desperate for some rest after a wearying day, we tried to sleep, but were constantly awoken by the Italians moaning '*Mama mia*' and '*Acqua – Acqua!*' They had been examined by our captain and when we dressed their wounds we had discovered that none of them could speak English. I only knew a very limited amount of Italian, but they seemed relieved when I announced '*Domani Andare Ospedale!*' – roughly 'Tomorrow you going hospital.'

Our water was running very low with no certainty about a refill, but we gave them drinks in small sips, hoping supplies would last out. When dawn broke the following morning, still weary from our lack of sleep, we began to load the prisoners into Cliff's ambulance, having shared what biscuits and water we had with them. As the last stretcher was lifted aboard and we were retiring into our shelter we heard another vehicle draw up with a resounding roar. Captain Pomfret gave a weary groan of anguish. 'Go and have a look, Hough. See what they've sent us this time!'

Billy peered out, turning back to us with a face as white as a sheet. 'Bloody 'ell, sir – it's a German armoured car!' We stared as a German officer climbed out and came towards us, pistol in hand.

'Good morning, Herr Doktor,' he said to Captain Pomfret. 'I am Major Maurer – Panzergruppe Achte. I did not think your British Army placed its *Hauptverbandplatz* – what you call advance dressing station I believe – in front of the fighting troops.'

'Why – have you come to give yourselves up?' said Captain Pomfret with a grin.

'I see you have not lost your English sense of humour,' rapped the German major. 'It happens that you are three kilometres ahead of your own tanks, and this spot is going to be a most unhealthy place in a very short time. My Unteroffizier, who is in the SS, says I should shoot you as we do not have the time to take you prisoner. However, I tell him that in the Wehrmacht we are not such barbarians as to shoot English Red Cross soldiers who are carrying out their proper duties.'

So, what do you want us to do?' asked Captain Pomfret wearily.

'I can allow you five minutes – no more – to get out of this place. After that you are likely to come under fire from both my tanks and your own. As you prepare to leave, Herr Doktor, perhaps you could apply a dressing to this wound on my arm. A shell splinter caught me as I stood in the turret.' For the first time we noticed that his left sleeve was torn and smeared with blood.

'You heard him, lads – get cracking!' said Captain Pomfret, as he set to work cleansing and dressing the German major's arm.

The rest of us dismantled the great canvas sheet, folding it and tying it to the truck superstructure, and throwing the stretchers inside. Tiredness was forgotten as the adrenalin flowed through our bodies. Four and a half minutes later we scrambled aboard as Bert started up and revved the engine.

'What about the Italians in the ambulance?' our captain asked.

For the first time the German officer's face broke into a tiny smile. 'You may keep them, with my compliments,' he murmured. 'Thank you for treating my arm. *Auf Wiedersehen, Herr Doktor* – maybe we shall meet again some day.'

Before jumping into his staff car, the captain called to Cliff to guide us to our main dressing station, a journey that the ambulance had made several times the day before. With a roar all three vehicles raced away from the armoured car with the black crosses on it, at full speed over the ridge. As we stared out of the open rear of our truck we saw puffs of black smoke and dust blossoming up from the area we had just vacated. We passed through a line of Valentine tanks heading towards the enemy, and further back still another line of newer, larger tanks, probably part of the convoy we had travelled in – all hull down, firing over our heads and over the Valentine tanks. The whoosh of their shells sent a shiver through our spines.

'Bit of a close call, that!' shouted Corporal Wallace, when we had put enough distance between ourselves and the noise of battle to hear ourselves speak. 'I thought we'd had it that time. Fancy that German bloke letting us go!'

'Well, he did get his arm dressed in exchange,' said Alan dryly. 'Not a bad deal from our point of view.'

We rattled along as fast as the rough terrain would permit, and after about twelve miles the thumps and explosions became less noticeable. Captain Pomfret's staff car manoeuvred in front of the ambulance and he waved us to halt. 'Comfort stop, lads. This desert looks a bit dry, anyway.'

As we were climbing back into our vehicles, Sergeant Ross chuckled, 'Four and a half minutes flat to strip the shelter down and move off. I knew we could do it with a little incentive!' The sound of our vehicles starting up again drowned our replies, which were short, pithy and rather rude.

We continued our journey for another hour, with clouds of dust rising from soft, sandy stretches, until a solitary shelter came in view with a staff car and an ambulance beside it. Captain Pomfret advanced on the shelter, and we saw the short stocky figure of Captain Gemmel striding out to meet him.

'Mornin', Pomfret,' he said with a broad grin. 'We thought that you lot might be in the bag – glad to see you safe an' sound. Our main HQ's been ordered back a further forty miles while we hang on here as Number Two Advance Dressing Station. You're to continue and rejoin them. You look just about all in – what about a brew of tea before you carry on? I think our rations will stretch to that. Come inside, all of you.'

Thankfully we clambered down and trooped into the shade of the shelter. Sergeant Summer, Corporal Bird, and the rest of the section team crowded round, slapping us on the shoulders, happy to see that we had not been taken prisoner. The primus stove was lit, and we were soon drinking the most welcome mug of tea in our lives.

'What about these Italians?' asked Captain Pomfret, throwing open the ambulance rear doors to be immediately greeted by cries of '*Acqua – Acqua*'. 'Can you take them in here?'

'No – take 'em on with you. Save our stretchers for our own casualties. We've got two ambulances forward now: we thought it was them when you arrived. We'll give these fellows a drink of water, and then you can be on your way.'

'We've none of us had any proper sleep since yesterday morning,' said Captain Pomfret, 'but I think we should join up with the unit before we attempt to rest.'

Corporal Wallace noticed that the Italians were cringing away from us in fear, so I tried to reassure them by quoting that bit out of 'Dante's Inferno' that goes '*abbandona speranza chi entrava qui*' – which I thought meant 'Forget your fears and come with us'. Captain Gemmel roared with laughter. 'There's no wonder they look scared – you told them "abandon hope all ye who enter here"!'

We thanked our comrades in Number Two ADS and continued our journey, led by our staff car and following the directions given to us by Captain Gemmel.

After travelling across a bare, rock-strewn plain, climbing a sharp escarpment and dropping down the other side, through a wadi overgrown with greeny grey desert scrub, we emerged on to a wide sandy track, the surface churned up by the passage of many vehicles. Remembering the choking experience of our first journey up the blue, we spread into arrow formation to avoid the billowing dust clouds. Alan, riding on top, banged on the cab to tell us that he had seen an aircraft in the distance. Fortunately it never came near us, and we continued unhindered.

After another hour and a half of dusty progress we entered an area piled high with wooden crates, oil drums and square five gallon petrol cans, well separated from the rest to lessen the risk of accidental ignition in the burning sunshine. The whole was contained within a large barbed wire enclosure, and a long line of queuing trucks was moving slowly from dump to dump and driving out of the opposite side. 'Looks like an ordnance store,' shouted Alan from above, 'and further on there are shelters with red crosses on.'

Ten minutes later our staff car turned in through a gateway. The RASC driver on guard duty called out, 'Didn't expect to see you lot again – heard you were in the bag! Glad you got away,' he added.

'Not half so glad as we are, Tommo,' called out Alan as we came to a halt.

Captain Pomfret walked over. 'Drive to the far side of the camp, park the truck and come straight back to the cookhouse for a proper meal. I'm on my way to organise it now. After that go back to your truck, get your blankets out and your heads down – and that's an order.'

The wounded Italian prisoners were handed over to the main dressing station to be checked over. The next day they were to be sent further still down the line to finish up, after recovery, in a prisoner of war camp.

The news of our return had not spread round the camp so, barely able to keep our eyes open, we drifted back to our truck as soon as we had eaten. We dragged out our bedrolls, threw them down in the vehicle's shadow, collapsed upon them, closed our eyes and drifted away into much-needed oblivion.

Suddenly a harsh and strident voice raised a surge of rebellion in my sub-consciousness, penetrating the thick dark mist of sleep. I had no desire to listen to the bawling voice – only for the unwelcome interference to cease. But the voice became more insistent, and then something prodded me in the ribs. I managed to force an eyelid open, to discover RSM Menham standing over me. The gist of his tirade seemed to be that we were a bunch of lazy layabouts, lying stinking in bed when we ought to be up and about, and carrying on with our normal duties.

Alan and Arthur, two shapeless bundles in blankets either side of me, showed signs of uneasy movement, and a muffled voice cried out in exasperation from the far end, 'Hey, sod off and play a tune on your mouth organ!'

By now I was completely awake, and the blood froze in my veins as the RSM's cheeks flamed and his eyes seemed likely to pop out of their sockets. He strutted to the end of the line and barked, 'Who said that? Out of bed, man, immediately. Do – you – hear – me?'

I waited with baited breath for the explosion that would surely follow. The figure slowly levered itself up on one elbow, and observed wearily, 'Look, Archie, I wish you'd just go away and exercise your noisy authority somewhere else. We've been working flat out without sleep for at least twenty-eight hours, and Captain Pomfret ordered us to get our beds down and catch up on some sleep. So far we've managed all of a quarter of an hour. If you want to argue with our section officer just wake him up, but in the meantime – BLOODY WELL LEAVE US ALONE!'

The RSM's jaw dropped, the purple flush drained from his cheeks and the anger from his voice as he stammered 'Oh – er – it's you. I thought this was one of the stores trucks: I caught its men asleep here at ten o'clock this morning. I'm really sorry I disturbed you. We heard what a rough time you were having, and I'm glad you managed to get back. Get to sleep again, and I'll make sure no one else bothers you.' As the sergeant major finished speaking I felt myself drifting back to sleep once more.

CHAPTER

13

'Wakey, wakey!' said the voice in my ear.

'What time is it?' I growled.

'Six-thirty,' the voice answered as I forced one eye open.

'It can't be, it's too light. You can't kid me – it's always dark by six-thirty in the evening.'

'That's right, but it's six-thirty in the morning. You lot have practically slept the clock round!'

I sat bolt upright, to discover that one of our RASC drivers, obviously on guard duty, was standing over me with a huge grin on his face. Alan and Arthur were sitting up as well, and the breakfast gong had begun to sound. Corporal Wallace, John and Billy roused themselves, and we made a concerted dash to grab our washing and shaving kit, hoping to use what water we had left in our bottles for the purpose. It came as a very welcome surprise to find that these were now full, as were the section's water containers.

As we left the cookhouse truck carrying our breakfast 'burghou' and fried bacon (tinned, of course) with beans in our mess tins, we bumped into Bert. 'Have you seen anything of Sergeant Ross?' Corporal Wallace asked. 'He was in his blanket by our truck yesterday when we finally managed to get to sleep.'

Bert laughed. 'He was up and about early, and he went off with Cliff Rigg's ambulance and the Italians to pick up some more medical stuff, dressings, bandages, antiseptics and so on, from the casualty clearing station. He'd been on the radio to them beforehand. Your stuff must have been just about cleared out after the last few days. They had an early breakfast before they set out, as did Captain Pomfret.'

'Has he gone down there as well?' asked Billy.

'Oh no – he got on the radio to the ordnance point. He'd heard they've got some new bigger, stronger water containers, German ones that the Ities left behind. He's gone to see if he can wheedle some out of them for us – and if you're wondering how your water bottles got filled up, I persuaded Jack Turner to bring his water cart and replenish you while you were in the land of nod. I do have some uses, you know!'

A little later on in the morning Captain Pomfret's staff car returned in a swirl of dust as his driver pulled up alongside our section truck. The captain stepped out, opened the rear door and lifted out several strong black oblong metal containers, almost like suitcases except that they stood on the narrower side, with strong handles on the narrow upper side. 'Jerrycans!' he exclaimed. 'The Germans carry water or petrol in these. They fasten up securely and don't leak. They're just what we need. Our ordnance chaps are so impressed with them that they've sent a sample down to Cairo to have a load more made – only ours will be green, not black.'

'We were afraid we might get the order to move off again while you were away, sir,' said Corporal Wallace. 'Any news about how things are going up there?'

'From what I can gather there's been a rare old tank battle raging day and night on the spot we vacated in such a hurry. At the moment both sides seem to have drawn back a little to lick their wounds. On the coastal sector, though, where the Italians held the high ground, the Australian troops, backed by Ten Corps, managed to make a breakthrough and pushed on up the coast road as far as Bardia. Captain Clark's Number Three ADS has gone up there with them. So far we haven't seen anything of their ambulances, so we don't know exactly what's happening. As far as we're concerned we wait here until we get further orders.'

Towards teatime Driver Smith and Cliff Rigg returned from the casualty clearing station with Sergeant Ross, who was highly delighted that he had been able to cadge quite a load of dressings and medicaments, enough to keep us going for quite a while.

★ ★ ★

We stayed put for several more frustrating days as the action around the Egyptian border simmered away in a series of local skirmishes. In the coastal sector the Germans rushed to support the Italians, and managed to halt the Allies' advance just beyond Bardia.

On the evening of our fifth day back with our main unit Captain Pomfret and Sergeant Ross called us together to tell us that on the following day we would be on the move again. The whole unit, with Captain Gemmel's ADS joining us on the way, was to travel to a wadi twenty miles short of the wire separating Egypt from Libya, to sit behind our armoured column – which had already slipped into position there. All vehicles were hidden by camouflage netting, as we would be, until the column's new tanks and Armour were given the order to break through the wire and dash straight for Tobruk, with the intention of relieving our troops who had been under siege there since the enemy breakthrough at El-Agheila, and also relieving the pressure on our lads in the Bardia sector. 'As soon as our armoured column gets through the wire we follow on, hell for leather!' exclaimed our captain.

We moved off in the early morning light, before the sun rose above the horizon. When we reached the wadi we squeezed into place behind the Armour, then quickly spread the camouflage netting over everything, so that reconnoitring enemy aircraft would not spot us. 'Remember, no naked lights at night; not even a cigarette's glow,' Captain Pomfret warned us. 'We can't afford to run the risk of being trapped here.'

'I'll be glad when we move out of this flaming wadi, sir,' said Billy, knocking a green scorpion off his boot. 'There's too much livestock here for my liking!'

Next morning we heard our Armour move forward in the early dawn light, leaving us, still under camouflage, waiting for the radio signal to follow. We kicked our heels all day, and as we laid our blankets as far from the patches of desert scrub as possible, Captain Pomfret wandered by to inform us that the next day we should be on our way. 'Our column's met little resistance so far.'

During the night I stirred. Was it gunfire I heard, or had I imagined it? I listened again, and faintly heard some sort of thudding and banging. There were no flashes in the sky, so I drifted off to sleep again.

Next morning our RASC guard wakened us as the first grey fingers of light were creeping over the horizon. We stowed our blankets, stripped away the camouflage nets and waited, pulses racing, for the order to move. After an hour with no signal from the radio truck,

Billy said, 'I'm going to climb up the wadi bank – see if I can see any sign at all!' He'd only been gone a few moments when he came racing back. 'There are an awful lot of vehicles on the track,' he said, anxiously.

'Well, there would be' said Corporal Wallace. 'Fuel and ammo trucks moving up.'

'No, not moving up – moving back. Eastwards at a hell of a lick. I can't see a single one going towards the west.'

We found out what it meant a moment or two later, when Captain Pomfret came racing around in his staff car. 'Move off in five minutes!!' he shouted, 'Get down to the track and move east – fast! Jerry's broken through to this side of the wire and is moving down the coast road. All non-armoured stuff has to get out of the way, the other side of our artillery!' Even as he finished speaking the CO and the major's staff cars and the radio truck moved off, with the rest of the unit's vehicles joining the mass exodus.

As we tagged along, Arthur shrugged his shoulders and shouted above the noise of hastening vehicles, 'I think we've had this carry-on before. It's getting to be a bit of a habit. isn't it?'

There was no stopping and starting now. All vehicles raced east, with scant regard for the great clouds of sandy dust flying up around us. After thirty miles of hard going we approached an escarpment that stretched north as far as the eye could see. As our vehicles rattled and growled their tortuous way up the hard rocky track and reached the top, the barrels of twenty-five-pounder guns, well dug in, pointed menacingly at the desert over which we had just raced. Once over the escarpment we continued our journey, though not in quite such fevered haste. 'It's a relief to see that our mates in the artillery are on the job!' murmured Alan, with a wry grin. It was a sentiment we all concurred with.

Around midday our unit vehicles drew off the track for a short break. The cookhouse truck dished out mugs of tea, dry biscuits and pilchards, and then we were on our way once more. By late afternoon we had travelled roughly ninety-eight miles east, and I was doing my turn on the roof of the truck when I called out to my comrades below, 'I'm not sure if my eyes are deceiving me, but wouldn't you say that white smoke looks as if it's coming from a moving railway train?'

They stared ahead. 'It certainly looks like that to me,' agreed Corporal Wallace, 'and I'll tell you something else. Over there on the left there's a massive stores dump!' We gazed in the direction indicated, fascinated by the vast array of equipment, rations and other stores stacked in wooden crates, but before we could confirm the source of the white smoke we had veered south, bumping along a narrower dusty track and halting on a large open sandy stretch, devoid of any treacherous greenery.

Minutes later Captain Pomfret's car came around. 'Our CO's just had word on the radio truck that our twenty-five-pounders gave Jerry's tanks such a pasting that the few still capable of moving turned round and headed back through the wire.'

'What went wrong, sir?' asked Corporal Wallace.

'Same old thing. It seems that Jerry's new tanks can still outshoot ours. It's only when they come up against our artillery that we get the upper hand,' said the captain.

'What happens next, sir?' said Sergeant Ross, leaning out of the cab window.

'Park your truck two hundred yards over there, fix your bivouacs, then put up our shelter, Sergeant. Make a good sound job of it, because it seems we're likely to be around here some time while our Armoured units are re-equipped and regrouped.'

'What about Captain Clark's ADS – anything fresh yet, sir?' asked Sergeant Ross.

'Not a word so far, but things in that sector are equally mixed up and hectic. We can only wait – and hope.'

'Was that a train I saw a few minutes ago, sir?' I asked.

'You spotted it as well, did you?' the captain replied. 'The Royal Engineers have been slogging away extending the line up beyond Mersa Matruh ever since we first moved up. Now it's doing a first-class job getting our vital requirements to us sharpish.' With a word to his driver, he moved on to explain the situation to everyone else.

Being so close to the supply depot spreadeagled either side of the new railhead meant that our unit ration truck could collect fresh and varied rations, even including bread in place of the hard and tasteless biscuits we had endured during the recent action. But we gained most satisfaction from a water pipe that had been laid alongside the railway line and connected to a small pumping station, which meant that our water truck could be filled twice daily, affording extra water for drinking and washing. It still tasted of the chlorine purifier but we had got used to that. The cookhouse truck was putting on proper cooked meals. Despite being out of tins, compared with cold bully beef or pilchards it was *haute cuisine*.

★ ★ ★

'We start doing sick parades again tomorrow morning, Sergeant Ross,' Captain Pomfret announced on our second day at the railhead site. 'Make sure everything's laid out ready to start – and put out a few stretchers in case we need to give bed care.'

'No problem, sir. How about a brew of tea? We've just made one.'

'I wouldn't like to insult you by refusing,' the captain replied with a twinkle in his eye. 'Don't forget – two sugars!'

'Hey!' exclaimed the burly Ordnance Corps soldier, 'just go easy with those tweezers if you don't mind. Talk about bringin' ruddy tears to your eyes!'

'Sorry, mate,' chuckled Arthur, 'but in this job we have to be cruel to be kind. If I don't get rid of all that nasty stuff on your desert sore it'll never get better.'

The normal treatment session that followed the morning sick parade was coming to a conclusion on our fourth day by the railhead when we were interrupted by a lot of shouting from across the camp. After our recent experiences any unexplained noises were regarded with suspicion, so Billy ran out of the shelter to discover what was going on. He poked his head back in through the flap, shouting, 'I'm sure Captain Clark's lot are back! There's no sign of their section truck – they're all climbing out of the back of a small fifteen hundredweight. They look as if they're about all in, and haven't had a wash for days.'

We dashed across to where a knot of people was gathering, and indeed it was Captain Clark, Sergeant Colston and the rest of Number Three ADS climbing out of the vehicle, their faces reddened by days in the hot sun, their clothing covered in fine white particles of sand and streaked with dark patches where perspiration had dried.

'What happened to you lot, Jim?' Alan asked the tall ginger-haired orderly.

Jim grinned, and the sand mask on his face cracked. 'We got nabbed by Jerry and taken into Bardia, where they gave us some rye bread and fresh oranges. Then some of our planes came over and dropped some bombs, and in the confusion Captain Clark helped us to sneak away. He led us on foot through the open desert until we ran into a small detachment of blokes wearing Arab clothes and riding in this fifteen hundredweight. Turns out they're a special mob of our troops who go miles behind the enemy, wrecking their stores and blowing up fuel dumps – LRDGs they call themselves. And if you're wondering why Captain Clark has no shirt on, he lost it as we were taken prisoner. If they'd known he was an officer they'd have kept him in a different place to us.'

A couple of days later Billy had been across to the QM stores truck and came racing back with an excited beam on his face. 'Guess what! Mail – stacks of it! I've just seen a whacking great bag arrive with our ration truck. The orderly office truck lot are going to dish it out in about twenty minutes.'

'That's good news,' I said. 'I was beginning to think it would never catch up with us, the way we've been racing around!' In truth, I had suffered agonies of doubt as to how my new postal address – simply name, rank, number, and 'Middle East Forces', issued to us during our first days in El-Tahag, which I had immediately sent home – could possibly work in all this turmoil.

'I'm going over to the orderly office truck with our daily sick bay roster,' called out Corporal Wallace, 'so I'll collect any mail for us.'

A quarter of an hour later he was back, his face one beaming smile and a pile of letters in his hands. 'Look at them!' he chortled, 'just look at them. There's something for every single one of us.' During the next half hour the only sound in the shelter was the tearing open of envelopes and the rustling of pages as we eagerly scanned, with a lump in our throats, the long-awaited contact with our loved ones.

'. . . such a wonderful relief at last to have an address where I can reply to all the letters you have sent me since you went away, love,' wrote Edna. 'Now, I will be able to tell you about things here at home, about how much I miss you and wait with an aching heart for the day when we can be together again. I can imagine, from your address, that you are probably in the desert where the fighting is going on – so please take what care you can. I pray every night for your safety, and your safe return . . .'

I read the letter through for the third time, swallowed the lump in my throat, folded the letter up and placed it very carefully in my wallet.

★ ★ ★

With the news being of nothing more than local skirmishes, our section was kept busy providing sick parades and sick bay facilities for our own unit and others nearby. Number Two ADS, under Captain Gemmel, had gone a few miles down below the railhead, and was doing the same there. Captain Clark and his team were resting and recovering as they waited for replacement of all the equipment that had been taken from them by the Germans, including their truck and canvas sheet.

It was round about then that Sergeant Ross came up with a bright idea. 'Instead of having the canvas anchored to the top of our truck when we're in action,' he said to Captain Pomfret, 'why don't we just fasten it with two ropes, one each side of the driver's cab down to the front mudguards, and keep a sharp knife hanging nearby. Then if there's an emergency all we have to do is slash the ropes and drive out from underneath, leaving the canvas to be reclaimed later, when the action moves away.'

'You know what, that sounds brilliant,' said the captain. 'We'll try it out next time we're up the blue, and I'll pass the idea on to the others.'

Enemy aircraft made sporadic raids on the nearby rail terminal, and although One Five One remained unscathed the planes were always a little too close for comfort. Sometimes we saw the bombs falling, followed by huge spurts of sand, and heard the dull crump of explosions. Sometimes one of our ambulances had to go over to pick up casualties.

It was while we were at the railhead that I was party to one of the strangest encounters in all my time in the desert. It had been one of those mornings, busy right up to lunchtime, and Arthur and I had just dealt with the final two patients. We had no bed patients in our shelter that day, Captain Pomfret had gone off to the officers' mess and Sergeant Ross to his. The rest of the team were collecting their lunch, and we would go for ours when they got back. Arthur had just lit the primus for tea while we waited, when a vehicle squealed to a halt outside. Peering out I saw a fifteen-hundredweight truck adorned with the jerboa insignia and the words 'Military Police', obviously en route for the large barbed wire enclosure erected nearby where enemy POWs awaited transit to the Nile Delta POW camps. A British infantryman carrying his rifle in the lowered position helped a German POW down from the open rear of the truck and marched him inside. As they entered, the guard asked, 'Could you dress this bloke's arm, please? We're escorting a bunch of these POWs, and the train's due to leave very soon.'

'What's he done?' I asked.

'Torn his arm on the barbed wire. It's just a scratch – but a bit messy.' I had been applying a dressing at the far side of the shelter, so I led the POW round there as the guard accepted Arthur's invitation of a mug of tea.

I turned to the slightly built POW. '*Sehen Wunde,*' I asked, in my schoolboy German.

He held out his forearm, displaying a four inch long scratch, mostly superficial, with blood oozing gently. ''ow do,' he said softly. I stared in amazement, sure that I had misheard.

'*Was sagst ihr?*'

''ow do,' the POW repeated patiently.

'I've just heard you say "'ow do" twice in an unmistakeable Yorkshire accent! Please can you explain what's going on!'

I went ahead with the cleansing and dressing of the wound as he told me his tale. 'Yer see, me father were a First World War POW in a camp in England, an' decided to stay there when it were all over. He bought a butcher's shop i' Manchester Road i' Bradford, brought his German fiancée over to Bradford an' married her. I were born an' brought up i' Bradford but still visited our relatives in Stuttgart. I were actually visitin' 'em when war were declared, an' they wouldn't let me return to England on account of both my parents bein' German born, an' what's more they bunged me into the Wehrmacht an' I got sent out here. I'm mighty glad ter be a POW, I can tell yer. Maybe some day I'll get back to Bradford, even though me papers call me Soldaten Schmidt!'

By now I had finished dealing with the wound, and the prisoner's infantryman guard had returned from drinking his tea. 'Come on – back to the truck!' he ordered. 'Got to have you on that goods train!' He helped the POW into the back, and the truck accelerated away with a mighty roar. As they left the prisoner gave me a little wave with his uninjured arm.

'What was that you were muttering about?' asked Arthur. 'I could hear you nattering on, but I couldn't tell what you were saying.'

As we drank our tea I related the story to him, and he shook his head in incredulity. 'I'd keep that to myself if I were you!' he said, 'or they might think you've been drinking the surgical spirit!'

I have often wondered if the tale was true and, if so, whether 'Soldaten Schmidt' was ever reunited with his parents.

★ ★ ★

'Hello, what's in the wind now?' muttered Alan one lunchtime as our captain came striding back to the shelter he had only left a few moments earlier.' I bet we're on the move again. I thought this quiet spell was too good to last!'

Corporal Wallace looked up as Captain Pomfret entered. 'Anything wrong, sir?' he asked. 'Are we moving?'

'Some of us could be, Corporal,' he answered with a straight face.

'They couldn't . . . they wouldn't split us up, sir?'

The ghost of a grin flitted across the captain's face. 'Might do – for a short time.' Suddenly he could contain his mirth no longer. 'All right, relax. We're all going to enjoy a few days' leave in Alexandria.'

'What about the patients in the sick bay?' asked Sergeant Ross.

'That's just what I'm talking about,' laughed our captain. 'We can't all go at once and leave the patients to fend for themselves. Over five weeks everyone can fit in a seven day leave period. You lot will have to go two at a time, while the rest keep things working normally. I'm giving you advance notice before it goes up on Part One Orders, so work out a rota – who goes together, and in what order.'

'That's great news, sir,' said Billy. 'I can't wait to surround myself with lots of glasses of foaming ice-cold beer!'

'You watch you don't get lured down Sister Street, young Hough,' grinned Captain Pomfret. 'There are ladies, and I use the term loosely, just waiting to pounce on innocent, well-brought-up young chaps like you.' He was still chuckling as he strode off to the officers' mess tent.

'What a stink!' exclaimed Bill Kershaw, a tall slim, ginger-haired lad who was wrinkling his nose in distaste and frowning fiercely with unconcealed disapproval as he gazed around the carriage of leave-taking troops being transported east. From our unit there were Bill and his mate, Charlie Hanson, from our main dressing station team, Cliff Rigg and Jack Morgan, ambulance orderlies, Arthur Copley and me, and four RASC drivers. We were among a crowd from nearby units, all anticipating a short but well-earned break.

I winked at Arthur. 'It's Alex,' I said.

Bill turned to me. 'Who is this Alex? He needs fumigating, he does!'

'No, Bill,' I laughed, 'Alex, short for Alexandria, the place we're heading for.'

'You mean we've got to put up with this for seven days?' he asked, aghast.

'No – it's a leather tannery several miles west. And before you ask, the REME blokes at Tahag, who told me about it, promised that the prevailing winds always blow towards the desert. They said that even if you're blind you know when you're a few miles from Alex . . .'

The six of us from the One Five One stood on the kerb of a palm tree-lined main street, watching a confused mass of traffic whizzing by in all directions with a total lack of road discipline and a cacophony of horn sounding such as we had never experienced before. We wondered how we would ever find the Regal Hotel, our specified accommodation. A horse-drawn cab lumbered along, unheedful of the honking mêlée around it, and the cab driver 'whoad' his steed to a stop beside us. 'You want Gharry, sirs?' he asked, in a thick guttural accent. 'I take you Sister Street – show you many strange things,' he added with an evil grin.

'No, you'll not take us to Sister Street,' growled Arthur, 'you'll take us to the Regal Hotel. Do you know where it is?'

'Oh yes sir, very quick. How many, pliz?'

' Six,' replied Arthur with a fierce glare. 'We go straight there, understood?'

'Oh yes sir. Pliz to climb in gharry,' replied the driver in alarm.

We clambered aboard, and with a flick of the driver's whip the horse drew them away.

'Hey, I say, what's this Regal Hotel like?' asked Charlie Hanson. 'I hope it's not some crumby, flea ridden pension.'

'Calm down, Charlie,' grinned Arthur. The lads who stayed here before say that the beds have clean cotton sheets, the food's good, and they don't charge the earth.'

It proved to be only a short distance away. We could probably have walked had we not been lumbered with our back and side pack webbing equipment. As the driver halted and we climbed out, Charlie said 'I'll pay!' and said to the driver 'How much?' He pulled some ten piastre notes from his wallet, and handed over six of them in response to the driver's request. He was about to follow us into the hotel when the driver grabbed his arm and leered, 'I wait for you – take you Sister street – you see exhibish – you see donkey and . . .'

'Get off my arm, you filthy old reprobate, and be off with you!' snapped Charlie.

A couple of REME soldiers came out of the hotel. 'Is yon misbegotten son o' a camel botherin' ye?' one of them asked. Charlie nodded. 'Leave him tae me!' exclaimed the tall red-headed Scot, who strode up to the driver, and let fly with a string of Arabic words. They had an immediate effect: the driver backed away in alarm and jumped aboard, urging his horse away at a trot.

'Thanks, mate!' said Charlie. 'What did you tell him?'

'Nuthin' much. Just threatened to chop off portions o' his anatomy if he didna' skedaddle fast. Ah tek it this is yer first time in Alex?' Charlie nodded agreement. 'Never gi'e them mair than a hauf o' whit they ask,' said the Scotsman as they moved away.

In the meantime the rest of us had presented ourselves at the reception desk in the foyer of the hotel, where a swarthy-skinned and portly man in a pale grey suit introduced himself as the manager. After entering our names in his register he banged sharply on a brass bell, whereupon two Sudanese porters in white robes, tasselled fez on their heads, appeared. Muttering something to the porters, he turned to us. 'These boys will escort you and your luggage to your room.'

The two porters picked up all our packs as if they were featherweights, and the tallest said, 'You come, pliz.' The room they showed us into was light and airy, with six single iron bedsteads with spring mattresses, clean white cotton sheets and pillowcases, and two folded woollen blankets at the foot. The tall one pointed to blackout blinds beside the two windows and said, 'Before making light, pliz be putting up blackout. If enemy plane come – boom, boom.' He rolled his eyes and showed his teeth in a wide grin as they left the room.

'Hey, this is a bit of all right,' said Bill. 'Did you notice the shower room as they brought us up? That's where I'm going right now!' Agreeing with him, we rummaged in our haversacks for soap and towel and made a dash for the showers.

Fifteen minutes later we were back in our room, with the grime of the desert swilled away, and changed into clean slacks and shirts before making our way down to the dining room, pleasantly surprised to see tables for four or six and cutlery set out on white tablecloths. Cliff sat down, smacking his lips. 'I wonder what's for dinner.'

'You mean lunch,' grinned Charlie. 'If we're going to live like gentlemen for a spell let's try to talk proper while we're here!'

One of the Sudanese porters told us that lunch was chicken, chips and green salad. 'Sounds fine to me – how about you lot?' said Charlie.

We all agreed, and the waiter disappeared towards the kitchen, returning with six plates piled high with half a chicken each and a mound of chips, the whole buried in lettuce, tomatoes, cucumber, radishes and spring onions.

Unable to wait a moment longer, Cliff grabbed his knife and fork, impaled a couple of chips and, with an expression of delighted anticipation, popped them into his mouth. He chewed for a moment or two, and his expression of delight was gradually replaced by one of disbelief, and finally distaste. 'These . . . these chips,' he spluttered. 'They're not real chips – they're ruddy well *scented*!' He spat the word out as if it was an obscenity. The Sudanese waiter backed away in alarm, as Cliff turned on him angrily.

I thought it was time I stepped in. 'Hold on, Cliff. It's no use attacking the waiter – he didn't prepare the food. When we came out of the shower, I was talking to one of the REME lads who's been here a few days, and he warned me about the chips. They're made out of yams – sweet potatoes – as they're the only kind available here. He said you get used to them eventually.'

Cliff resumed his seat, the wind taken out of his sails. 'All right,' he said, pulling a face. 'I'll eat 'em if I have to – but it doesn't mean I have to like 'em!'

I couldn't say I was wildly enthusiastic myself about the faintly sweet 'parsnipy' tang of the chips, but they were properly cooked and everything else about the meal was excellent, as indeed was every meal served up during our stay at the Regal.

We spent our days exploring the town, and nosing around the little back street stalls where brass and copperware objects of surprising beauty and intricate pattern were being fashioned by craftsmen crouching crosslegged on the bare ground and working on the metal with primitive tools. I thought it might be a nice idea to send a little present home to Edna, though I wasn't sure if that was a possibility until one day when we were strolling through one of the posher areas. A large shop window draped entirely in rich red velvet had a silver framed notice in the middle, which read, 'British Serviceman. May we have the privilege of assisting you in the choice of a gift for your Girlfriend or Wife from our exclusive range of World Famous Oriental Perfumes.' We entered, to be greeted by a rotund Egyptian clad in a lightweight suit, with a burgundy fez upon his head.

We asked if we could test some of the aromas available, and he led us to some deeply cushioned chairs, and clapped his hands to summon one servant with cups of coffee and another bearing a large tray filled with stoppered bottles. We sniffed at the different aromas, and I finally chose a gentle fragrance redolent of woodland violets. I enquired how the present could be dispatched safely to my wife, and the Egyptian produced a form that he completed in triplicate, with her name and address. He handed me a copy as I paid the (quite expensive) price, and assured me that if the present was not received within three months I would be refunded on production of the receipt.

For the rest of our leave, which was now nearly at an end, we travelled each day to a nearby luxury coastal resort with miles of clean yellow beaches. Wearing our blue gym shorts, we swam in the clear blue sea and lazed on the sands, along with the population of what appeared to be a millionaires' playground. But of course like all good things it came to an end, and we had to return to our unit.

CHAPTER 14

We were on our way up the blue once more. Lots of things had happened since our leave in Alex. Allied troops, outnumbered and underarmed, had been evacuated from Greece and then from Crete, and now the only place we were facing the enemy was in the Western Desert. Another attack was mounted by our still sadly depleted forward troops, with the intention of relieving Tobruk, but after two days of vicious conflict Operation Battleaxe had to be abandoned, with heavy losses of our tanks. By the end of the second day our forces were back to the positions they had been in before the operation began, and our unit was moving to take up a position somewhere behind them – for what purpose we did not know.

After several hours of uneventful and bumpy westward travelling, our convoy turned due south and continued for ten miles before coming to a halt in an area of undulating sand, a tight valley between two rocky outcrops. 'Is it 'shelter up and ready for business,' sir?' asked Sergeant Ross as Captain Pomfret came striding around.

'No, actually it's not. Roll out the camouflage nets and peg them over your vehicles, then dig in your bivouacs well down so that they don't throw a shadow. If you hear an aircraft come over keep under cover, or lie down if you're in the open, and don't move until it's gone.'

'I don't know how long we're expected to hide here like this,' said Alan, several days later, as we returned from the cookhouse truck carrying our regular breakfasts of biscuit burghou, 'but one of the cooks told me that the Germans have invaded Russia and are making deep penetrations. He said he heard it on the canteen truck radio first thing this morning.'

'If it is true, they've certainly taken on the unknown,' said Corporal Wallace. 'Look at what happened there in the past . . .'

'I wish I knew why we're stuck here, dashing into our hidey-holes every time a plane comes over,' said Billy. 'It's like a cat and mouse game. I've got a funny feeling that something's just waiting to happen.'

'I've noticed that too,' said Arthur, 'but I didn't want you lot to think I was scaremongering.'

'It's not as if there's any increased air activity,' I said, 'but I agree it's there – a kind of foreboding.'

We didn't have to wait long. Towards midday we heard it – the sound our senses had anticipated: the rumble of distant gunfire. It was not the explosions of anti-aircraft fire but the sound of battle, all the more disquieting because we were at least seventy miles east of the border wire. It continued all afternoon, and as darkness fell we discerned flashes and flares on the northern horizon. Our stomachs twisted into knots of anxiety as we anticipated the order to drive away at top speed.

'What's going on, Sarge?' said Alan. 'It looks as though things are going wrong!'

'Keep your nerve, lads,' said Sergeant Ross. 'We'll get word to move if necessary.'

We stood there in the darkness, with only a tiny sliver of moon in the sky, trying to understand why we were making no contribution to a situation that was far from normal. Eventually the noise faded, and no more flashes were to be seen.

'You know what I think,' said Billy. 'Jerry could have broken through and be bypassing us at this very moment.'

'No, you're wrong,' muttered Corporal Wallace. 'If there'd been any danger of that Captain Pomfret wouldn't have kept us in the dark.'

'What's that about me keeping you in the dark?' The familiar voice of Captain Pomfret came out of the darkness. 'I assure you I've no control over the moonlight!'

'It's just that we've been standing around like cats on a hot tin roof with flashes and bangs coming from all around us, and we don't seem to be doing anything!' muttered Corporal Wallace.

'That's what I've come to talk to you about,' chuckled the captain. 'There's nothing wrong. In fact it's all worked out easier than was expected. Our Intelligence chaps got word that a German armoured column was about to make a reconnaissance raid into our territory to check out the disposition and strength of our Armour. All today that column's been allowed to penetrate further and further, coming up against only minimal resistance from a couple of light armoured car squadrons, who egged them on by hitting and running, while the main body of our Armour has remained, like us, out of sight. The enemy column was lured into range of a battery of our twenty-five-pounder artillery, and took fright and disappeared rapidly when several of their tanks went up in flames. They'll now be telling General Rommel how thin on the ground we are, and how unlikely it is that we'll be able to mount any further large-scale attacks against them in the near future!'

In mid-November 1941 our unit was racing westward again. A lot of things had happened in the last few weeks. Our Commander in Chief Middle East Forces, General Wavell, was transferred to India to take over as C in C of British Forces there, and a new C in C, General Auchinlech (who had been C in C India), had taken over. Determined to take advantage of the quiet spell, he had launched Operation Crusader with the intention of catching the enemy unawares, linking up with our beleaguered Garrison at Tobruk, and pushing on to Benghazi, El-Agheila, Tripoli if possible. We, the One Five One, were with the Seventh Armoured Division, who had been re-equipped with new British tanks that had a rather longer range of fire. We followed them through the wire in the very south of our region, and I will never forget my first glimpse of that often-discussed phenomenon. It was like a long grey snake stretching from north to south as far as the eye could see, several rows of vicious intertwined barbed wire six feet high. We reached a gap in the fence with a pathway wide enough to allow a tank or a truck to get through. At each side of the path a single strand of barbed wire attached to wooden posts bore the ominous warning 'Danger – Mines', with a skull and crossbones painted below. The single strand wires continued beyond the fence, as did the signs, indicating a massive minefield; and the signs changed to 'Achtung – Minen' and 'Pericolo di Morire'. Holding our breath, at last we reached the open desert again. Now we were heading pell-mell towards Tobruk in Libya.

'It looks just the same here in Libya as it did in Egypt,' said Billy. 'I thought it might look a bit different.'

'Why would it look different?' asked Corporal Wallace. 'The great big North African desert was here long before warlike men decided to install barbed wire fences and lay hundreds of explosive mines.'

'If we reach Jebel Akhdar on the western side of Tobruk you'll see a difference,' said Arthur. 'One of the REME lads told me that for quite a long strip around Derna it's all red-brown earth with grass, trees, vegetables and fruit.'

'Sounds like a mirage to me,' snorted Billy. 'I'll believe it when I see it.'

We rattled along for many a mile, over sand that seemed to have borne nothing heavier than a camel's foot, until a warning shout from Alan perched up above informed us that an unidentified aircraft was paying us some attention. 'It's all right – it's a Spitfire', came the reassuring cry, 'but the pilot's behaving a bit oddly. He keeps waggling his wings and swooping down in front of us.'

'Probably greeting us,' said Arthur.

'I doubt that,' shouted Alan. 'He's firing his guns into the sand about ten yards in front of the CO's car! He's trying to tell us to stop.' As we watched, the CO's car halted and he climbed out.

Having achieved his object, the Spitfire departed with a waggle of its wings, and as if in explanation an armoured car and several bren gun carriers, all bearing the red Jerboa sign and packed with infantrymen, came streaking over the higher ground ahead and halted beside the CO's car. An officer jumped out, waving and gesticulating at the high ground behind him and directly in front of us, and spoke to the CO for a few brief moments before climbing back into his armoured car and zooming away the way he had come, with the bren gun carriers close behind.

Lieutenant-Colonel Swindale strode to the radio van, where he was joined by Major Forsythe and Captain Pomfret, and an argument seemed to be taking place.

The staccato crackle of machine gun fire and the dull crump of mortar shells could clearly be heard from over the hill as Captain Pomfret's car came crawling round, and he ordered us to break out the bully and biscuits and drink the tea, which each truck was now carrying in a substantial vacuum container. 'It's a good job the Spitfire pilot spotted the enemy column ahead or we might have been in a spot of bother. That armoured car officer asked the CO if we'd like to take on the enemy by ourselves, seeing we were doing an outflanking move ahead of our Armour. I believe his language was most colourful, and quite upset our CO.'

'What's the latest info, sir?' asked Corporal Wallace anxiously.

'Apart from the minor fracas taking place just over the hill, our divisional column's come up against unexpected fierce resistance just south of the enemy airfield at El-Adem, which has delayed our dash towards Tobruk – and our movements aren't secret any more. We've been ordered to hang on here to await further orders.' Saying which, our captain drove on to the next truck.

We hung on for the rest of the day for orders, which did not materialise, and with the coming of darkness we tried to sleep. Guards were quickly appointed by RSM Menham, in case of any need for rapid movement during the night – which was punctuated by noises of conflict, varying in volume.

Shortly after first light Captain Pomfret's car came nosing round again. 'Our tanks and the rest of our Armour's managed to break through towards Tobruk again. Be ready for off in half an hour!' he called out.

Soon we were heading north-west again, the way the armoured car and the bren gun carriers had gone, with the sounds of battle echoing and reverberating much closer than before. It was daylight enough to see clearly ahead, and John, on lookout overhead, suddenly bawled out, 'There's something happening just a few hundred yards ahead,' and spurts of grey smoke sprang up round a cluster of heavy trucks, accompanied by the crackle of small arms fire. A warning shout of ' Enemy aircraft!' from John had us huddling down amid the equipment and stores. A couple of Messerschmitt aircraft swooped past, spraying machine gun bullets as they attacked the cluster of Allied vehicles ahead. We stared open-mouthed as the infantrymen in the light trucks that were nearest jumped down, lay on their backs and blazed away with their rifles. So heavy was the hail of fire that one of the planes was hit, the engine spluttering for a moment before the aircraft plummeted to the ground in a plume of smoke. The white circle of the pilot's 'chute drifted down as the black smoke and flames arose from the burning wreck. The second plane circled around, intent upon making another strafing run, but at that moment a Spitfire came screaming across out of the morning sun, and the moment the German pilot saw it he headed away as fast as he could, with the Spitfire closing on him. We had been so intent watching the sky that we were shocked to realise that our

CO's car had performed a U turn and was heading back through our convoy, waving wildly for the rest of us to follow suit. In moments we were racing back the way we had just come. We must have gone at least a dozen miles when the leading car signalled another halt, and Captain Pomfret came round again.

'Got a bit too near the sharp end that time, chaps,' he called out. 'The CO says stop for a brew, but be ready to move at a moment's notice as things are pretty fluid.'

We had just made it back to the truck when utter pandemonium broke loose, with the whirring sound of bullets all around us. We looked up, expecting to see another attacking aircraft, only to realise that the bullets were coming horizontally; a hundred yards to one side we saw the muzzle flashes. The CO's car streaked away, the rest of us following closely in a fashion that would not have disgraced the Le Mans racing circuit. After a few miles our assailants gave up the chase, and we halted once more. Bert held up his mug – minus tea but with a bullet hole in it. Apart from that, everyone in our section seemed to have escaped unscathed, but when Captain Pomfret eventually came round his normal grin was replaced by a grim frown. Sergeant Ross enquired if everybody was all right.

'No, I'm afraid not. Several men on that side of the convoy have been hit. They're being whipped into the ambulances now, and I'm going round to check their wounds.'

'Do you want us to come along and give a hand, sir?' asked the sergeant.

'There isn't time. You stay put with your section, because we'll need to move again very quickly. The ambulance orderlies will do the dressings as our medical officers examine the wounds, so we can get them to the casualty clearing station for operating as quickly as possible. Most of them seem to be quite severe abdominal wounds.' Captain Pomfret raced away to the waiting ambulances.

After ten anxious minutes our convoy moved off again, the ambulances immediately behind the CO's car and the radio truck, with the officers' cars in close proximity. Five miles further and we halted again, as ten light trucks armed with bren guns barred our path. Our CO climbed out and spoke to an infantry officer, and after a few moments of gesticulation towards the east the ten trucks formed up like an arrow in front of us, and we all moved off once more at increased speed. The reason we had been stopped soon became apparent, as a line of unfamiliar vehicles appeared ahead; their Italian markings left us in no doubt. Our convoy raced towards them, led by our arrowhead of bren gunners, and the line of Italian armoured cars parted in the middle after one or two shots had been fired in the air. We raced through the gap, and our infantrymen fanned out behind, to deter any notions the Italians might entertain about pursuit. We sped on out of harm's way, waving thanks to our saviours as we went.

After another forty miles we began to pass stores dumps and concentrations of heavy vehicles, and our leading staff car turned off the track on to a rock-free area and halted. We all followed, and Captain Pomfret drove up. 'Shelters up! Major Forsythe will show you where. I'm going down to the CCS with the ambulances to make sure our lads get the urgent surgery they need.'

Can't we do anything for them here, sir?' asked Sergeant Ross.

'Wouldn't be fair to them,' replied the captain. 'They've mainly got serious abdominal injuries, so we need full general anaesthetic to operate and proper aftercare. Doing the extra twenty miles is their best chance. As I said, shelter up. I'll be back soon.'

We moved into the position indicated by Major Forsythe, whipped our canvas up and set out the equipment ready for action. The sounds of battle raged in the west, and we knew that casualties would soon be with us.

'We managed to get them all to the CCS,' said Captain Pomfret as soon as he returned. 'They were taking the first one, young Bill Kershaw, into the operating theatre truck as I left.'

'Is Bill in a bad way, sir? I asked, remembering our recent leave in Alex.

'Not good, I'm afraid – probably a ruptured spleen,' replied the captain, frowning.

During the next few days we worked non-stop, ambulances arriving like a shuttle service from the various battles raging in the area south of Tobruk. The idea of a rapid link-up with the garrison had gone amiss, and there was just a confused mêlée of attack and counter-attack.

An infantryman whose shell splinter wound I was dressing said, 'I saw you lot the other day – when we shot that Jerry plane down. It's a good job you got out of the way sharpish. There's been one tank attack after another there until this morning, when Jerry threw everything into it and we had to let go. The reason why that area's so important is that it dominates the way to El-Adem airfield and onward to Tobruk. Believe me, that place, Sidi Rezegh, will be remembered long after this lot is over.'

The confused conflict continued for another month, ground taken and lost and retaken again, until with one supreme effort the Allied column succeeded in linking up with the beleaguered garrison at Tobruk, and the enemy began to slip away along the coast road to Benghazi. Because of the tremendous battering our Armour had suffered, only a small force could continue to harry the retreating enemy, which fell back beyond Benghazi to make a stand at Agedabia, a hundred miles short of the Tripolitanian border; here our troops met their first real resistance since Tobruk.

It was now 23 December, and an uneasy stalemate hung over the desert conflict. The Seventh Armoured Division, our 'Desert Rats', had taken the brunt of the savage fighting around Tobruk, and were pulled back to a rear area to re-equip and replace lost armour and men. Captain Pomfret strode into our shelter with a frown on his face. 'Leave everything – it's shelter down, patients in the ambulance, and back through the wire into Egypt.'

'Don't say we're on the run again, sir,' said Corporal Wallace. 'I thought things had quietened down up there.'

The captain's face broke into a smile. 'No, we're not on the run – not this time. We've been ordered back for a rest, to restock our stores and equipment, besides getting replacements for the lads we had to rush down to CCS.'

'Any news about Bill Kershaw, sir?' I asked.

'Sorry, Hill,' he answered sadly. 'Kershaw didn't survive his operation. He was too badly injured. And the rest of them are likely to be out of it for a long time yet.'

The One Five One unit moved that day, and by the evening, after a journey untroubled by enemy troops or aircraft, we found ourselves beside a huge supply depot on the outskirts of Mersa Matruh. 'Do we put it up, sir?' asked Sergeant Ross, waving his thumb towards the massive canvas as Captain Pomfret came by.

'We certainly do. Ours is the only section capable of functioning properly at the moment, and we'll be up to our ears in sick parades once the local units know we're here.'

On Christmas Day, having dealt with a huge sick parade made up of men from nearby units and some of our own with various abrasions and ailments, we were sprawled around outside the shelter, our mess tins filled with the bully beef and potato stew conjured up by the cookhouse truck. Since hearing the news about Bill Kershaw I had felt as if a heavy grey cloud was hanging over me. I didn't fancy the food, and I didn't feel like joining in the banter of my comrades. I wandered round to the far side of the shelter, to sit and ponder. Captain Pomfret approached the others, asking with his usual humour how they were enjoying their 'turkey and Christmas pud'. He must have noticed my absence, because he came round and asked quietly, 'What's the matter, Hill?' I didn't answer, and he glanced at the uneaten food in my mess tin. 'Are you off colour, or is it something else?'

'It's all so bloody futile, sir!' I burst out.

'What does?' he murmured softly.

'It's us, sir, what we're trying to do. As soon as we set up and start treating our wounded comrades we get chased away like a bunch of kids caught stealing apples in an orchard.'

'But that isn't all, is it? Come on, get it off your chest instead of letting it eat you up.'

For a moment I stared at the desert sand, as if the words would not come, and then it came pouring out like a torrent released. 'I feel so bloody useless, sir. I studied and trained and I couldn't even save one of my own mates. It's only a few weeks since I was on leave with Bill Kershaw in Alex – and now he's dead.'

'You can stop right there,' said Captain Pomfret quietly. 'First of all, we don't save anybody. We use our training and skill to ease their suffering and help them to recover, but sometimes their injuries are just too severe. I travelled down with Bill in the ambulance, and he was apologising to me for being a nuisance and taking up my time when I could be dealing with others. Do you reject courage like that, Hill?

What you're suffering from is the shock that comes from the harsh realities of war. Just think of the many hundreds you've helped – and be proud!'

'I think I feel quite a lot better now, sir, thanks.'

As he went he murmured, 'Do you know, I never heard you say you were useless!'

I emptied the fly-infested contents of my mess tin into the sand, rinsed it out and went to the cookhouse truck to collect some more, explaining that the flies had got at my first helping, then walked back and joined my comrades, feeling as if a weight had been lifted.

'You all right, George?' said Arthur.

'I'm fine, thanks. I was feeling a bit off, but I'm all right now.'

On 28 December the mail caught up with us, bringing instant rejoicing. We learned that in early December, while we were chasing up and down, the Japanese had attacked the American navy in Pearl Harbor, the USA and Britain had declared war on Japan and the Germans had made massive advances in Russia, reaching the outskirts of Moscow – but were now bogged down by the snows of the Russian winter.

As the weeks went by we remained just beyond Mersa Matruh, being brought up to working strength again. Fresh nursing orderlies were sent to take the place of the injured ones, trucks were repaired or replaced, and medical stocks arrived to replenish those depleted during our long spell up the blue.

The most unexpected change was when Lieutenant-Colonel Swindale was suddenly recalled to HQ in Cairo, to be promoted to Deputy Assistant Director of Medical Services, Middle East Region, and a new commanding officer arrived to take over our unit. Whereas Lieutenant-Colonel Swindale was tall, thin and balding, old-fashioned in outlook and known by most of the 'Geordies' in the unit, his replacement was a younger man, Lieutenant-Colonel 'Tommy' Thomson, of medium height, tubby – almost rotund, and with a liking for bawdy tales that would have horrified his predecessor. He was also possessed of an extremely powerful voice, which echoed around the unit when he summoned his long-suffering batman. It was not long before a story began to circulate that our new CO didn't need a radio to communicate with HQ – all he needed to do was shout! His main eccentricity was an old-fashioned hip bath, which he carted around in the back of his shooting brake-style staff car. Each morning he instructed his batman to put his allowance of ablution water in the bath outside his tent, then stripped naked and with a bristly brush scrubbed himself all over. Unit comics hinted that if Rommel saw this he would abandon his attempt to conquer North Africa.

At the same time the other long-term stalwart, RSM Menham, received word of his promotion to the rank of lieutenant quartermaster, and departed to take up his appointment with a unit near Cairo. It was Billy who summed up our feelings for the departing RSM. 'I'll miss the old so and so,' he murmured. 'For all his bark there was no venom in his bite.' RSM Menham's replacement was also younger, tall, heavily built and lacking the impish sense of humour of his predecessor.

On 21 January 1942 Alan came back from the canteen truck with news: the radio had spoken about a fresh attack from Rommel, which had broken through at El-Agheila and was now belting along the road to Benghazi. 'You know what that means,' he added.

'Yes, it means some of the new lads up there will get their first taste of "pack up and run",' grunted Corporal Wallace.

Snippets of news filtered through all day, but by the evening the radio announcer was able to reassure his listeners that we had a series of defensive positions in the area south of Derna, and that after a skirmish with our tanks that had been rushed up from Egypt the attack had petered out, and an uneasy calm prevailed once more.

The Desert Rats, rested and re-equipped with new tanks after their mauling in the battle for Tobruk, moved up again, joining the new defensive screen to the west. Our new CO settled in very quickly, his flamboyant style the object of some discreet mimicry. Fortunately he was a sensible man, who recognised that the unit was efficient and well trained, and he allowed us to get on with our job with no interference.

As further units of the Seventh Armoured Division moved up the desert once more, the One Five One were ordered to follow. After three days of gruelling transit along the old desert tracks we reached the map reference point where we had been ordered to set up our shelters, with Captain Gemmels going on a further ten miles to establish the forward ADS. Our transit had been better organised this time, with regular stops for meals, which were now prepared while we were at a standstill and carried in 'hot boxes' – vacuum containers that continued the cooking of the contents – and at night time we quickly put up our bivouacs.

A little while before we reached our destination John, on lookout, called out, 'There's something familiar about this place.' We crowded to the open front, trying to work it out. Suddenly realisation dawned.

'It's that place where the infantry shot that plane down,' I exclaimed. 'It's Sidi Rezegh!' As we passed by we saw the twisted, broken, burnt-out relics of that fierce confrontation lying in the rough sand.

After we had put up our shelters as directed, our new CO called us all on parade the next morning to inform us that as a large number of American Grant tanks had been sited in two large defensive boxes ahead of us we need fear no disturbance by the enemy. From now on there was no need to dodge back: we would just stay put and carry on looking after the sick and injured, as we had been trained to do.

'This new CO's a ruddy optimist,' said Alan as we returned to our shelter. 'As far as I'm concerned, I suggest we still keep the rope knife handy.'

'I don't know why, but I've never felt as uneasy as this,' said Arthur several days later. You mark my word, something's brewing!' With a conspiratorial wink Sergeant Ross hung our knife beside the single rope tethering the overhead canvas.

An hour later our forebodings were vindicated. It started with the single sharp crack of an explosion, followed by a plume of grey smoke rising in the centre of our parked vehicles and shelters. In a moment explosions, smoke and the whirring sounds made by fragments of red hot metal flying through the air were all around. Corporal Wallace dashed out of the shelter to catch sight of the muzzle flashes of a line of huge German tanks creeping over the high ground to the south. 'It's a Jerry tank attack,' he bawled. 'Let's get the hell out of it!'

It was almost a relief to know that our forebodings had not been imagined, and we swung into action as trained. Within seconds our patients had been bundled into the ambulances, medical stores pushed back off the tailboard, and the tethering rope severed with one quick slash of the knife, leaving the canvas to sink to the ground as we leapt aboard. The lightning departure of all our vehicles must have thrown the German tank gunners off their aim, because the puffs of smoke began to drop further behind us as the instinct for self-preservation lent us wings.

Soon we were out of range, but we continued for at least twenty miles before our CO's car, which had somehow manage to get to the front, halted. He stepped out and held up his hand. 'Some silly so and so forgot to tell Rommel that our CO promised we'd never need to run away again,' said Billy, with a wry grin.

'Hey, what date is it?' asked Corporal Wallace.

'The 26th of May 1942,' I said. 'Why?'

'Could be a date to remember,' Billy said, grinning in spite of the tension. 'The day when the Afrika Korps disobeyed Lieutenant-Colonel "Tommy" Thomson.'

As we spoke, our CO was holding forth in no uncertain manner to Major Forsythe and Captain Pomfret, waving his hands and pointing at the tops of our trucks, minus the canvases we had left behind. Eventually he climbed back into his car, slamming the door violently, and Captain Pomfret began moving around our vehicles, shouting instructions. When he reached us he climbed out, grinning. 'Our CO thinks it's exceedingly bad form for the German tanks to attack us like that, particularly as our top brass had assured him we were in a safe position well out of the way. He's also unhappy about the canvases we've abandoned, and hopes we might get them back.'

'What about our men, sir? Anyone hurt?' asked Sergeant Ross.

'No. Thanks to the training that our ADS thought up everybody got clean away, and the only damage was to my car, which was the last away.' He pointed to the roof, where a deep gouge ran the full length from front to back. 'It's a good job it wasn't an inch or two lower.'

'What went wrong, sir?' asked Corporal Wallace.

'It seems that Rommel wasn't very impressed by our defensive boxes, and decided to send a roving column way round to the south to come up and attack and destroy our "soft skins" – the vehicles that carry rations, fuel and munitions, without which our Armour's useless. We just happened to be the first lot they encountered as they struck north. Some of our Armour's moved in to engage them.'

'What do we do now, sir?' asked Sergeant Ross.

'We sit tight and wait for further orders. Maybe they're right and these new Grant tanks are a match for theirs, but we'll have to make sure the enemy doesn't do any more nipping round the back and cutting off our lifelines. Anyway, in the meantime our cookhouse is going to dish out some of that tasty stew, so out with your mess tins and join the queue.'

Later that day Captain Gemmel's ADS rejoined the unit. 'There weren't any casualties getting through to us on our sector,' said Charlie Hanson when I saw him standing in the teatime cookhouse queue. 'It was just too dangerous, so we were ordered back to rejoin you. When we got back to where they said you were we found your three big canvases lying on the ground. We picked 'em up and brought them along. Tell your lads to come and fetch yours.'

'Did you see any sign of the Jerry tanks which chased us off?'

'No, nothing just there – but there was plenty of noise so we didn't hang around. We weren't sure if we could find you but we struck lucky. Anyway, I hope the cookhouse has got some of that stew left – our rations have very nearly run out.'

So that is how we got our shelter canvas back. We went over after tea and reclaimed it, anchoring it firmly to the roof of our truck once more.

As darkness fell we wrapped ourselves in our blankets and lay beside our truck in the bright moonlight, trying to ignore the distant sounds of battle, seeking sleep and wondering what tomorrow would bring.

CHAPTER

15

With the first streaks of dawn filtering across the skies the guard on duty was round, calling out urgently, 'Get up you lot, there's another flap on.'

He was closely followed by Captain Pomfret in his car. 'Shelter up, ready to receive casualties, is it, sir?' said Sergeant Ross, sleepily.

'Like hell it is!' exclaimed the captain. 'We've got to be away from here in no more than twenty minutes. Those new Grant tanks are no match for the German Tigers, with their eighty-eight millimetre guns, and our defensive boxes have been completely cut off. Now it's an almighty dash back to prepared defensive positions on the other side of the border wire, and it'll be a race to beat Jerry to them. Run across to the cookhouse truck and pick up one of those vacuum flasks of tea, then be ready for a sharp getaway.'

'Oh, no, not that again,' said John. 'Off we go on this crazy see-saw up and down the desert again. It's been like this ever since we came out here.'

'Too right,' snorted Alan. 'It's been push forward, have a big battle, win some bare patch of desert that nobody wants, fight another battle, lose the ground you've just gained, and end up with stalemate. I tell you, we'll still be chasing up and down this ruddy wilderness when we're ninety.'

The CO's car moved off eastwards in twenty minutes, with the radio truck and the rest of our unit following him in close formation. Towards late afternoon we halted as he consulted our radio operator, and then turned south to follow a single strand of barbed wire attached to a line of posts punctuated by occasional notices warning 'Achtung Minen'.

It did not look like the point we had passed as we travelled west, and we could see no sign of the border fence. I was on lookout, and when I caught sight of an Italian fighter plane diving down towards us I shouted out 'Enemy aircraft!' Our vehicles halted, and we threw ourselves to the ground as far away from the trucks as we could get. The aircraft flew over us, banked round and started another run, spraying bullets as he approached. As I lay there, buried as deeply in the soft sand as possible, I heard another sound – and thirty feet above the ground a Spitfire came hurtling towards the enemy plane, firing as it went. Catching sight of the Spitfire, the Italian pilot veered away. The Spitfire disappeared in hot pursuit, and returned moments later with a waggle of wings to indicate that it was now safe to continue.

I raised myself to my knees, spitting the grit out of my mouth and gingerly moving my limbs, half-expecting to feel the mounting pain of a bullet wound and relieved to find that I was unhurt. Astonishingly no one else had been hurt either, and our journey recommenced, with the great border fence soon coming into view over a slight rise in the ground. With infinite care we traversed the narrow pathway through the fence with minefields on either side, and it was with a feeling of great relief that we spread out over the open ground on the Egyptian side.

We journeyed on over atrocious terrain, descending steep embankments like minor cliffs and passing through patches of soft sand where our vehicle wheels spun helplessly and we had to jump out and heave with all our might to get them moving again. After emerging coughing and spluttering from our endeavours, we found ourselves on a rock-strewn plateau of firm ground, where our CO signalled a halt. Still up above on lookout, I watched as Captain Pomfret was driven across to the cookhouse truck. 'It looks as though we're stopping here,' I informed my mates below. 'The cooks have just been told to get cracking with some food.'

The captain rode around the rest of the vehicles, pointing out where they should park. 'We're here for the night,' he called out as he approached us, 'unless anything crops up. Just dig yourselves a shallow trench to sleep in, not too far from the truck.'

'Must be expecting trouble if we need to dig slit trenches in this hard stuff,' said Billy, as we climbed down, hungry, thirsty, exhausted and covered from head to foot in fine yellow dust.

'I dare say it's in case any enemy aircraft come nosing around,' said Sergeant Ross. 'We aren't all that far inside Egypt.'

We dragged the spades out of the truck and set about the back-breaking task of hacking ourselves shallow depressions in the rock-hard surface, just deep enough for us to lie down below the surface. The jangling of a serving spoon against an empty shell case signalled the arrival of our evening meal. We were delighted to discover that our cooks had come up trumps again, with a stew concocted from tinned ingredients thickened with pulverised dry biscuits, together with a dixie of hot tea.

Our water truck had not been replenished because of our hasty departure, and most of what it still had was needed in the cookhouse, so the precious supply in our water bottles had to be used very sparingly. We moistened a large piece of lint and passed it round to wipe our faces. Shaving could wait.

Darkness swiftly closed in, and we crawled into our shallow trenches in our blankets. I felt as though I had barely closed my eyes when I felt a hand roughly shaking my shoulder. 'Come on, come on, get up!' I opened one eye, vaguely making out the face of the unit RASC mechanic who had been detailed for guard duty. 'A German column's bypassed what few tanks we have left. They're only seven or eight miles away, and moving in this direction!'

'What, in the dark?' asked Arthur, stirring.

'It isn't dark, it's brilliant moonlight if you open your ruddy eyes!' growled the mechanic. 'And anyway, the CO's given the order that we move off immediately.'

We jumped out of our trenches, snatching up our blankets as we hurled ourselves into the back of the truck. 'Are we all aboard?' called out Sergeant Ross as Bert started the engine.

We were startled as a vehicle drew near without its lights on, but as it drew near we heard Captain Pomfret. 'Listen, all of you. No lights, no smoking, and drivers, keep moving in very close formation and only stop if the vehicle in front of you halts. If you get stuck in soft sand then get out and push it clear. If your vehicle breaks down completely abandon it and jump into one of the others. Whatever you do keep moving. There won't be any going back to pick you up. Is that quite clear?'

With a muffled roar the One Five One vehicles moved away in the moonlight, following the CO's car with the radio truck travelling by its side, ready to pass on any further directional orders. After we had rolled, jerked and bumped along for what seemed like an eternity, the sound of revving engines and muffled shouts suggested that all was not well in front. As we were the last truck in the convoy it took quite a time for us to reach the source of the trouble. Tyres were losing their grip on a steep escarpment of soft, shifting sand. If the driving wheels rotated too quickly they were bogged down, so those travelling in the truck had to jump out and push and shove until firmer ground was reached. We, like the rest, found our transport sliding sideways. Bert shouted to us to jump out and keep pushing as he drove on very slowly, and he managed to keep going at a snail's pace.

We had been travelling for three or four hours when the last rays of moonlight disappeared below the horizon. In the total darkness that followed it became impossible to maintain contact between the vehicles, so we came to an abrupt stop.

Captain Pomfret's voice was heard in the darkness. 'We'll halt here. Scratch yourselves a bit of a trench and get down in your blankets. We must be on our way again as soon as dawn breaks.'

No sooner had we closed our eyes than there was the sound of aircraft quite close overhead. They did not sound like German planes, because the 'wha, wha' beat of the engines, which we had come to recognise and dread, was absent, and they also appeared to be approaching from the East. Immediately after they had passed over us and a small high ridge to the north-west, a red flare was released followed by a cluster of white ones, illuminating the sky. In the glow we made out RAF roundels and the unmistakable shape of Wellington bombers. The first one dropped a stick of bombs over the hill, and this procedure was repeated by each aircraft. The last one released a green flare, after which they all disappeared back to the east.

'Hell's flames!' said Billy. 'Nearly being duffed up by our own planes – that's just about the limit.'

'Shut up and lie perfectly still. There'll be another lot over in a moment,' hissed Captain Pomfret. 'They're after the enemy armoured car column five miles away over that hill, and neither the Germans nor our bombers know we're here. Let's hope their navigators and bomb aimers are accurate, eh?'

We froze as another flight passed over us, with the release of flares and the 'crump, crump, crump' of exploding bombs over the hill.

Finally the air attacks ceased, and all that was left was the flickering glow of fires from the burning enemy armoured cars over the hill.

Captain Pomfret stood up. 'I'm certain we won't be troubled by that lot for the rest of the night,' he said, nodding in the direction of the flickering glow. 'Back to your blankets again – but remember, the moment the first faint light of dawn breaks we're on our way again. The guard will call you, and the CO wants a quick word with everyone before we set out.'

It seemd that we had barely closed our eyes before the first faint fingers of dawn were creeping over the horizon and the guard was shaking us awake.

We hurried across to the CO's car, joining the rest of the unit. 'Listen carefully, all of you,' he said, his normal boom reduced to a hoarse whisper. 'We were supposed to head for Mersa Matruh, but another enemy column has raced down the coast and beaten us to it. I've received a radio message telling us to make for our final natural defence position at El-Alamein on the coast road, where just twenty six miles inland lies a vast area of impassable quicksands known as the Qattara Depression. It's still one hundred and forty miles away. Extensive minefields have been set up and lots of artillery has been dug in, waiting to blow apart any enemy incursion – but we've got to get through the minefields before Rommel's lot reach them. From now on each vehicle is on its own – it's your own responsibility to get through. If your vehicle breaks down there's no time to repair it. Set it on fire and jump aboard another. We're heading for a rallying point ten miles east of the El-Alamein railway halt. Do not stray from the marked path as you cross the minefields. Do I make myself clear?' We nodded dumbly as the implications sank in. 'Then off we go – and the best of luck to us all!' He waved us back to our vehicles and we all scrambled aboard, moving off quietly but quickly gathering speed as we hastened on.

This time we were not the last vehicle in the convoy; Dave and Cliff's ambulance was beside us. This was just as well. Alan noticed it first – a hesitation in the firing of our engine. 'Something's wrong,' he exclaimed. We sat tensely as the engine hiccuped and stopped.

'What's up, Bert?' called out Dave, halting beside us.

'Run out of petrol,' said Bert, shaking his head in anguish.

'Come on – that looks like a landing strip over there.' Dave pointed to our right, where a windsock fluttered in the breeze and the broken remains of a crashed reconnaissance plane stuck up at a drunken angle. 'I'm sure I can see some petrol cans: jump in and we'll go and see.' Bert joined him in the front seat of the ambulance and they hared away, returning moments later with three or four large cans.

'It's aviation high octane stuff, but beggars can't be choosers,' Bert said with glee, pouring it into the tank.

'Come on then, let's get cracking,' said Sergeant Ross. 'We've wasted enough time as it is. The others will be miles away by now.'

The powerful aviation spirit lent wings to the engine. We raced onward for another hour, till suddenly we braked to a stop again and Bert jumped out as clouds of steam poured from the bonnet. 'Overheating,' he shouted. 'The cooling system's short of water. Any spare in the truck?'

Sergeant Ross shook his head. 'We've had no time to fill up our containers. What about you, Cliff?' he said, as the ambulance halted beside us.

'We've got a drop – maybe not enough, though,' said Cliff, carrying a container over and pouring the contents into our radiator.

'It's not,' said Bert. 'Has anybody got any more?' We shook our heads in dismay.

'Then we'll have to burn it and ride in the ambulance,' said Sergeant Ross, 'and it's no use you pulling a face, Bert. It's our only chance. Grab your kit, and out we get.'

'Hang on a minute,' I said. 'If our engine's sick we can treat it. What about those bottles of medicines and lotions in our treatment pannier? They've all got lots of water in them.'

Bert looked at me with tears in his eyes. 'George, you're a genius!' Wasting no time, we poured the bottle contents into the radiator, and with a whoop of joy Bert pulled the starter. After two attempts the engine coughed, then roared into life, and we scrambled aboard again – aware that the distant sound of mortars and machine gun fire indicated how close on our heels the enemy was.

After a couple more hours of hard and uncomfortable travel we reached the guard fence of a huge minefield. As we headed for the clearly indicated gap, a solitary red-capped Military Policeman standing beside a small truck waved us to halt. 'What mob are you?'

'One Five One Light Field Ambulance.'

'Cutting it a bit fine, aren't you?' he said with a grin. 'The rest of your lot went through hours ago – in fact there's only our infantry rearguard between you and Jerry, so off you go, sharp as you can, and report to the military checkpoint a mile to the north of the minefield exit. It's on the coast road beside the El-Alamein railway halt.' He waved us on our way, and Bert carefully steered us between the two boundaries of bright orange ribbon that marked the safe pathway. We hardly dared to breathe – but suddenly we were out and away, and the release of pent-up emotions had us cheering like football supporters whose team has just scored the winning goal.

As we wound our way towards the coast road we passed areas of high ground bristling with well-dug-in heavy artillery. As we reached the tarmac road a roadside notice informed us that 'All vehicles must report to CMP Checkpoint and Information Unit', with an arrow pointing down the road. We veered away from the coast up another ridge, which again was bristling with guns, then dropped down beside the railway line. The nameboard of a small halt read 'El-Alamein'. Another fifteen-hundredweight truck close by displayed a notice proclaiming 'Information and check point. All vehicles halt.'

Sergeant Ross poked his head out of the truck window as we halted beside the Military Police corporal. Noting our sergeant's RAMC cap badge and the following ambulance, the corporal said with a grin, 'Left it a bit late, didn't you? Were you going to bombard Jerry with your number nine pills? Tell me who you are and I'll tell you where to go.' After searching through his papers, he said, 'It's ages since they went by. Just keep going till you spot them, or ask again at the next checkpoint, twenty miles further along.' Thanking him, we moved on, but a couple of miles further on a horrible grinding noise beneath our bonnet had Bert braking. He freewheeled on to the sand at the roadside as clouds of steam poured out. Throwing open the bonnet he saw a great crack in the engine block. 'That's it – she's had it,' he cried. 'What can I do now? She's brought us all this way – I can't just leave her. I ought to stay.'

'Don't be daft – we can't go on without you,' said Corporal Wallace.

Just at that moment we espied a large RASC recovery vehicle travelling westward with an armoured car on the back. Seeing the steam arising from our engine, it halted and the driver approached us. 'What's up, lads? Having trouble?'

Bert showed him the damaged engine block.

'Don't you worry. Give me your full unit name, and when I've dropped off this armoured car up the road here, me and my mate will load it aboard and take it to our repair HQ – they'll let you have it back eventually.' There were tears of joy in Bert's eyes as he scribbled our unit details on a scrap of paper and handed it over.

We collected our personal kit, piled into Cliff and Dave's ambulance, and were on our way again. We had only travelled a few miles when we screeched to a standstill. Sergeant Ross, who was riding in front, shouted, 'Captain Pomfret's staff car! I'm certain it just whizzed past us – going west. Yes, he must have spotted us. It's turning round and coming back.'

Moments later our captain joined us. With a huge grin he said, 'Dodging off again eh? I can't let you lot out of my sight for a few minutes without you wandering off and getting yourselves lost. Honestly, though, I'm so glad you got through. I brought some biscuits and bully and a big container of water. You must be ready for it.' His driver was unloading the food and water as he spoke, and we quickly shared it out. As we ate ravenously and gulped the water, Captain Pomfret continued. 'Now I've found you, my next job is to guide you to our unit.'

'Where are they, sir?' asked Sergeant Ross. 'Did they all manage to get clear?'

'We didn't lose any more men, but our vehicles are in a parlous state and need a great deal of attention before we do much more desert roaming. As for where they are, this morning they commenced the journey down to a big rest camp – Qassassin it's called, down in the Nile Delta south of Cairo. It's close to Ishmalia, a large green area on the banks of the Nile, where we're going to rest, recuperate and have our transport brought up to scratch. If you're ready, gentlemen, I suggest we continue. It's quite a distance, and I suggest you take the opportunity to catch up with some of the sleep I'm sure you've missed.'

He led us away, down the coast road, and as we relaxed tiredness overcame us. Dozing intermittently, we journeyed on for what seemed like forever, hearing only occasional traffic noises, until at last we swerved sharply off the road through a gateway marked 'Qassassin Camp' and came to a halt outside a large hut, the camp office.

CHAPTER

16

But for the name on the gate it could have been Tahag all over again. Same blue and white cotton tents, Shafto's Shufti's, rickety NAAFI canteens, dhobi wallahs wanting to take our washing, the early morning call of 'Shai – NAAFI – Shai' – and, of course, the pestering flies. But they had been with us up the blue, so why should they surprise us?

Along with Corporal Wallace we had managed to get together in a tent for six, and were making the most of our period of rest. Captain Pomfret's assertion that all our vehicles had managed to get through without loss – apart from ours – proved to be over-optimistic. Two of the large three ton trucks had been abandoned, one with a broken axle and another which had rolled on to its side, slightly injuring the men travelling in it. Our unit was in no fit condition to return to action for the time being.

We were returning from our evening meal a day or two later when we found our captain talking to a small crowd on the flat ground beside our tents. He saw us approaching. 'I've just been passing on the latest info about Alamein. This morning an enemy column made a probing thrust through the minefield, was allowed to penetrate our first artillery screen without a shot being fired, and continued on to what appeared to be a deserted plain. A tiny force of light tanks and armoured cars put up sufficient resistance to prevent them going further and push them back across the minefield. Rommel should be convinced that there's hardly any opposition between him and the glittering prize of Cairo, apart from a few remnants of our Western Desert Force.'

'Can we really withstand a determined attack, sir?' asked Alan.

'Make no mistake about it, the situation's well in hand, but everything's so well camouflaged that I bet even you didn't notice it!' chuckled Captain Pomfret.

The Allied strategy was put to the test a week later. Rommel, with his heavy Armour poised for what he confidently expected would be a short sharp engagement followed by a swift and victorious swoop straight into the heart of Cairo, sent off a telegram to Mussolini, inviting him to fly to North Africa to lead the triumphal victory parade into the capital of Egypt. The Italian dictator, still smarting from the defeat inflicted upon his forces by the first Allied advance, gleefully boarded a plane bound for Tripoli and Rommel launched his offensive. He easily penetrated the defences on the first ridge beyond the minefield, chasing away a small force of light tanks on the plain, and gathered his heavy Armour together for a quick thrust to Cairo. It was here that things started to go wrong, as the Armour was surrounded by a massive collection of hidden artillery which hammered the Germans mercilessly for three days and nights without let up. And when the pounding paused it was taken up by the Allied air forces, flying from well-established airfields a short distance away. With more than half his Armour destroyed, Rommel tried to fall back across the minefield, only to find he was within the range of more concealed Allied artillery, and only a few battered remnants of his force regained the safe side of the minefield. Mussolini, on hearing of the Axis setback, hysterically ordered an Italian column to make a direct thrust across the Qattara Depression and capture Cairo. Despite having been warned by their chiefs of staff they still went ahead, and became totally bogged down: the Italians stood by helplessly as their tanks, guns and supply trucks sank down into the quicksands.

After the total collapse of the offensive that he had boasted would clear the British out of North Africa, Rommel was curtly summoned back to Berlin to give an account of himself, and Mussolini scurried back to Rome, his tail between his legs. The badly mauled Afrika Korps meanwhile set up a defence line on their side of the minefield, discovering to their dismay what it was like to suffer immensely long lines of communication, constantly under heavy and prolonged attack from the air.

Despite our success in thwarting the attack, our mobile forces had not yet re-equipped sufficiently to dislodge the enemy from Egypt. For the time being the only activity was daily exchanges of artillery fire, and an ever-increasing number of raids by our aircraft on the German supply line.

As we waited at Qassassin a rumour circulated that General Auchinlech was to be replaced by a new man straight out from England. 'A chap's been telling me in the NAAFI,' Billy said one evening, as we sat in our tent, 'that this new bloke's called Montgomery – and he says that if it's the same officer he served under in the south of England he's a keep fit fanatic who doesn't touch alcohol, doesn't smoke and believes in everybody taking a two mile run before breakfast!'

'Sounds like a made-up tale to me,' said Corporal Wallace.

'I don't know – he's a regular with a few good years of service, this chap I was talking to, I mean, and he says the last they heard of this Montgomery he was getting pretty high up among the brass hats.'

It was lunchtime on 12 August when Billy came dashing back with the news. 'What did I tell you?' he said excitedly. 'This General Montgomery bloke arrived in Cairo this morning, and he's taking over the Desert Campaign under GOC Middle East General Alexander. I've just heard it on the canteen radio.'

'Better get out your gym. shoes and PT shorts,' I said. 'When he hears how fond of fags and booze you are, he'll single you out for a very concentrated keep fit course, starting at five o'clock in the morning!'

Two days later our CO had us all on parade on the tarmac square in front of the camp orderly office. 'Men of the One Five One,' he boomed, holding aloft a sheet of official-looking paper and his jaw jutting forward, rather like Charles Laughton's Captain Bligh, 'Today I've received a personal message from our new field commander, General Montgomery, requiring me to introduce a regime of physical training in which everyone, officers and men alike, will participate. These exercises are to be enjoyed for an hour at first light each morning, followed by a further two hours after breakfast. The only deviation will be on Sundays, when half an hour at first light will suffice. In the afternoons all will take part in some sporting activity such as soccer, rugby, cricket or netball. He states that his aim is to determine that all officers and men of the

Eighth Army, as this fighting force will now be known, are fit, alert and totally capable of carrying out the tasks he will demand of us.'

A faint groan arose from the men on parade, prompting the new RSM to bark, 'Silence in the ranks!'

'I have instructed the guard to waken you all at five thirty a.m., starting tomorrow morning, under the guidance of our new unit PT instructor, Sergeant Spring. That is all I have to say. You may dismiss them now, Sergeant Major.'

'Did he really get a personal letter from the new general, Sarge?' I asked Sergeant Canning, our orderly office sergeant.

'Well, it was a copy of the personal letter sent to all commanding officers in this region,' grinned Sergeant Canning, 'but you know our new CO has a fine sense of the dramatic.'

'What's he up to, this General Montgomery, sir?' gasped Billy to Captain Pomfret as we all completed our first early morning run. 'Does he want us to fight with our bare hands and chase the Germans on our feet?'

'I wouldn't like to say,' chuckled the captain, also panting for breath, 'but if he does we're going to be a hell of a lot better able to do it.'

'What about the CO in his vest and short shorts?' grinned John in the showers a few moments later. 'There he was, struggling to keep up with Sergeant Spring in front – every bit of fat on him wobbling like jelly.'

Nevertheless, after a few days of the muscle toning exercise, followed by a swift cold shower, the dull tiredness began to leave our bodies, and the spring came back into our step. We even began to look forward to the afternoon games, surprised to find we could run around in the heat without being drenched in sweat and our energy flagging. With the better rations and meals our appetites increased, and the exercise turned our food into solid muscle rather than flabby fat.

Sitting in the NAAFI one evening, we were discussing the state of things. 'I see we've got some American bombers and crew knocking the stuffing out of Jerry here,' said Arthur. 'Do you think we'll be having another bash soon?'

'I've heard that our new general has refused to make a serious move until he has all the Armour and equipment necessary to finish the job off properly,' said John, 'and he insists on everything being planned down to the last detail.'

'Not before time, either,' said Billy. 'Our lads have struggled on for too long with tanks with pea-shooters for guns, compared with Jerry's eighty-eights.'

Soon replacement vehicles turned up to replace those that had been lost, and ours came back with a brand new engine – much to Bert's delight. Then our injured men returned from Base Hospital. Now we were up to strength again it seemed certain we would soon be moving up.

The line of trucks and ambulances stood on the road inside Qassassin Camp waiting for our CO's signal to move out. Captain Pomfret's car came slowly down the line. 'New engine all right, Bert?' he called out. Our driver gave him an enthusiastic 'thumbs up'. Turning to the rest of us, the captain said, 'We've had a bit of a break, but I'd like to think we won't be visiting this area again. If things go according to plan we'll be seeing places a bit nearer home in the next few months.'

'Is the balloon going up right away, sir?' asked Corporal Wallace.

'No, not quite yet. General Montgomery has made it abundantly clear to the "chairbound warriors" that he'll start when he knows he can go all the way.' With a wave, he stepped back into his car, which drove forward to take its place with the other officers' cars behind the CO and the radio truck.

We moved to a sandy patch fifty yards from the seashore and thirty miles east of El-Alamein, and were ordered to continue our early morning exercises. At the first glimmer of light the guard came around, banging on the bivouacs, urging us to crawl out and trot briskly to the beach with its white coral sand where Sergeant Spring waited, bounding about with unseemly energy at that unearthly hour and impatient to put us all through our paces.

'Come on, Hough, put some energy into it!' he said, grinning as we shivered in the keen wind blowing off the sea. 'Intelligence sources in Cairo say that Jerry might try to land raiding parties on these beaches at first light. One glimpse of your ugly mug will have them running back, screaming, into the sea.'

One of our replacements, newly out from England, asked nervously, 'What do we do if a raiding party does come out of the sea?'

'Why, lad – invite them to join our exercise group and offer to hold their guns for them while they take part!' chuckled Sergeant Spring, with heavy sarcasm.

As soon as the camp was established our CO decided it would be good training if each section learnt to be self-sufficient in preparing its own meals. Having persuaded our QM stores to issue a small petrol stove to each section, he instructed us to collect our ration issue each day and get on with the job. With the greater variety of rations now available, thanks to our closeness to the main storage depots, we managed to concoct some interesting meals. It was Sergeant Ross who suggested that we should take turns in pairs to prepare meals. My partner was Arthur, who said, 'If only we had a simple oven, I'm sure I could make a meat and potato pie.'

'Nothing ventured,' I replied. 'Let's have a go.'

Where a stony bank rose up from the surrounding sand we managed to lever out of the stones, making a hollow chamber. Here we stood a large stores tin, sideways on and resting on two stones under either side, leaving gaps around the sides. We collected a pile of dried desert scrub, doused it liberally with petrol, placed underneath the tin and, while Arthur was preparing the pastry and filling it with tinned meat and potato, I lit the fire. It burned with a lot of smoke, which when it cleared left bright glowing embers under our makeshift oven, needing only an occasional handful of scrub to maintain the heat. Arthur carefully put his pie in. Against all odds it was a success and we used that Heath Robinson affair often while we stayed in that spot.

We had not been at our new location many days, when, completely unexpectedly, word was circulated that we were going to be allowed to take a week's leave in Cairo in groups of forty. I was convinced that this was just a wild rumour, but when I mentioned it to Captain Pomfret he confirmed it, saying that our CO would hold a parade that afternoon to announce it.

'What about the big push we're going to make, sir?'

'I've told you before. When General Montgomery decides it's the right time we'll all know about it – make no mistake about that.'

Because we were not committed to holding sick parades, the whole ADS section as well as Captain Gemmell's opted to go on leave together, with several of the ambulance crews, and we were dropped off a few days later at a very small railway halt to board empty goods wagons on their way back to Cairo.

'I hope we can find a hotel with better grub than that Regal place in Alex,' said Arthur, as we trundled along towards Cairo. 'I never really developed a taste for those sweet potato chips!'

'That reminds me,' I said. 'While we were in Qassassin I mentioned to a Pay Corps bloke I met in the NAAFI that we'd just been given leave in Cairo, and he told me about this Toc H leave hostel. It's run by the wives of three British church ministers, and they prepare and serve all the meals – which are all superb, proper English dishes. And another thing he said was that all the beds have soft, fully sprung mattresses.'

'Did you get the address?' asked Corporal Wallace. 'It sounds too good to be true – there must be a snag somewhere.'

'Well, you could call it a snag for some of the troops. They won't entertain the slightest hint of unruly behaviour, fighting or drunkenness, and they won't allow anyone to smuggle a woman in, like some of the sleazier places do. The slightest hint of any of that and you pack your bags and go. And yes, he did give me the address.'

The others from our section agreed that this sounded an ideal place to stay, and it proved to be one of the happiest choices we ever made.

We found the hostel just off the main street, and all six of us stepped up the four steps to a large wooden door. This was wide open, and a short passageway led to the reception desk at the end, where two ladies waited to greet us. The first one, who had a round face, neatly waved brown hair and a twinkling smile in her eyes, introduced herself. 'Good afternoon, boys. I'm Mrs Freeman, and I'd like to welcome you here. I expect you're all a bit weary after a tiresome journey, so if you wouldn't mind giving me your name, rank, number and regiment, I'll have you shown to your rooms. Mrs Hardy here, and Mrs Willis, who's in the kitchen, and I want you to enjoy your stay and would like you to feel at home. There's plenty of hot water if you feel like taking a bath – or perhaps you prefer a cold shower. There's a bathroom on the same landing as your bedrooms.'

We gave her our particulars for the register and signed our names.

'We try not to impose irksome restrictions, but we'd like you to be in for eleven o'clock at night if you don't mind. Cairo can be an unwholesome place for young men at that time of night. If you like an alcoholic drink please come in quietly. Apart from that, enjoy your time with us.'

'Don't we have to go to church or anything?' asked Billy uneasily. 'I mean, with you being . . .' he faltered.

'You mean because we're connected with the church?' she chuckled. 'Bless you, no. There's a short service on a Sunday morning that you're welcome to come to if you wish – but there's certainly no obligation.' She turned to the other lady, who was even smaller, with tiny birdlike features surmounted by a mop of frizzy, greying hair. 'Eva, will you get Yusef to show these gentlemen to rooms four and five, please.'

'Welcome to our little home, boys!' Mrs Hardy said in a clear, musical voice. 'If you'll just follow me.' She led us towards a flight of stairs. 'This is the dining room – breakfast eight to nine thirty, lunch twelve to one thirty, dinner six to seven thirty.' She clapped her hands 'Yusef!' As if by magic a white-robed, maroon tarbush-hatted, dark-skinned houseboy appeared. 'Rooms four and five, Yusef,' she commanded – and he led us up the stairs and along the landing, to throw open the doors of two facing rooms at the far end.

'Have you stopped panicking about coming here, Billy?' I laughed as Yusef disappeared down the stairs.

'I got it wrong,' he admitted ruefully. 'I thought they'd be stern ladies in black dresses who wouldn't allow any laughing and joking.'

The accommodation proved to be every bit as good as the Pay Corps man promised, and the food was a revelation. All the meals were cooked to perfection, tasting exactly as they had at home before the war. Even the potatoes were proper white ones. Yusef brought the steaming dishes to the tables under the watchful eyes of Mrs Freeman and Mrs Hardy.

We did not see much of Mrs Willis, the lady who was responsible for everything in the kitchen, but she appeared in the dining room one morning as we were about to go out. She was a tall, angular lady with a deep contralto voice, and straight grey hair combed straight back on her head and tied behind. 'Mornin', boys,' she said. 'Enjoy your breakfast?'

'We enjoy every meal you've put in front of us,' said Corporal Wallace, with a smile.

'Why don't you try a visit to Ezbakhia Gardens this morning?' she said. 'It's a lovely public park, and there's a hut with tables and chairs outside where you can get a cup of real home-made tea. If you hang on a minute I'll lend you my camera, so you can take a picture of yourselves and send it home to your loved ones. I'll get it developed and printed for you before you leave.' She dashed away to return bearing a box camera. 'Just point and click.'

We visited Ezbakia Gardens, and found them as delightful as Mrs Willis had promised. We managed to take some snaps of ourselves sitting round a table with fine china cups of tea in our hands and a big beams on our faces. We also fitted in an afternoon visit to the local sports stadium, where two Egyptian teams were playing a basket ball match. To our dismay a foul move on the pitch developed into a brawl that was joined by the spectators. We made a hasty exit.

Like all good things our leave came to an end, and after paying a very reasonable bill considering the food and the comfort provided, for which we thanked the three ladies from the bottoms of our hearts, we travelled back on the railway goods wagons on the last day of August 1942 with the rest of our leave party. The driver of our unit truck, which picked us up from the rail halt, told us that the enemy had just mounted another major offensive at El Alamein. Surprisingly we stayed put well away from the conflict, which raged on for four days, during which time our Boston light bombers attacked the enemy columns round the clock, and with equally devastating effect his supply dumps and his transport, which was bringing his fuel, ammunitions and stores down that long and vulnerable coast road.

The enemy attack was a two-pronged effort, one column coming through on to the plain, the other coming up from the south as the Italians had done earlier. They threw everything into it, determined to break through to Cairo, but General Montgomery – 'Monty' as he was now affectionately known – had studied the lay of the land, and whichever way the attacking columns turned they were met with a devastating hail of artillery fire, which no Armour could withstand for long. In addition the newly boosted numbers of American Bostons and British Wellingtons kept up their daily and nightly pinpointing of the vulnerable targets with devastating results. Eventually a whole column of the deadly Tiger tanks was immobilised for lack of fuel within the range of our artillery, which proceeded to pound them to destruction. Finally the German commander had to concede that this further attack was not going to restore the Afrika Korps' superiority, and the remnants of his Armour and battle-weary troops limped back over the minefield, leaving behind a mass of shattered equipment and a host of bewildered Italian troops, most of whom were relieved to find that their fighting days were now over. General Montgomery resisted the temptation to send his forces racing after the weary Germans: he was not quite ready yet for his 'Big Push'.

While all this was going on, the final party from our unit had taken their week of leave, which underlined the confidence now manifested in the situation at El-Alamein. For the next three or four weeks we remained on the coast, performing our early morning exercises and swimming daily in the sea. Then the signal came for us to move forward once more, ending up ten miles short of the plain where the recent enemy attack had been so completely overwhelmed. From the amount of Armour and equipment that was moving into positions around us, and the air of suppressed expectancy, it was clear that something was going to happen, and very soon. The Desert Air Force was now operating a 'bus service' of attacks against the enemy, and as a consequence of the daytime swoops on the supply trucks on the coast road, the German vehicles had started making the hazardous run at night. This was where our Wellington bombers came into their own, with their precision night-time forays leaving the coast road ablaze with enemy fuel and ammunition. We hardly ever saw an enemy plane overhead, and if we did it was usually racing to escape pursuing Spitfires.

One morning, towards the end of the third week in October, Captain Pomfret came striding over to the section truck, carrying his map board with some papers clipped to it. 'I guess you're fed up with hanging around all day with nothing to do,' he said casually as he leaned against the truck bonnet. Immediately all eyes and ears were upon him: knowing him as we did, it was obvious that he had important news to impart.

'Oh, I don't know, sir,' ventured Billy. 'It's healthier than driving through minefields.'

'Not half as exciting though,' chuckled our captain. 'You must admit we've trailed to and fro in this dusty wilderness for too long. It's time we did something towards getting home.' He paused, the silence broken only by the petrol stove hissing away under a dixie of stew and the distant roar of a flight of Bostons returning from a raid. The captain carefully removed a sheet of paper from his map board. 'I was away yesterday, as you know, with the CO and the rest of the officers. We were at HQ being briefed about our attack. I have here a personal message from General Montgomery to every serviceman out here in the desert, which I, as your immediate officer in charge, am required to read out to you. "The Allied troops are without question the finest in the world, struggling for too long against an enemy with more powerful equipment. That situation is about to be reversed, and with Armour now available to us and the equipment to back it up we are more than a match for anything that can be put up against us. We are therefore going to knock him for a six, clean out of Africa. There will be no stopping, and no turning back. In the future, mankind will remember this impending battle as the turning of the tide in our fortunes of war. Remember, every step forward is a step nearer home."' The captain looked round at us. 'That's the kind of talk we need to hear, and believe you me, he means every word of it!'

'What's our job this time, sir?' enquired Corporal Wallace. 'Part of the usual quick left hook around the south?'

'No, not this time. We're with a support group, which will stay in reserve until ordered forward – a sort of rear party.'

'Do you mean we might not move at all, sir?' asked Sergeant Ross.

'Whatever gave you that idea, Sergeant?' chuckled Captain Pomfret. 'It means that we move up behind our Armour instead of finding ourselves mixed up with it – or even in front of it!'

'Is the balloon going up right away, sir?' asked Arthur quietly.

'Not today – probably not even tomorrow. I won't keep you in the dark: as soon as we get the word I'll let you know.' With a cheery wave, he wandered off in the direction of his tent.

All that day the procession of Allied bombers overhead went on relentlessly. Sometimes the targets were near enough for us to hear the distant rumble of explosions. At other times the interval between outward and return journey suggested a more distant rendezvous. The next day was the same, and the one after that, and we never saw a single enemy aircraft, as if our fighters had literally swept them from the skies.

On the afternoon of the third day after he had passed on General Montgomery's stirring message, our captain was back with a twinkle in his eye that foretold more news. 'This is it, chaps,' he said as we gathered round. 'At dusk tonight we move to a position five miles behind our artillery, and dig ourselves shallow trenches to sleep in within the ring in which our trucks will form up. At a pre-arranged time the barrage will commence, and it'll be the heaviest concentration of artillery fire ever to be directed towards a specific area in the history of warfare. I suggest you grab some cotton wool to stuff in your ears when the bombardment commences, because the noise will exceed anything you've ever experienced before. Once we're in position none of us must stray outside our ring of trucks, because under cover of the barrage a huge armada of newly arrived American Sherman tanks and mobile guns, which have been kept camouflaged and well hidden in the wadis around here, will be moving through, ready to strike the enemy hard as soon as the barrage lifts. All this Armour will be passing within a few yards of our ring in complete darkness apart from the flashes of the guns. They'll be heading on a compass bearing, so be warned – don't move outside your trucks.' He looked around intently as the import of his words sank in, then added, 'I don't think any of us will sleep much tonight. Any questions?'

Sergeant Ross said, 'Are we likely to move during the night, sir?'

'I doubt it. As I told you, we're with a support group that won't move until our Armour has gained complete control of the area, and that will probably take a day or two.'

'What about casualties? Will we be dealing with them, sir?' asked Arthur.

'Not in the early stages, because fully staffed ambulance trains are standing by to transport them away from the battlefront. Our orders are to stand by in readiness to move as soon as we're ordered to do so. This time we're really going to make it – you'll see.' A trace of his familiar grin flitted across his face.

Later that afternoon a padre turned up and invited us to join him in a short service. 'It doesn't matter whether you're C. of E., Methodist, Presbyterian, RC or nothing at all. Just come and sit quietly while I ask for a blessing upon us in the days that lie ahead.' He spoke quietly and sincerely for a few moments, reminding us that we were striving for a return to a more peaceful life, then called a blessing upon us. As he departed I felt better for his words, as if an inner tension had relaxed.

We ate our evening meal – tinned stew and bread baked by the mobile field bakery which had now joined the ration supply centre, and as dusk began to fall we stood beside our loaded trucks, waiting for the signal to move to our designated position. There was an ominous calm, and even the sky looked dull and leaden. We saw the radio operator hurry across to the CO's car and watched as our CO followed him back to the radio truck. A moment later he emerged, and signalled us all to climb aboard and follow his car. In five more minutes we were moving towards the setting sun.

It took less than half an hour to reach our ordered location, and in the last glimmers of daylight we were marshalled into ring formation by a couple of Military Policemen, immaculate despite the impending battle. Soon we were in position and they departed, leaving us to scratch out our shallow holes in the sandy desert.

CHAPTER 17

Suddenly a single star shell lit up the sky, then another and another. Then there was a series of individual bangs as our artillery started to fire, building up into a barrage like thunder that rolled in from every quarter as all the batteries joined in, increasing all the time in intensity and swelling into a mighty crescendo of mind-destroying sound, as if all the drums of hell were beating out a fierce tattoo to the destruction of the world.

We had lain there in the darkness, waiting, hardly daring to whisper, surrounded by an oppressive silence that had almost shouted in its intensity – as if the whole world had held its breath waiting for something to happen. And now it had.

The sky to the west was a blaze of light almost as bright as day, with the muzzle flashes merging into one massive torchlight of fire from that massed orchestra of explosive and flying steel. The noise was so intense that I was experiencing physical pain even with my ears stuffed with cotton wool, and the ground around us trembled to the maelstrom of sound. Soon there came an additional noise – a rushing, clanking, squealing sound. A mighty horde of huge grey shapes, banging, clattering and kicking up fearsome clouds of dust: an armada of fighting vehicles surging past, like a massive herd of buffalo on the stampede. The mighty monsters went on rolling by, sometimes so close that without the protecting ring of trucks we would surely have been crushed by the flailing tank tracks. For an eternity the artillery barrage continued unabated as the Armour rolled forward – and then it ceased as abruptly as it had begun, leaving the more familiar noises of battle: the rattle of machine gun fire, the whoosh of flying tank shells and the peculiar singing howl of German multiple mortars in reply.

On the night of 23 October 1942 the great battle of El-Alamein was joined. The lumbering tanks halted all around us, waiting in reserve to be called on as needed. That mighty battle, which raged with days of bitter, unrelenting and often hand to hand conflict, has been well recorded, but for us in the One Five One Light Field Ambulance it was like waiting in the dressing room at some bizarre theatre for our cue to go on stage, unable to see any of the performance. We could not even speculate on the progress of the battle, as we had to rely on the short and vague bulletins broadcast each evening on Cairo Radio, together with any snippets of information that Captain Pomfret passed on.

After days of frustrating inactivity, as we sat in the back of the truck eating our breakfast of bread and marmalade, John said, 'I'm sure I can sense a change in the "noises off". They seem to be further away this morning.'

Suddenly Billy shouted, 'Captain Pomfret's running over. There's something going on.'

Our captain leaned on the tailboard panting for breath with a expression of glee on his face. 'We've done it, lads – we've ruddy well done it. Monty's made the breakthrough he was after, and now we're pouring through the gap that's been blasted in the enemy positions. Stay close to your vehicles: we'll be on our way very soon. And they say Tripoli's a good place to spend your leave!'

'Is it a limited breakthrough, sir?' asked Corporal Wallace.

'Like hell,' snorted our captain. 'Jerry's abandoned a whole battlefield of equipment and left thousands of Italians in the lurch. He's high-tailing it up the coast road as fast as he can go.'

It was two more days before we moved, thanks to something that was utterly unpredictable and inexplicable. It started to rain! In fact, rain is too moderate a term to describe the deluge that descended upon us. Whether the tremendous artillery barrage had anything to do with it is hard to say, but it was such a rare occurrence in that part of the desert as to be almost unheard of. All the vehicles specifically designed for the desert were at a disadvantage, struggling to extricate themselves from the thick yellow desert mud that was up to their axles when they should have been pursuing the enemy up the coast road. Fortunately the rain stopped after two days as abruptly as it had begun, but it had given the battered remnants of the Afrika Korps two days' start on our Armour.

An event of even greater import occurred on the day the desert rains ceased. It was 8 November, and units of our Allied First Army began to make landings in Casablanca on the Atlantic coast of North Africa, and from then onward the days of the Axis forces in North Africa were numbered. Landings at Oran and Algiers followed two days later. News of the landings spread like a forest fire through the pursuing Eighth Army, convincing them that this really was it. There would be no more going back, and now, after months of travail in the desert, the Eighth Army would be the first Allied troops to enter Tripoli.

It was Captain Pomfret who brought us the news of the First Army landings, at the same time informing us that we were heading for the westbound coast road in an hour. 'No hold-ups this time,' he grinned. 'As soon as we hit the main road we keep going. The Royal Engineers are repairing the way ahead all the time.'

We sped along the hard tarmac until we reached the El-Alamein minefield, now completely cleared in the area surrounding the road, and passed into the region that the enemy had held until a few days before. All around was the evidence of the ferocity of the recent conflict, and also the frantic haste with which the Afrika Korps had pulled out. Smoking, black cross-emblazoned armoured vehicles, still smouldering, exploding ammunition dumps, great mounds of equipment scattered around, and among all this vast groups of bewildered Italian soldiers, looking lost and forlorn now that the fleeing Afrika Korps had commandeered their transport and left them stranded. As we sped along the road a group of hollow-eyed Italian POWs with just a lone British infantryman in charge waved to us, and one of them cried out, 'Hey, Inglesi! – you catcha Tedeschi pronto!'

'I'll tell you one thing,' observed Corporal Wallace, 'the Italians aren't too pleased at being abandoned by the Germans!'

The true extent of the defeat became more apparent with every mile we journeyed westward, with huge burned-out enemy oil tanker vehicles lying at drunken angles on the roadside where they had been heaved out of the way, and the shattered remains of ammunition trucks, their torn and twisted contents scattered far and wide – in silent witness to the accuracy of our Wellington bombers.

As we passed the small airfield near Fuka, light RAF aircraft were already landing there, waiting to be re-fuelled from a waiting bowser with the familiar RAF roundels plainly visible on its side.

A few miles further on our convoy halted, and Captain Pomfret drove down the line of trucks. 'Pull in to the roadside and have your food and drink. We'll be here for about thirty minutes!' he shouted as he passed. We clambered down, stretching our cramped limbs as Alan dragged out the large vacuum flask of tea, and started to fill our mugs. Billy returned from the far side of the truck after attending to a call of nature. 'I'm sure I saw somebody move in that ditch,' he said, pointing to a hollow across the road. As we looked, a man wearing a bedraggled German uniform scrambled out, hands held high, croaking 'Kamarad'.

'Hell's bells – we've got a prisoner,' said Corporal Wallace as the figure stumbled towards us, hesitantly croaking 'Wasser. Geben trinkwasser, bitte.'

'That's a fine howdy-do,' muttered Sergeant Ross. 'Can't tell a word he says.'

'He wants a drink of water,' I said.

'Can you talk to him?' asked Sergeant Ross.

'I did German at school – but I've forgotten most of it.'

Slowly and haltingly I questioned him. He told me he was a storesman with a ration truck, and when he had stepped down to answer a call of nature his comrades had driven off and left him. For four days he had been hiding without food or drink. I told our sergeant, who passed him a water bottle and watched as he drank ravenously. 'Better give him a slice or two of bread as well,' the sergeant said. The look of gratitude in the prisoner's eyes had to be seen to be believed as Arthur handed him a couple of slices.

'What on earth are we going to do with him?' said Sergeant Ross. 'We can't take him with us.'

Our problem was solved a few moments later as a fifteen hundredweight truck with a Military Policeman in the driving seat came along the road. Sergeant Ross signalled him to stop, explained our problem, and he agreed to take the POW off our hands. In my schoolboy German I explained to the prisoner what was happening, and he grabbed both my hands, crying 'Danke, danke, danke' as the Military Policeman led him away.

Minutes later we moved off again, grateful to be travelling on tarmac without the swirling dust of our previous desert journeys. Because of the efficiency of our desert airforce we saw not a trace of enemy aircraft. As we drove we watched for places on the coast road that had only been names before: Sidi Barani, Solum Pass, Bardia. We bypassed Tobruk and eventually came to a halt in the fertile strip of land around

Derna in Jebel Akhdar. Our CO's car led the way along a path marked 'Clear of Mines', over a hill into a wooded paddock carpeted with green grass, which sloped gently down to a farmhouse from which the Italian inhabitants had long since departed.

As soon as Bert had manoeuvred our truck into the position indicated by Major Forsythe, who was organising the layout, we climbed out, and Arthur ran his fingers through the soft green shoots. 'Grass,' he crooned softly, 'real green grass – yet only a few miles east of here it's sand and rock and desert scrub.'

'This is further west than our unit's ever been before,' said Corporal Wallace, 'and I honestly didn't believe those tales the Desert Rats were telling in Qassassin Camp about the tiny green area that reminded them of home. I thought they'd been out in the sun too much.'

'Yes – and proper trees, not palm trees,' I said. 'And proper earth as well. Look, you can crumble it through your fingers.' I let the reddish brown soil trickle through on to the grass.

'Bit like a Garden of Eden, did I hear someone say?' said Captain Pomfret as he strode into view. 'I wouldn't wax too lyrical about it if I were you, because there's no welcome sign on the mat. We've just had a warning on the radio to keep well away from the buildings. It seems that the unfriendly fellows in the Afrika Korps have booby-trapped some of them with anti-personnel mines. You might find it difficult to shave with both your hands blown off. Apart from such minor details, yes, I agree, it's certainly a wonderful change after all that desert.'

The next morning, as we returned from the cookhouse truck with our breakfast, Billy remarked, 'Did you hear that dog barking during the night? A real dog's bark, not the howl of the desert pyards. I thought we were back in Yorkshire.'

As we prepared to move on again, Captain Pomfret appeared. 'Take a good look round at the greenery, lads,' he said, 'because this morning we're striking into the desert again. Our Armoured column's making a dash south-west for the coast road at Agedabia, with a view to cutting off the Germans at Benghazi.'

'Where's Agedabia, sir?' asked Billy.

'A hundred miles short of El-Agheila on the Libya-Tripolitania border.'

'El-Agheila – that's where our earlier campaigns came to grief, isn't it?' asked John.

'Yes, but not this one,' said the captain. 'Remember, we've got our First Army knocking at Rommel's back door now. Oh, incidentally, we've just learned that when this offensive started Rommel was back in Berlin, and a General Georg Stumm was the temporary commander of the Afrika Korps. He suffered a fatal heart attack during that first terrific barrage. I'm sure that helped to set the cat among the pigeons. Rommel's back again now, by the way.'

Our convoy moved off, plunging deep into the desert once more. The terrain quickly changed to a series of rough sandy boulder-strewn wadis and ridges, slowing our progress to a bare twenty-five miles an hour. Alan was up top on lookout when he called out, 'There's a hold-up ahead. I can see a line of vehicles stopped in front of us.'

Our CO's car signalled the rest of us to halt, and as we looked out we saw Major Forsythe's car heading towards the stoppage and Captain Pomfret's driver bringing him round the convoy. 'Cookhouse truck serving lunch in ten minutes,' he shouted, 'and Major Forsythe is off to find out what the trouble is. It can't be Jerry – they haven't got anything as far inland as this. We're on an ancient camel track that's a short cut to the southern camel track from Siwa Oasis to Agedabia, where our Armour's hoping to cut off the Afrika Korps who've started falling back from Benghazi. There's a detachment of our Long Range Desert Group standing by on high ground overlooking Agedabia, but they only have light weapons.'

It was a good hour before Major Forsythe returned, and at the same time the congestion began to clear. Within minutes we were on our way again and the cause of the delay became apparent. The rough track led over an escarpment, descending in a series of twists and hairpin bends. Part-way down a large tank transporter had slithered sideways, completely blocking the way forward. It had taken all this time to shift it out of the way.

As we reached the bottom of the escarpment the hard track deteriorated into sandy dust, and our whole column moved into desert formation to reduce the dust clouds. We kept going for several hours, and I was sitting on top when I caught sight of unmistakeable battle smoke on the horizon. At the same time our CO gave the signal to halt at a wave from the radio truck. The radio operator stepped out and hurried to our leading car. The Armoured part of the column continued in the direction of the smoke, and soon we clearly heard the cracks, bangs and rattles of a conflict ahead. After half an hour the sounds died away and the smoke cleared as we moved forward once more, running out on to the coast road a few miles further along. A dozen or more black cross-emblazoned tanks and half-tracks lay scattered about, twisted, torn and still smoking, a large one hundred millimetre mobile enemy gun overturned in a ditch, and an armoured car with the turret completely blown off gave silent witness of the battle that had taken place.

We moved on a little further, then our CO's car drove off the road on to a large flat area, followed by the radio truck and Major Forsythe's car. A discussion took place, and then the major's car moved down the line ordering us to pull over for the night. Soon Captain Pomfret was round. 'We got word that no mines had been laid in this area – they didn't have time. Our cooks are going to get cracking with our evening meal.'

'What's happening, sir?' asked Sergeant Ross.

'Quite a bit of what's left of Rommel's Armour managed to squeeze through before our column turned up – the Long Range Desert Group chaps just couldn't hold them. Then when our heavy stuff turned up the few who hadn't managed to get through shot back to Benghazi. Don't worry, they're well surrounded and will soon be flushed out. Our pursuit column's close on the tail of those who managed to get through, and we think they may try to make a stand at Mersa Brega, twenty miles this side of El-Agheila. There's a natural defensive position there with some minefields. As for us, we stop here tonight and follow on tomorrow morning.'

After an early breakfast we formed up into a convoy and waited. Three hours went by, with our CO making several trips to the radio truck, then Billy said, 'There's a conflab going on between our CO and the rest of our officers.'

Moments later Captain Pomfret was with us. 'Lunch first, then move off. Jerry's trying to make a stand behind his minefields, but he's desperately short of fuel and ammunition. He's not going to hold us up for long.'

Later we travelled on for about fifty miles, then pulled off the road near a sheltered cove on the sea-shore, where a milestone on the roadside held an arrow pointing west and the words 'Mersa Brega'. The distance marking had been chipped away. We stayed put for several days, which would have been completely frustrating but for our heavy armour and supply trucks that continued to pour past, heading west. Then on the morning of 16 December our captain came racing round. 'Ready for off in one hour!' he called out.

'Where, sir? We haven't heard any sounds of action,' said Corporal Wallace.

'Forward, of course. There were no sounds of battle because the New Zealand Division did a two hundred mile left hook round the enemy defences, hoping to cut them off while we battered them from this side. Unfortunately Jerry took fright and managed to slip away during the night, but never mind, every move takes us a step nearer Tripoli.'

Once more we were on the move, relieved that we could travel on the tarmac road again: the Royal Engineers had done a rapid job of clearing the mines from the road and verges, and filling holes made by shellfire. A few miles more, and a road sign brought the realisation that we were now in Tripolitania, beyond the barrier where both General Wavell and General Auchinlech's attempts had come to grief.

Billy, on lookout, called out to us to see a huge white marble arch towering more than thirty feet high at the roadside.

'It looks like a ruddy great tombstone to me,' said Corporal Wallace, 'but I can't work out what the inscription says.'

'You won't,' I said, 'because it's in Italian.'

'Well, go on then: you're the language expert.'

It was true that I had bought some Italian and German dictionaries in Cairo, which I had studied during our spells of inactivity in the desert, but by no means did I consider myself an expert. However, as our truck drove slowly past the towering monstrosity I managed to work out 'Il Duce – Triumphal Arch – Tribute – Heroic – Italian – Settlers'. 'It's a tribute to the brave Italians who invaded this country and settled here, and it was erected by Mussolini.'

A few miles later our convoy turned off the road again to park on an open sandy plain. 'Do we put the shelter up, sir?' Sergeant Ross asked the captain.

'No. We're likely to be here for just a few days, and we can do any sick parades and treatments from the truck tailboard. But by all means put your bivouacs up – it's getting chilly at night.'

Christmas crept up on us as we waited there, and to our incredulous delight we discovered that our supply system, which now included a fleet of Dakota transport aircraft, as well as shipping that was able to deliver at Benghazi port, had brought simple Christmas fare – all in tins, of course. We enjoyed turkey, potatoes, carrots and peas, and Christmas pudding and custard. But the greatest joy of all was a sack of mail, which arrived on Christmas Eve. After eating the unexpected Christmas meal I sat there with a lump in my throat, reading and re- reading the precious letter from Edna that recalled the Christmas we had spent together with the Hansons in Warsop. The vision of her sweet loveliness filled my mind, and an aching longing for her welled up inside me. I blew my nose loudly, secretly wiping away a tear which was running down my cheek. I glanced around embarrassed that someone might have witnessed my show of emotion, but everyone was engrossed in their own private thoughts.

On the same day the news filtered through that the Axis forces had retreated from their shaky defence position at Sirte to a new defence line between Homs and Tarhuna to the west of Beurat, and the Eighth Army was pressing them hard.

A couple of weeks into 1943 our Armour started to press forward again. with the Desert Rats and the New Zealand Division setting out on 15 January to make a wide detour deep into the desert to outflank this latest enemy defence position. The going was atrocious, from rocky hills to soft shifting sand. Meanwhile the Highland Division launched an all-out frontal attack, but the Afrika Korps hung on grimly. It took four days of bitter hard fighting to dislodge them, and even then they resisted every inch of the way.

Meanwhile our column, trying to achieve a lightning encirclement, had to dig their vehicles out every few miles. The Highlanders fought their way forward yard by yard until they reached a point thirty miles from Tripoli, where a ridge of high ground was only a mile inland from the coast road along which the Highlanders were fighting. This was where the Germans had dug in their artillery and mortars, and they threw everything into the attempt to knock out the Highlanders. Attack and counter-attack followed until, mounting their final greatest attack, the Highlanders struggled in hand to hand combat from gun position to gun position along the full four mile stretch. Finally the last gun was silenced, the last mortar knocked out.

Suddenly our two divisions managed to reach firm ground and came racing to Tripoli. The enemy troops took flight, heading for the Tunisian border a further hundred miles to the west, closely followed by our two divisions. This cleared the way for the Highland Division to enter Tripoli, and on 23 January 1943 the town officially fell to the Allies. The Highland Division was chosen to lead the victory parade in recognition of their final blood-drenched battle, following which they were to take up garrison duties there. The Highlanders had their own field ambulance following closely, and all the casualties were rushed into one of the town hospitals, which they took over until an Army field hospital unit, already on its way from Egypt, could take over.

The One Five One, along with the Support Group, who had been helplessly held on the gridlocked coast road, moved on beyond Tripoli, and we set up our shelters on a flat strip of land on the Tripolitanian side of the border with Tunisia.

The rest of the Support Group moved on to take up positions along the line of communication up to Medinine, in Tunisia, where our Desert Rat Division and the New Zealanders faced the latest enemy defence position; it was said this had some salt flats rather like Qattara, though not as extensive. Captain Gemmel's ADS took over sick bay duties, leaving us at rather a loose end, but we needn't have worried because towards the end of the third week on the site Captain Pomfret came over to our truck with a broad grin on his face. 'I bet you chaps are bored to tears with having nothing to do,' he said casually.

Corporal Wallace looked up with suspicion from the sock he was darning. 'What did you have in mind, sir?'

'How do you fancy taking these five first class nursing orderlies down to Tripoli for a day or two, Corporal?' he enquired.

'Sounds to me as if there might be a catch in it,' said the corporal.

'No catch – it'll keep you busy, though. They desperately need some fully trained nursing orderlies to help out at the military hospital. The number of casualties suffered by the Highland Division during that last battle has had them working night and day without a break.'

'I thought they had the field ambulance that was attached to the Highlanders working at the hospital, sir?' I said.

'Oh yes – but they moved on somewhere else when the proper field hospital lot turned up – before the full extent and serious nature of the casualties was appreciated.'

'What if our unit moves on?' asked Alan. 'Do we stay in Tripoli?'

'No way,' said Captain Pomfret. 'We'll call you back again, don't you worry.'

We piled our kit into the fifteen hundredweight truck that was to transport us down to the military hospital. 'Off again, you lot?' asked the driver, an old friend from the early Newcastle days. 'I don't know how you do it, but you always seem to get the best jobs.'

'You mean like being between our Armour and the Germans first time up the blue?' said Arthur with a wry grin.

The drive into Tripoli took about an hour in the fresh morning sunshine, and the Italian civilians seemed to be going about their lives in a normal fashion; some even waved to us as we went by. There did not seem to be a great deal of damage to the town itself, but it was a different matter at the harbour – where sunken ships and wrecked port facilities made it look as if an earthquake had struck. However, a team of Royal Engineers, helped by some Italians, was hard at work clearing things up. Already one jetty was in action, with shallow-draught lighters drawn up beside it. A human chain of civilian workers was manhandling boxes and crates of supplies to the quay.

The military hospital stood half a mile inland, a large white two-storey building approached through a square courtyard. On the side of the yard nearest the road stretched a single-storey building with a archway in the middle through which we entered, halting outside a large open door where a freshly painted sign said 'Reception'. We climbed out with our kit and went into the entrance hall, at the far end of which a door marked 'Office' stood open. 'Hang on here,' said Corporal Wallace. 'I'll nip in there and tell them we've arrived.' He knocked on the door and disappeared inside. Five minutes later he was back. 'Grab your kit and follow me,' he said, picking up his webbing equipment. We followed him back across the courtyard, where he inserted a key into a lock and threw open a door which led into a narrow passage. We followed him through another door into a large airy room. 'This is it! Our quarters while we're here.'

The room had a clean, well-scrubbed wooden floor with ample space to lay down our kit and bedding, and a smaller room at the far end housed a toilet and ablutions. A light bulb dangled from the ceiling, and as John tried the switch on the wall the room was bathed in light. Heavy curtains at the window offered blackout, and a small table and two chairs stood by the window.

We spruced ourselves up and reported back to reception, where a corporal clerk ushered us into the office of the senior medical officer, a RAMC lieutenant-colonel. Corporal Wallace introduced himself and the five of us.

'I'm very grateful to your CO for allowing you to give us a hand,' said the SMO. 'We're desperately short of trained medical staff on our wards, particularly the two major surgical ones, and until we get the extra field hospital staff promised from the Nile Delta Base Hospitals your help's invaluable.' He pressed a bell push on the desk. 'I'm going to hand you over to the senior nursing sister, who's in charge of all the wards.' A side door opened to admit a slim, middle-aged, medium height lady, whose dark hair had silvery threads in it. She wore the distinctive grey and red uniform of the QAIMNS. 'Morning, Matron,' continued the SMO. 'These experienced first class nursing orderlies and their corporal from a field ambulance, with lots of desert battle service, have been loaned to us to help out in our present crisis.'

The lady turned to us, and her slightly forbidding appearance was lightened by a charming smile. 'That's the most welcome news I've heard for many a day. My poor overworked ward staff will be so pleased to see you.'

'Good. Let's waste no more time. Why not take them along to Surgical One and Surgical Two, Matron, and see if we can ease some of the strain.'

As she led us along a corridor she remarked, 'After all your time in the desert battles, I expect you'll be accustomed to dealing with serious injuries.'

'True – but we never knew what recovery they made,' I said.

'Well, you'll have an opportunity to see that here.' She led us to a small office between two wards packed with patients, and introduced us to the young QAIMNS lady. 'Sister Davidson, here are six well-trained young men who are going to help us with our problems.'

To our relief we settled into the ordered routine of the surgical wards without any difficulty, helped by Sister Davidson's sense of humour and quick wit. It reminded me of our early days at the Royal Victoria Infirmary, and with three of us to each ward on either day or night duty we soon managed to make a difference.

With some time off duty, we were able to catch up with news of how the war was progressing elsewhere. We learned that in the First Army front in Tunisia our troops and the Americans were making very slow progress against the German forces under General von Arnhim, where the terrain hindered every mile of hard-fought advancement.

On the Eighth Army side of the Tunisian front, Rommel's Afrika Korps was holding its own so far. On the Russian Front the Germans, having captured Stalingrad, found themselves in a massive Russian winter counter-attack, surrounded and vastly outnumbered. In the Pacific British and American forces were engaged against the Japanese, and German aircraft were still making raids on Britain, though our vast airforce and the Americans were causing havoc in Germany in return.

On the morning of 8 March we were busy on the wards when the SMO came striding along accompanied by Captain Pomfret.

'Hello, it looks as though we're on our way again,' said John, who was helping me change dressings. The two officers stepped into the sister's office, and we saw her appealing to them. Then Captain Pomfret knocked on the office window and waved us to join them. We all went over.

'Back to the unit is it, sir?' asked Corporal Wallace, rather sadly.

'Well, that was the general idea, but I've had an impassioned plea from Sister Davidson here to let you stay until the permanent field hospital replacements turn up. They're already on their way from the Nile Delta region. I've agreed to let you stay until they arrive. Our unit's moving up into Tunisia tomorrow. I've accompanied Captain Price down in one of our ambulances – he runs ADS Four and has some sort of a bug – so I'll look after his lot while he's laid up. I'm sure he'll be fit enough to come back with you in a day or two when you're relieved.'

Up in Tunisia the New Zealand Division managed at last to make contact with the enemy to the south-west, while the Eighth Army Armour doggedly hammered away until on 26 March the sheer weight of the Allied thrust overcame enemy resistance, and they broke through to link up with the New Zealanders. A large number of the enemy managed to escape, falling back to Sfax.

It was the SMO who brought news of the arrival of the long-awaited new staff.

'So it's back to our unit, is it, sir?' asked Corporal Wallace.

'Afraid so. There's an ambulance bringing casualties down this morning, and it'll take you and Captain Price back to your unit. Thank you for all your help. We'll be sorry to see you go.'

We said our sad farewells to Sister Davidson and the matron, and climbed aboard Cliff Rigg's ambulance; Captain Price was already waiting for us. We gazed out of the small rear windows as the hospital dwindled in size behind us, gradually blending in with the harbour and the town. It was dark by the time we pulled into a grassy field south of Sfax where the One Five One shelters were set up.

Captain Pomfret was there to greet us. 'Put your bivouacs up and settle in for the night, then you can fix up our shelter in the morning. The enemy's been flushed out of the Sfax area, and has fallen back to Sousse – but don't worry, I don't think they'll be there much longer.'

He was right. On 13 April the Seventh Armoured Division joined up with the First Army Sixth Division and on 12 May General von Arnhim surrendered. The next day Africa was freed from the grip of the Axis forces. Whatever else happened, the One Five One could pack up and move on, adapting to different needs for as long as men cried out for succour.

CHAPTER

18

It was 4.30 in the afternoon in the latter part of June, and our unit had been travelling since mid-morning from Sfax, where we had provided our usual sick bay facilities for units camped nearby. The last half-mile was over a rough track leading off the coast road a short distance outside Tunis, and we finally drew into a small sandy enclosure bounded by a six foot high prickly cactus fence.

Our CO stepped out of his staff car, bellowed 'Officers!' and waved them to congregate around him. 'This'll do,' he boomed. 'The hedge will keep the draught away at night. Tell the men to put up their bivouacs in the shelter of it.'

'I don't fancy being near that lot for long,' muttered Major Forsythe, gazing at the ugly foliage with a shudder of distaste.

'Only here until we get further instructions, Major,' said the CO. 'You, Captain Pomfret, away and do your usual trip around the trucks. Tell them to park facing the hedge, but leaving enough space for their bivouacs.'

'Will do, sir,' said our captain, 'though I'm not sure about that hedge.'

'Natural windbreak, Pomfret, natural windbreak, shame to waste it. Where's that wretched batman of mine? BENSON!' he bellowed in full voice. 'WHERE ARE YOU?'

Grinning to himself, Captain Pomfret drove around to pass on the details about parking, and where the CO thought we should put our tents.

'I'm not putting mine anywhere near that cactus stuff,' said Alan. 'It looks as if it could hold some nasty surprises.' His forebodings proved well justified. As daylight faded and we were eating our evening meal, a wicked-looking black spider crawled out of the hedge and bit one of our drivers on the arm. In a blind panic he leapt to his feet, convinced he would die. Within minutes he was shivering violently and complaining that his arm was numb. Captain Pomfret heard the commotion and hurried over. Noting the red inflammation an inch around the bite, he took a small scalpel from a sealed container and made a small incision, allowing the blood to flow naturally for a moment or two, before saying to Sergeant Ross, 'Take him and put an antiseptic dressing on that, Sergeant. He'll be all right now.'

At that moment an outraged bellow from the CO's tent had our captain hastening away. He was away for a few minutes, then his car came round again. 'Tents down, everybody into the trucks again, and shake your bedding and tents well before putting them aboard. There's rather too much natural life in this spot for us.' We could see his shoulders shaking with laughter. 'And another dressing, Sergeant.'

We carried out his instructions, and when I wandered over towards the CO's tent I heard the captain say, 'There, I'll just put this dressing on now sir, and then it will be fine. It was the hedge. I said I felt uneasy about it, didn't I?'

'Well, it seemed such a natural windbreak, Pomfret.'

'Perhaps you didn't break enough wind, sir,' the captain chuckled. 'That would have stopped it!'

Our trucks and ambulances followed the officers back along the stony path and three miles along the main road before halting at a bare and grassless plain. It was almost dark by the time our bivouacs had been put up once more.

'Something was making you laugh, sir,' said Sergeant Ross. 'Was the CO bitten on his arm as well?'

'Well, no – not exactly. I'm not at liberty to divulge precisely where, but he's had to borrow one of Major Forsythe's air cushions.'

'Quick move, that one, sir,' chuckled Arthur. 'Even Rommel never had us moving away so quickly .Where next, I wonder?'

'I can give you a little snippet of information. There's a Special Services corporal coming to do a bit of work on our vehicles in the morning – probably be with us a couple of days.'

'What we want to know is where we're going, sir,' said Billy.

'Going? Oh, a spot where there's plenty of fresh fruit,' chuckled the captain, beating a hasty retreat.

'Well, I'm off to my bed,' muttered Sergeant Ross. 'We can only wait and see.'

'Sarge,' called out Billy, 'tell the RASC bloke on guard duty to shoot any of those spiders if they come marching up the road.'

'They wouldn't bite you. They'd die of alcohol poisoning.'

Corporal Hodges turned up the next morning with 'Special Services Division – RASC' stencilled on the door of his fifteen hundredweight truck. In the rear were an assortment of tins, jars, rubber and metal pipes, rubber sheeting and various small tools. 'I've come to do your vehicles,' he announced. 'I need to see your transport officer.'

The guard escorted him to the officers' tents, where they were joined by Lieutenant Landon and MSM Pugh, officer and sergeant major of our RASC, and after a few moments' discussion they all came over to our ADS truck and spoke to Bert, who was tinkering around with his beloved engine. After a short discussion the lieutenant and the MSM went away, leaving Bert and the corporal to pore over the truck engine. Finally Bert said, 'OK, Corp, you get cracking. She's in good fettle so you shouldn't have much trouble.'

He left the corporal to fiddle around under the bonnet, and came across to the rest of us, where Billy was saying, 'I tell you, that truck's loaded up with tins of thick grease, jars of sticky, gluey stuff and some kind of mastic – you know, like they put round the glass in windows.'

'Come on, Bert,' said Corporal Wallace. 'What's going on?'

'Oh, nothing much,' murmured Bert, trying to appear casual. 'He's come to waterproof our vehicles, that's all.'

'Why? Are we expecting a lot of rain?' asked Arthur, suspecting a legpull.

'No, the engines,' said Bert, enjoying his moment of glory. 'He has to make them watertight so they can drive ashore from a landing craft without it having to go right up on to the beach.'

'Landing craft? Beach? Where?' yelled Arthur and Corporal Wallace.

'What's all this about going ashore from a landing craft?' came the voice of Sergeant Ross, breaking off from his task of checking the contents of the medical pannier.

'Corporal Hodges is going to stop the tide swamping our truck when we go invading, Sarge,' answered Bert with a huge grin. We shot around to the front of the truck where Corporal Hodges was lighting his pipe, puffing out clouds of pungent smoke into the air.

'Come on, out with it, Corporal,' said Sergeant Ross. 'Where are we bound for?'

''T ain't no manner o' use you arstin' me them questions,' grunted the corporal stolidly, blowing out another great cloud of smoke. 'I don't know nothin'. All I do is go round bungin' up 'oles as directed. It just 'appens to be your turn to 'ave your 'oles bunged up today.' And we had to be content with that. We watched him as he went round all the vehicles, brushing on his sticky compounds, filling up holes with his black mastic, sealing the gaps in the cab floors where the pedals came through with his rubber sheeting, and finally fastening a right-angled pipe to the exhaust so that the open end was level with the roof. 'There y' are,' he said, with a satisfied nod. 'That should get you to dry land without splutterin' to a standstill.'

Once the corporal had finished treating our vehicles we did not have long to wait. The day after his departure, 10 July, 'Fergie' Ferguson, the canteen truck orderly, came rushing across in high excitement. 'Hey, lads,' he exclaimed, 'I've just picked up a news bulletin on the truck radio that said our North African forces have landed on Sicily this morning, and have managed to establish a bridgehead.' The canteen truck became our focal point for the next few days, as we struggled to hear the newsreader against the background of static. It sounded as though things were going well for us.

Four days later Captain Pomfret came striding across to our section truck, and we could tell from his expression it was important news. 'We're on our way directly after lunch,' he announced. 'We drive to a loading point on the coast a couple of miles away. Check that everything's safely aboard the truck, because if you forget anything there's no coming back.'

'Sicily, sir?' I asked.

'I'd say that's a fairly safe bet. I did say we'd be going to pick some fresh fruit, didn't I? I hope you all like tomatoes and grapes.'

Our vehicles reached the embarkation beach in the early afternoon, joining a long line of trucks and cars already waiting there. 'Hey, fellers, just look,' called out Billy. We crowded to the open front of the truck and stared in amazement at row after row of long, low-profile landing craft coming up to the beach, dropping their doors down on to the hard shingle like gaping mouths anxious to swallow up the waiting vehicles.

As each vessel accepted its quota the doors were raised and it moved swiftly out to sea, with another empty vessel moving in to take its place. Soon we reached the front of the queue and hastened aboard one of the three vessels taking our unit. By late afternoon all the waiting vessels were filled, and the small flotilla was on its way.

As the shoreline receded Captain Pomfret sought us out. 'Any more for the *Skylark*?' he said. 'What more could you desire than a nice Mediterranean cruise – all expenses paid?'

'An even nicer cruise to Blighty, sir,' said Corporal Wallace.

'All in good time, Corporal, all in good time. For now I have to pass on to you some instructions from the naval officer in charge. You're to wear your steel helmets all the time, in case we receive any unwelcome visitations from the skies. After the first couple of days enemy air activity has been fairly light, but you never know. Better safe than sorry.'

'Which part of Sicily are we heading for, sir?' asked John.

Our captain produced a large map of the island and pointed to a red cross on the eastern side. 'There it is – a small harbour named Augusta about half-way up. The latest news has it that our troops have pushed ten miles inland, and it'll take another two days before we arrive. So, as I said, enjoy your cruise while you can.'

Rations had been issued before we set out that morning – not the bully and biscuits of our desert days but something new called 'Compo', which had been brought out when the First Army landed in Tunisia. They were boxed, pre-packed meals with crispbread, butter, cheese, jam and meat pastes, all sealed in individual foil wrappings and issued in a separate box to each man; our large vacuum tea flasks had been filled as well.

We did not have much room to move around, and spent our time close by our vehicles. At night we wrapped our blankets around us to keep out the very cool breeze.

Shortly after our midday meal on the second day of our voyage Alan, gazing ahead, shouted, 'Land – away in front of us. I'm sure it is.'

'Pull the other one,' grunted Corporal Wallace. 'I can't see anything.'

'No, he's right,' said Billy. 'It's just a tiny grey smudge, but it's land all right.'

During the next hour the smudge grew in shape and form, filling the whole horizon. The green of the land, white buildings with red roofs, and white roads up the rising ground behind the port were quite clearly visible. Then the harbour came into view, with a couple of Royal Naval escorts nestling against the quay and beached landing craft up against the sloping concrete ramp, to allow vehicles to drive ashore with no need to plough through the water.

'Pity Corporal Hodges went to all that trouble,' muttered John. 'At least we won't get our feet wet.'

As soon as our turn to disembark came round our three landing craft nosed up to the ramp, our vehicles were driven ashore and we followed. As soon as we were reunited on the quay our CO, who had been consulting a red-tabbed staff officer, climbed back in his car and waved the rest of us to follow.

'Well, what do you make of that?' said Corporal Wallace, as we drove smoothly away. 'I think I expected enemy guns firing and their aircraft dropping bombs – not just coming ashore nice and peaceful.'

'Don't speak too soon,' said Billy. 'That's asking for trouble.'

As we drove along the quay some local fishermen spreading out their nets waved to us, and as we drove along the cobbled streets with their white-walled, red-roofed dwellings we saw children playing beside the doorways. We found it hard to imagine that this had been enemy territory just a few days earlier. Beyond the tiny harbour town the white road climbed up the hill, lined with cactus bush hedges white with dust. On all sides were greenery, flowers and fruit trees. After the drab monotony of the desert it seemed like a Garden of Eden. However, before we could develop a rosy-tinted false sense of security, our peace was rudely interrupted by the hair-raising whine of diving planes and the staccato chatter of machine gun fire, which had us desperately leaping from our trucks to find what cover we could among the hedgerows. Fortunately we were not the target, but a tell-tale plume of black smoke rising from the harbour indicated that this Garden of Eden still had some serpents.

'Hey, fellers, what about these?' breathed Billy as we scrambled back into the truck. In his hands were three tomatoes almost as big as pomegranates, beautiful, ripe and red. 'They sort of fell off the plant into my hands as I lay there.'

'Whoa – stop. Don't eat them!' said Corporal Ross. 'They need a good soaking in a sterilising solution to kill off all the bugs, or you could find yourself laid low with something quite nasty. That goes for all of you. Are you listening?'

'All right, Sarge,' chuckled Billy. 'I know all about typhoid and dysentery and stuff. I wasn't really going to put them straight in my mouth. Let's get a big basin of pot. permang. solution ready. We're going to need it.' As the trucks moved on again Billy carefully placed his prizes into a large kidney dish to await further treatment.

Our CO led the way up the hill for a further two miles, then turned on to a wide path through the hedge, on to a grassy orchard, which was set within a fence of stunted cactus bushes, on the far side of which, through a narrow pathway, lay a cultivated area of tomato plants, laden with ripe red fruit. Through the fence on the other side was a small vineyard, with line after line of grapes ripening in the sunshine. Captain Pomfret's car came bumping across. 'Move over there and set the shelter up,' he called, indicating a spot thirty yards further along. Glad to have something positive to do after our inactivity of the last few weeks, we soon had the great canvas sheet unfolded and pegged around our truck, among the lemon trees where the fruit was turning from green to yellow and the almond blossom was drifting on to the grass like snowflakes. The wide spaces between the trees allowed plenty of room for our trucks and shelters.

As soon as we had everything fixed up Billy set out on a tour of investigation, to return shortly with a large cloth filled with ripe red tomatoes and another with ripened grapes. Corporal Wallace brought out an enamel bucket half-filled with potassium permanganate, observing sarcastically, 'I guessed you were doing a good neighbour act, helping to remove some of the ripe fruit before it rotted on the trees.'

Sergeant Ross added, 'We know you had the most pure and unselfish motives in mind!'

After ten days ashore in Sicily the noise of battle receded as the Allied task force continued to press inland, encountering pockets of resistance from both German and Italian troops that slowed the forward advance, and over on the far side of the island, where American troops had landed, there were reports of heavy fighting. So far the number of casualties from our region was small, but we were kept quite busy providing sick parades and sick bay treatment for the various service units located nearby. At the end of the second week our ration truck returned from its daily run with a large object draped in tarpaulin almost filling its back. The driver, 'Jacko' Jackson who had completely recovered from his spider bite, said 'You'll never guess what I've got in here!' as he pulled up beside our shelter.

'I know,' said Billy. 'It's a distillery, and we are going to start making brandy out of all these grapes.'

'It's a railway engine, and we are going to start a mountain railway,' said Arthur.

'Huh, think you're clever, don't you?' snorted Jacko. 'It's something better than that. It's it's a generatin' set – you know – electric, and a whole lot of cable, lampholders, lamps and stuff to go with it as well.'

'I hope you didn't pinch it!' said Sergeant Ross, frowning.

'No, it's official. Our transport officer organised it all. There's even a little petrol engine that drives it. It's all there, nice and compact on a baseplate. Jack Yardley, one of our mechanics, used to be an electrician. He'll have us all lit up in no time.'

For the next couple of days Yardley, with the help of a couple of his mates, worked hard laying cables around the camp and fixing lampholders in the shelters, so that the lamps would not throw direct light outside the canvas. When the time came for the great switch on the petrol engine was started and the switches were flicked, and the shelters were bathed in brilliant light, or brilliant compared with the faint glow of the hurricane lamps we had been accustomed to.

As the fighting continued, with the enemy putting up fierce resistance on all fronts, our shelters were in constant use dealing with casualties and providing sick bay facilities as a regular stream of ambulances continued to bring us new patients, and take down to the casualty clearing station now opened in southern Sicily those who needed more extensive treatment.

One day, having completed our morning sick parade, we were sitting enjoying our mid-morning brew when the sound of heavy hammering from the far side of the orchard had Arthur gazing in curiosity out of our shelter flap. 'Something's going on over there,' he said, 'but I can't make out what it is.'

Alan, who had been over to the QM stores for medical equipment, returned, and to Arthur's query replied, 'Tents. There are half a dozen Service Corps blokes working like mad putting them up.'

'We don't need any more tents,' said Arthur.

'What sort of tents?' I asked.

'Like the one the officers use for a mess, big enough to accommodate more than one person.'

The next time we saw Captain Pomfret, Billy asked, 'Are we expecting to hold on to a lot more patients, sir?'

'More patients? Not that I'm aware of.'

'So what's the idea of the tents, sir?'

'Ah, those tents,' grinned our captain. 'I wasn't going to mention them . . . let it come as a pleasant surprise to you all.'

Even Sergeant Ross and Corporal Wallace stopped what they were doing, and the sergeant asked suspiciously, 'What sort of a surprise, sir?'

'Nurses,' said the captain with a bland expression.

'Nurses? What nurses?' we shouted.

Captain Pomfret was enjoying himself. 'All right,' he chuckled, 'I suppose I'll have to put you out of your misery. Later today a small party of Canadian military nurses, newly arrived out here, is going to stay with us for a few days before going down to join the casualty clearing station staff. The idea is to give them some idea of how we go about our work in the forward areas. They'll help us in our shelters while they are with us.'

'What, real female, feminine nurses?' asked Billy, sceptically.

'Yes, real female, feminine nurses, as you put it. I understand they're quite good lookers, but before you start letting your imagination run riot I must warn you that they're under very strict supervision. The sister in charge is a real battleaxe and stern disciplinarian – so be warned, absolutely no hanky-panky.'

That afternoon an ambulance drew up, followed by a fifteen hundredweight truck carrying suitcases and bedrolls. The vehicles came to a halt outside our orderly office tent, where the CO and Major Forsythe were waiting to greet them, as a masculine-looking nursing sister with iron grey hair stepped purposefully down from the ambulance and strode towards our two officers. She was dressed in olive drab slacks and shirt, in place of the familiar grey skirt, cape and white blouse worn by British military nursing sisters. She had a hatchet face, and she directed a steely gaze at them. 'Good afternoon, Colonel Thompson, Major Forsythe,' she said in clipped tones. 'I am Sister Blenkinsop, presenting my nurses to you.'

'Told you,' grunted Billy. 'Our boss was kidding when he said good lookers. It'll be do this, do that, from morning to night – you'll see.'

'I hope you've arranged duty guards for their area during the night. I don't want my girls pestered.'

'Huh. If she's anything to go by they won't need guards,' said Billy, disconsolately.

The rest of the nurses began to step down, and Alan chuckled. 'You've got it all wrong. Billy, just cast your eyes over this lot. Every one a stunner.'

The nurses were dressed like the sister in charge, but the plain attire only served to enhance their natural youthful beauty. On the pocket of each shirt the red and gold motif of the Canadian Army Medical Corps Nursing Service glinted in the sunlight. They stepped across to reclaim their cases and bedrolls from the truck and, assisted by the two Service Corps drivers, followed their leader towards the newly erected tents.

'Hmm. They aren't sleeping wrapped in a blanket on a groundsheet,' said Corporal Wallace. 'They've all got big luxurious sleeping bags.'

'I wonder if they'll run out screaming for help at night if they see a creepy-crawly in their tent,' chuckled John with a wicked grin.

'You can forget that, lads,' came the voice of Captain Pomfret. 'They've done training under canvas in Canada, as well as a tough course in self-defence, so you might be the ones running about screaming.'

That evening Billy returned from a stroll around the orchard, which by strange coincidence took him past the nurses' tents. 'There's a couple of RASC blokes on guard patrolling the area between their tents and our camp,' he said, 'but what I'd like to know is who's keeping a watch on the guards?'

Next morning our captain escorted a petite brunette to our shelter. 'This is Holly. She'll be part of our team for the next few days. I am leaving her in your care, Sergeant Ross, and I expect you all to behave like perfect gentlemen towards her – or you'll have me to answer to as well as Senior Sister Blenkinsop.'

'Spoilsport,' murmured the young nurse, dimpling prettily as he moved out of earshot.

Sergeant Ross shook her hand. 'Where are you from, Holly?'

'Vancouver. I trained in the large hospital there, but when my guy came over to England to join the RAF I thought I ought to do something as well, so I joined the military nurses. And here I am.'

Our sergeant introduced her to each of us, and she grasped each hand in a cool firm grip. When we stepped inside the shelter there were stares of incredulous amazement from the stretcher patients, which brought another tinkling laugh from her. 'What's with you guys?' she chuckled. 'You been out here so long you forgot how a lady looks?'

This disbelief was matched by the sick parade patients from nearby units, who all tried to join the queue for treatment by this pretty, twinkling-eyed Canadian girl. 'Hey, you guys,' she said, 'I'm here to help out – not to treat the whole Allied Task Force.'

'Have a rest, Holly,' chuckled Sergeant Ross. 'Our lads will deal with the rest of them while Billy introduces you to the mid-morning tea ritual.' Gratefully she stepped aside as the rest of the queue glared in disappointment.

Holly proved to be a lively and intelligent girl, with an infectious and impish sense of humour. As well as lightening our workload she enlivened our day-to-day existence – that of Captain Pomfret included. The same could be said of the other shelters, where the rest of the young nurses were equally appreciated.

They had been with us about a week when there was an incident which reminded us that enemy aircraft raids should not be treated with complacency. There had been several sneak daytime raids on nearby Augusta Harbour, and just as one of these was quietening down a single enemy plane, flying very low, approached our orchard. Watching, cold with anticipation as it moved ever so slowly over our heads, we caught sight of a big black bomb caught somehow beneath it, swinging wickedly back and forth as the plane stuttered its way slowly, oh so slowly, over our heads. Holly was the first to recover as it staggered away. 'Gee fellers, what a whopper! Mom told me about guys when I was a nipper, but she never said planes had one as well.' Released from our icy fear we laughed until tears ran down our faces.

Sadly, two days later our lovely companions received orders to move down to the casualty clearing station where they were needed, and with aching hearts we were obliged to say farewell. Sergeant Ross thanked them. 'You've brought beauty, laughter and freshness into our lives for a short and precious time.'

CHAPTER

19

Several days after the Canadian nurses departed we heard that Palermo, the capital city of Sicily, was in our hands, and hard on the heels of that news we learned from our canteen radio that Mussolini had been arrested by Italian patriots up in northern Italy. With enemy resistance crumbling fast, Allied troops pushed the retreating remnants across the Straits of Messina to the Italian mainland. By late August the battle for Sicily was over, and in September the Allies launched an attack across the Messina Straits to gain a foothold on the mainland.

John came rushing back into our shelter one morning. 'Have you heard the latest about Musso?' he burst out. 'I've just heard it on the canteen radio.'

'You mean about the Patriots arresting him?' asked Corporal Wallace.

'No, that's old news. The Italian authorities have disowned him and thrown in their lot with us,' said John.

'Huh. I can't see the Germans taking that lying down,' snorted Sergeant Ross. 'If I know anything they'll try to reinstate him.' He proved to be a true prophet, because later that day we heard that the Germans had rescued the imprisoned dictator and spirited him away to a secret hiding place. Not surprisingly, they also declared their intention to fight on in Italy.

Our troops pushed forward in southern Italy with lightning speed until they were halted at a new defence line that stretched from Termoli in the east to south of Salerno in the west. Here the Germans were holding on grimly, with all roads to the north coming under the range of their artillery, dug into the steep hillsides. On the day following the declaration of the Italians' intention to join the Allies, we heard that the Fifth Army had begun a seaborne landing on the plain outside Salerno, hoping to make a quick dash for Rome. Unfortunately the Germans had been tipped off and had massed their forces there, so our landing force found itself up against very tough opposition. Our mainly unseasoned troops of the Fifth Army had to fight every inch of the way ashore, and the idea of a quick dash to Rome was dropped. We also learned that on the eastern side the Eighth Army, after recovering their breath following the rapid scramble northward and with supply columns re-established, was setting out to crack the artillery screen. By mid-September the Eighth had managed to reach Potenza at the same time as the Fifth, after a fierce and costly fight had gained Salerno, allowing our two forces to link up in a solid line, with a large portion of southern Italy completely clear of enemy troops.

We were still camping in the orchard near Augusta, anticipating the order to move onward at any moment. It came as no surprise when Captain Pomfret hurried over and said, 'Strike the shelter and pack everything on to the truck. At ten o'clock tomorrow we're all embarking at the wharf where we landed.'

'Which way are we heading, sir?' asked Sergeant Ross.

'Don't know for sure – but as it's a landing craft job I guess it's somewhere in Italy. But wherever it is we'll soon know.'

Next morning, with the unit trucks carrying loads of fresh fruit that had been quickly gathered and stored in every spare nook and cranny, we set out for Augusta harbour. Civilians had now returned to their homesteads, and some stood at their gates waving and cheering, making rather rude suggestions in Italian as to what we should do to their enemy. The landing craft were waiting for us, lined up with steel doors agape, ready to gobble up our transport. There was no waiting. As soon as everything was safely secured the vessels were on their way, chugging out of the harbour. We noticed that the Fascist and Nazi slogans which had decorated the walls had been hastily painted out and replaced with 'Viva gli Alliati'.

'What does that mean?' Corporal Wallace asked me.

'"Long live the Allies". It hasn't taken them long to change sides,' I chuckled.

Out in the open sea the landing craft headed northward, and Captain Pomfret came strolling round to check that we were all right. 'Drop of home-made lemon squash, sir?' asked Billy, proffering a bottle of cloudy liquid and a medicine glass. 'All prepared under the most hygienic conditions. We washed the bottles out with phenol gargling mixture before we used them, and boiled the contents as well.'

Our captain poured himself a glassful and sipped it with appreciation. 'We could have done with some of this when we were up the blue,' he said. 'I'll have another, if you have no objection.' He refilled his glass as he spoke.

'How about telling us where we're heading, now we're actually on our way, sir?' asked Arthur.

'Why not. It's the port of Taranto up on the instep of Italy, famous for the one man submarines they build and service there. And don't worry,' he added, seeing our look of alarm, 'it's already in our hands. It's going to be tomorrow morning before we disembark, before driving north towards Brindisi. I suggest we enjoy our sunshine cruise while we have the chance. I don't suppose you could spare me a bottle of this delicious squash? I happen to know that Captain Price has a bottle of gin tucked away – and it would go very nicely with that.'

'For you, sir, yes – a couple of bottles if you like, but please don't go singing its praises too much or we'll have everybody pestering us for some,' said Sergeant Ross, reaching into the medical hamper just inside the tailboard of our truck.

The morning dawned bright and clear after an uneventful night chugging northward. No moon had lit the sky, and only the gentle pitching and the slap of waves against the hull had given any indication of movement while we slept, wrapped in our blankets. As daylight increased and we began to stir, a large port appeared on the horizon, with warehouses and tall cranes becoming more distinct by the minute. It was not long before our shallow craft had manoeuvred into position, lowered their stern doors, and our vehicles were driving ashore. The first one out belonged to our CO, and as it approached the dock gates another staff car moved forward to intercept it; they ended up side by side. A staff officer resplendent with red tabs on his uniform stepped out of the larger car and beckoned our CO to join him. They walked a little way along the wharf deep in conversation, until the senior officer stepped back into his car and was driven swiftly away. Corporal Wallace, who had been gazing intently at the senior officer, said with a puzzled frown, 'That officer, the one with the red tabs, there's something familiar about him. I'm sure I know him.'

By now all our vehicles were out and waiting in a line for the signal from our CO. In response to his wave we all moved off in the direction of the midget submarine pens, which were alive with the noise of hammering and the flash of welding. A half-completed submarine stood in a bay beside the road. 'I've complained about life in the desert,' said John, 'but there's no way I'd go out to sea in one of those sardine tins, let alone go under in one.'

The Italian workmen waved to us as we passed, showing no signs of animosity, and soon we were out of the docks into the outskirts of the port. Looking back towards the harbour, we caught a glimpse of a large white ship with big red crosses on the sides moored about half a mile from the point where we had disembarked. 'A hospital ship,' said Arthur. 'I can't see whether it's one of ours or not.'

'Let's see if I can make it out,' said Corporal Wallace, peering out intently. '*Tosca* something or other. I can't make out the rest because of the bend in the ship's bow.'

'Sounds Italian to me,' said John.

We were moving through the town now, which was full of the normal hustle and bustle of everyday life. People thronged the pavements, and traffic moved along streets lined with shops. 'It all looks so normal!' exclaimed Alan. 'If I didn't know better I'd think we were at home.'

Soon we were travelling north on a good tarmac road through countryside still green in the autumn sunshine. After about five miles our CO's car turned off on to a side road that led to a large cobbled yard with a single-storey barn at the far end. It was the transport officer who came round this time, instructing us where to park, and telling us that the cooks were getting cracking with breakfast.

'Shall we be here long, sir?' called out Sergeant Ross.

'No idea,' replied Lieutenant Landon. 'All I know is that the CO's calling all the officers for an important discussion as soon as breakfast's over.'

We managed a quick wash and shave then dashed for our breakfast. As we came away we saw our officers congregating around the CO's car. Soon Captain Pomfret walked slowly towards us in deep conversation with Captain Price.

'Time for another little trip, chaps,' said Captain Pomfret with a broad grin as they joined us.

'Where are we off to now, sir?' asked Corporal Wallace.

'Not all – just the five nursing orderlies and you, Corporal.'

'Has this anything to do with the staff officer who talked to our CO as we came ashore, sir?' asked Billy.

'Staff officer? You mean to say you didn't recognise Deputy Assistant Director of Medical Services Colonel Swindale, our old CO in all his glad rags?'

'I wasn't sure, but there was something familiar about his build and slight stoop, sir.'

'Yes indeed. He informed us that he got such a glowing report about you lot from the CO of Tripoli Military Hospital that he wouldn't entertain anybody else for the job.'

'What job? Sounds a bit ominous to me,' muttered Corporal Wallace.

'Nothing of the sort. It'll be a piece of cake for you lads, and it'll only last two or three days at the most. You saw that hospital ship in the harbour? It's Italian, Ospedale Nave *Toscana*, complete with Italian medical officers, nurses and orderlies and an Italian naval crew. They did a runner out of Trieste in the far north before the Germans could impound the vessel and landed up in Taranto. The DADMS wants to use it to ferry a boatload of Allied patients and casualties down to the casualty clearing station at Catania in Sicily. He wants you lot and a medical officer to go with it to keep an eye on things. You'll be back in just a few days.'

'Aren't you coming with us, sir?' asked Corporal Wallace anxiously.

'No, but you'll be pleased to know that Captain Price is taking charge of your little party,' he said, indicating the little Welsh MO beside him.

A faint expression of dismay probably crossed our faces, for although he had only been with our unit for a short time we had all come to realise that what the officer lacked in inches he made up for in his rather bossy and officious manner. If he had a sense of humour he kept it well hidden. Captain Price took up the conversation. 'As Captain Pomfret has told you, my orders are to ensure that all our patients and casualties on board receive the proper treatment. I understand that some of the Italian staff can speak a little primitive English, and also that you, Private Hill, have been learning Italian and are fairly fluent.'

'I wouldn't say fluent, sir, but I can get by. I just hope this doesn't turn into a permanent posting, that's all.'

'Nothing of the sort,' snapped Captain Price. 'You heard what

Captain Pomfret said – just two or three days. I have no desire to be permanently involved with a bunch of jabbering foreigners.'

'Right, that's settled,' said Captain Pomfret. 'Grab your kit. My driver will run some of you down to the harbour, and the rest can go down with Captain Price and his driver.'

Moments later we were climbing into the two cars and were on our way, quickly covering the distance back to the harbour to draw up beside the gangway of the immaculate white ship. It seemed to be about as big as the SS *Northumberland*, which had brought us out from England, and the wisp of smoke drifting from the single funnel confirmed by its sharp tang that it was a coal-burning vessel. Captain Price marched importantly up the gangway and we followed, to be met at the top by the Italian first officer who welcomed us in a quaint and hesitant English, explaining as he escorted us along the deck that the 'good capitan' would be accommodated in a private cabin on the top deck among the ship's senior officers, and the rest of us in double cabins amidships on the main deck. With a muttered command in Italian he summoned a waiting cabin steward to accompany us to our quarters as he took the 'capitan' to the top deck.

We followed the steward to three cabins in line on the starboard side, with an adjacent small messroom which contained a long central table with upholstered seats down either side. He made gestures that indicated this was where we would have our meals, and left us to sort ourselves out. We had a look in the cabin nearest the messroom. It was comfortable and well equipped, with a bunk on each side with a soft mattress, white sheets and blankets. At the end of each bunk stood a large wardrobe and on the bow side were two portholes which could be opened to let in fresh air.

'This looks like being a comfortable trip,' said Corporal Wallace. 'Tell you what, you can share this cabin with me, George, because I'm going to have to rely on you to tell me what these Italians are jabbering about. The rest of you, sort yourselves out in the other two.'

We were putting our kit away in the wardrobes when the steward knocked and entered, and handed a menu to the corporal.

'NOT – UNDERSTAND – ITALIAN!' said Corporal Wallace loudly and slowly.

The young Italian tried by gestures to indicate what was on offer, with no success. Eventually Corporal Wallace relented. 'Put him out of his misery, George.'

I spoke a few words of Italian, and the look of relief that flooded the steward's face had to be seen to be believed. He launched into a flood of speech and gesturing, at such breakneck speed that I could only interpret about one word in three. I held up my hand to stem the flow.

'Parlare lento e semplice, vi prego,' I said, 'Slowly and simply, because I just learn your language. In that way we understand each other.'

Comprehending, the steward slowed down, and chose his words so that I could follow him. He had an ambition to emigrate to America, he told me, as soon as the stupid war was over, because he already had an uncle living there. His name was Aldo, and would the kind English soldier please teach him to speak the English?

'I'll do what I can, but as we're only with you for a few days it'll be difficult to make much progress.'

'So after all that Italian, what's on the menu?' asked Corporal Wallace.

'Minestrone soup followed by pasta bolognese, with fresh fruit for dessert. And he wants to know if he can start serving right away.'

'Good idea,' said the corporal. 'Let's have our lunch before they start bringing patients aboard. Tell him to go ahead, and I'll tell the other four to join us.'

The table had been set with a crisp white tablecloth and appropriate crockery and cutlery, and the soup and pasta were delicious. The fruit turned out to be small ripe pears, washed, peeled and halved. Finally the steward uncorked a bottle of red wine, pouring a little into a glass and handing it to Corporal Wallace.

'Is that little drop all we get?' he said, pulling a face.

'No, he wants you to taste and approve it,' I laughed. 'Go on, try it.'

He sipped, nodded and smacked his lips in approval as the steward filled the glasses.

Captain Price popped his head round the door as we were finishing, and Corporal Wallace called us to attention, knowing the captain's penchant for discipline. 'All right, at ease, men,' said the captain, gratified. 'It appears that you've got nothing to complain about, so let's talk about the job in hand. We expect patients to arrive this afternoon, and I want you all on the wards, and you, Private Hill, will move around using your knowledge of Italian to handle any misunderstandings that might crop up. I've been informed that the senior nursing sister, a lady thirty years of age, learned some English while in college in Rome, so between the two of you it should be possible to sort things out.'

'Nurses, sir?' asked Billy in feigned awe. 'Women, you mean?'

'Certainly, Private Hough. Why, do they frighten you?' asked the captain tartly.

'Oh no, sir, on the contrary. I was thinking how things have changed.'

'Are we supposed to apply dressings and give treatments, sir, as we've done in our own unit?' asked Corporal Wallace.

'Certainly not! Our job is to supervise, and nothing more. There are ample fully qualified medical officers, nurses and medical staff already. We'll have to sort out any problems, of course, but I'm in charge and you must rely on me. Although this is an Italian ship it's under British control.' He turned and trotted off to his cabin.

'We'd better wander round the wards – find out where everything is,' said Corporal Wallace. 'We need to know before the patients arrive.' He turned to me. 'You lead the way. You'll have to do most of the talking.'

Off we went, visiting each of the five wards in turn. The rows of beds stood empty, displaying immaculate bed linen. In each ward I explained who we were to the Italian nursing sister and her five orderlies, telling her that one of our group would be assigned to each ward, while I, with my rather limited Italian, would try to sort out any language misunderstandings. Finally we met the three Italian medical officers who would be seeing our patients, and again I explained my role.

Our tour was barely completed when the ambulances started to arrive on the quay. I hurried to the top of the gangway to find Captain Price waiting impatiently, with an Italian medical officer beside him. 'Ah, there you are, Hill,' he rapped out. 'You stay here with me as I look at each patient's documents, then you can tell this Italian chap what the injury or ailment is and he'll send him to whichever ward is appropriate. Will you explain that to him?'

It all sounded rather complicated, but as I passed on the instructions the Italian smiled and said 'Capito'. Turning to Captain Price, he said very slowly 'Un-der-stand.'

All went surprisingly smoothly, and as soon as the ambulances were empty the ship's gangway was raised, the ropes tethering it were released and we were under way.

'That went quite well, Hill,' said Captain Price crisply. 'We make a good team. I'm off to my cabin – number twenty-two if you need me.' And he strutted away up the steps.

All our patients were British, apart from six Canadians. They all seemed to accept that the Italians were fully trained medically, and that as I was around to smooth out any misunderstandings there was no point in worrying. One of the things I had expected to cause a little dissension was our British soldier's desire for a good cup of tea, something not wildly popular in Italy, but I needn't have worried. The senior nursing sister, a charming, intelligent young woman, said in hesitant English, 'Signor Giorgio, I learn the art of tea making the English way from my English tutor in Rome University, and I will supervise the brewing of patients' tea.'

The rations that had been hurriedly taken on board at Taranto were naturally Allied army rations, and I wondered how the galley chef would cope with them. I had met him as I went around the ship – he was a huge fat hulk of a man, Austrian by birth, who had lived in the Italian port of Trieste for most of his life and had an Italian wife. He had a volatile nature and uncertain temper, but despite his Austrian origin he bore no resentment towards the Englishmen who had taken over, choosing instead to vent his temper on the Italian stewards, who always approached him cautiously. Frequently we saw him chasing one or other of them out of his galley, bawling wild oaths at them in fractured Italian. When I first met him he asked in a mixture of English and German what we expected him to cook 'mit der tins of cow meat und vegetables'. I explained that this was a vast improvement on the bully beef and dry biscuits that our desert troops had endured. This seemed to strike a chord of sympathy with him, because he went out of his way to make the simple rations more palatable by adding herbs and spices. The serving of the evening meal in the wards brought no complaints, and we returned to our mess room, where Aldo was waiting to serve us. For all the Austrian chef's grumbles about our tinned stew, his addition of freshly cooked vegetables produced a very tasty and satisfying meal, and to our delight the steward produced another bottle of fine German wine. I asked who was supplying the wine, and he told me it had belonged to the German supervisory staff who had been left behind when the ship slipped away from Trieste.

'That was a brilliant meal,' said John, sitting back with a smile. 'I fancy a stroll along the deck now. Anybody else in favour?'

We all agreed that this was a splendid notion, and followed him out to the open deck, expecting to have to grope around in the moonlight as it was early evening.

We staggered back at the sight that met our eyes. The whole upper surface of the ship was brilliantly illuminated from stem to stern with floodlights that played on the red crosses which adorned the sides of the vessel. 'They must be stark raving mad,' exclaimed Corporal Wallace. 'If a Jerry submarine sees this he'll torpedo it.'

I stepped across to an officer who was standing nearby, and asked if it was not rather risky to be showing all this light.

'But, Signor, we always travel like this. We're a hospital ship and we show the red cross. No one will attack us.' I hadn't the heart to tell him of the time we were shot up by enemy tanks in the desert – in spite of the huge red crosses on our shelters and ambulances.

We stayed a little longer, enjoying the cool sea breeze, before making a final tour of the wards. Everything was going smoothly, so we retired to our cabins to enjoy the comfort of clean white sheets and soft mattresses.

I awakened next morning as a tap on the door preceded the entry of Aldo, who bore a tray on which stood two cups of steaming tea. 'Morning tea, sirs,' he said in halting English, adding in Italian, 'That is how Senior Nursing Sister Vincenza said I should announce it.' Corporal Wallace stirred in his bunk, and sat up with a beam of approval.

'We are almost arrived, Signor,' said Aldo, pointing through the porthole. 'There is Catania.' I looked out and saw pinky-white buildings shining in the morning sunshine about half a mile away. 'We wait for permission to berth, Signor Giorgio. I do not think we wait long.'

'You'd better ask him to serve our breakfast,' said the corporal, jumping out of bed. 'A quick wash and shave before we eat, and then we must do a trip round the wards, warning them to have the patients ready when the ambulances come to pick them up. You know, that's the best night's sleep I've had since our leave in Cairo,' he added. 'I could get used to this.'

A little later Aldo tapped on the door again to tell us that he was serving our breakfast, and we hurried next door to find the other four already sitting there. Our steward began to spoon porridge into dishes, and Billy picked up his spoon and had a taste. 'This is proper porridge, made with oats! How come an Austrian cook knows how to make real Scottish food?'

I asked Aldo, and he said that Fritz had been a cook on a Scottish tramp steamer before the war started. 'That's why he took a shine to us,' I said.

We finished off with beans and sausages – from the tinned rations of course, but cooked and presented with care and very appetising. We had just finished eating when Captain Price came along. 'I hope you've alerted the Italians and the patients that the ambulances will be along soon,' he said to me. 'Our captain, who speaks a little English, tells me we're about to move up to the quay.'

I assured him that everything was organised, and sure enough at 9.30 the sound of the anchor being raised and the feel of movement confirmed it. By 9.45 our vessel was nudging alongside the quay. Some of the ambulances were already waiting, and as soon as the gangway was lowered the stretcher-bearers came aboard. Captain Price stood with me at the top of the gangway and made sure that each patient had his documents correctly completed; this was a double check, because Corporal Wallace and the others were supervising each departure as they left the ward. Loaded ambulances drove away and returned empty: for a while it was like a busy bus terminal. By midday the last stretcher had been carried ashore and the last ambulance had trundled away, and an air of comparative calm settled over the ship.

'Well, that's that,' said Captain Price brusquely. 'We've done quite a good job. Any problems to report?'

'Nothing we couldn't handle, sir,' said Corporal Wallace, 'and the Italians seemed to deal with the patients very efficiently. What happens now?'

'According to the captain we lift anchor and make our way back to Taranto right away. It's likely to be the early hours of tomorrow morning before we get there, so make the most of your free time. Enjoy the fresh sea breezes while you can!'

CHAPTER

20

After another very comfortable night we were wakened once again by Aldo's knock and the rattle of crockery on his tray as he brought our morning tea, to find that we were already moored against the quay at Taranto. After the patients had departed the previous day I had spent time giving Aldo some very basic English lessons, and he said with a woeful countenance, 'I – sorry – today – you – go.'

'My word, yes, we'd better get a move on,' said Corporal Wallace, breaking off in the middle of a stretch, 'or else our truck will be here before we've had our breakfast.'

By 9.30 we were waiting at the top of the gangway, our kit beside us and on the lookout for our unit fifteen hundredweight truck. At 9.45 a vaguely familiar staff car pulled up, and a red-tabbed staff officer climbed up on deck and acknowledged the startled salute of Corporal Wallace. 'It's – er – you – Colonel Swindale, sir, isn't it?' he stammered.

'Good morning, Corporal Wallace,' said our original CO. 'How are you – all of you? Had a good trip, eh? Didn't expect anything else. I know my lads from the One Five One – capable of coping with whatever comes up. Now where is that Captain Price of yours?'

'In his cabin, sir,' said Corporal Wallace nervously. 'We'll get him for you right away.'

Aldo was nearby on the deck and I called out to him in Italian, 'Go and ask our captain to come at once, please. Tell him in English, "Important English officer wants you". Can you do that?'

He answered, 'Si, Signor Giorgio,' and hurried away.

Colonel Swindale said, 'I told them you would manage the interpreting job, Hill. And you, Corporal, why are you looking so nervous? I don't remember you being like that when I was your CO.'

'Well, er, no sir, but you didn't have all this then.' Corporal Wallace waved his hand in the direction of the red tabs.

'Hah, don't worry, Corporal. I still have a soft spot for my own lads.'

Captain Price came bustling down the steps, red of cheek and anxious of expression. 'I'm sorry to keep you waiting, sir,' he gasped. 'I had no idea you'd be coming.'

'Of course you didn't, Captain, how could you?' responded the colonel tersely. 'No need to get in a tizzy about it. Matter of fact, I want to congratulate you – all of you – on a well-executed mission. There's something I want to put to you. Mind if we all go up to your cabin for a little chat?'

Meekly, Captain Price led the way up the steps followed by the colonel, with the rest of us tagging along behind. The two officers entered the cabin but we hung back, uncertain if we should enter. 'Bring them in, Corporal,' boomed the colonel. 'Don't hang around outside!'

Corporal Wallace marched us in and saluted. 'All right, Corporal, at ease' said the colonel wearily. 'You're getting as bad as Staff Sergeant Menham when I first promoted him to sergeant major. Now, to the business in hand. What's your opinion of the standard of treatment on this ship, Captain Price?'

'To be honest, I expected the worst when we came aboard, but I was wrong. The standards of both treatment and catering are excellent, sir.'

'What about you chaps? Were you treated all right?'

'Couldn't be more comfortable – and the galley chef seems to have taken a shine to us, sir,' said Alan.

'Good. I'm glad to hear you say that,' said the colonel, a wintry smile flitting across his face. 'I need you to do one more trip for me – give you a chance to renew acquaintances in Tripoli. I've got some more serious longer-term patients who need transferring down there quickly, and there are some at Catania as well, so you'll need to pop in there on the way down. I've arranged for some more rations to be picked up there as well as some medical supplies. The whole round trip shouldn't take more than a week to ten days.'

Captain Price looked a little put out. 'Our unit CO will need to be notified, sir,' he said anxiously. 'I asked him to lay on transport to pick us up this morning.'

The DADMS raised an eyebrow, and this time there was a real twinkle in his eyes. 'It's all right, Captain. I've already informed him that I need you for a few days more. I knew I could rely on you to help me with my little problem.' He turned to me. 'Bit of a linguist now, Hill, eh? Where did you pick that up?'

'I bought an Italian dictionary when I was on leave in Cairo, sir, because we had a shelter full of wounded Italians up the blue and it's difficult to treat someone when you can't talk to him.'

'Hah, yes, good thinking, that. It's reassuring to know that someone can keep tabs on what these Italians are rabbiting on about.' He turned to Captain Price. 'I must have a word with the ship's captain – I understand he speaks passable English – so if you'd be good enough to escort me to his quarters. In the meantime,' he said, turning to us, 'why not whizz off round the wards and warn the Italian sisters to expect another load of patients very soon. Have a good voyage!' With that the senior officer stumped off towards the bridge with Captain Price struggling to match his pace.

'Well, what do you make of that?' exclaimed the corporal. 'Tthere we were feeling a bit sad about leaving the ship, and hey presto we're going on a trip to Tripoli.'

'That's all very well,' grumbled John, 'but what about when we've done this extra job? What's Colonel Swindale going to dream up next? He has a funny habit of saying "just one more trip, and that's it". Who's to know he isn't already cooking up another surprise for when we get to Tripoli?'

Sister Vincenza looked up in surprise as Corporal Wallace and I entered the ward. 'Your transport is very late! I thought you would be on your way to your unit by now.'

'It seems you're not getting rid of us so easily, Sister,' said our corporal. 'We've received instructions to accompany another batch of patients to Tripoli, calling again at Catania on the way. The ambulances are due to arrive at any time.'

'Oh – che sorprisa! I think that you, Signor Giorgio, must hurry round the other wards to let the Italian staff know. The beds need fresh sheets.'

Back on deck again I noticed the big staff car driving away, and moments later the first of a line of ambulances began to draw up at the gangway. Captain Price must have been on lookout because he came down, accompanied by one of the Italian medical officers. 'I understand that most of our new patients will already have been receiving treatment, so if you'll translate my comments about injuries and treatments to Dottore Verrezi here, he'll make notes on the patients' documents for the ward staff.'

The transfer of this relatively small number of patients to the wards was completed in a couple of hours, and before lunch was served the *Toscana* was heading south once more, making excellent time, and we heard the anchor being lowered in the calm waters outside Catania as we retired to our bunks that night.

The next morning, as the patients were being given breakfast, the anchor was raised and the ship moved in, to tie up at the same wharf as before. We noticed quite a number of wooden crates on the quay. 'They must be the rations and stores the DADMS promised us,' said Arthur. It was not long before a huge crane began lifting the crates up and lowering them through open hatch covers into the hold beneath.

Captain Price and Dottore Verrezi approached along the deck. 'The ship's captain has just passed on a radio message, saying that our patients are on their way,' said the Welsh captain with a frosty smile, 'so I suggest you report to your wards – all except our interpreter, who will of course stay with me.'

'Anything different, sir?' asked Corporal Wallace.

'Yes. This time we've got ten officer patients coming aboard. Sister Vincenza has a small extra ward under her care specifically for officers. Please ask her to get it ready.' The captain turned to me and as the first ambulance drew along to the foot of the lowered gangway added, 'Only just in time by the look of it.'

Soon the gangway was echoing to the clomp of the stretcher-bearers' boots as the patients were carried aboard. They were followed by a shorter line of men hobbling on crutches, some with plaster casts on their legs, others with arms immobilised at strange angles, others walking slowly but showing no outward signs of injury.

The Italian medical officer murmured something to me as the last few were being dealt with. 'What does he want to know?' asked Captain Price with a frown.

'He's saying how well organised we are. We get them into the wards quicker than they usually do.'

'Hmm, quite. I don't believe in a lot of palaver. Get them into the wards where they can be examined properly, that's my motto,' he said with a tiny smile of satisfaction.

By the time darkness fell we were on our way south once more, enveloped in our blaze of light. I was standing by the ship's rail enjoying the cooling breeze when I noticed a light flashing some distance away. When I turned round I was greatly relieved to see answering flashes from the bridge of our vessel.

'We must look like a pleasure steamer with all these lights blazing,' said Arthur from behind me. 'It still gives me the collywobbles.'

We sauntered down to the mess room where Aldo was setting the table for our evening meal. 'I come for more English lessons tonight, Signor Giorgio, at nine o'clock, bringing my notebook,' he said in Italian.

'Aldo, that won't do! Say it again to me – in English, please.'

'I come – for English lesson – nine of clock – please you – sir George,' he said slowly.

I couldn't help laughing. 'Not quite right. In our language you may call a man "sir" as a token of respect, but if you add his first name you imply he's been awarded a knighthood – and I certainly haven't!'

'Is molto difficile this English,' sighed Aldo, waving his hand in despair.

'The sooner you teach this chap to talk proper English the better it'll be for us all,' said Corporal Wallace.

'OK, Caporal, I speak you English,' said Aldo, with a grin. 'You like drink good wine for dinner?' He produced a bottle of marsala from behind his back like a conjuror performing a trick and filled up our glasses.

'Go on then, Corp. Give the lad a word of encouragement,' said Billy. 'You must admit he's trying his best.'

'Oh, er, yes. Vino molto buono,' the corporal announced in a loud voice, adding 'Wine very good' to avoid any misunderstanding.

Aldo winked at me and broke into a flood of Italian at breakneck speed, which left Corporal Wallace open-mouthed and speechless.

'What did he say?'

'Just "You're welcome" – or words to that effect,' I chuckled.

★ ★ ★

The following morning we were finishing our breakfast when the ward orderly from Sister Vincenza's ward came dashing in and said to me that Sister Vincenza was having a problem with one of the officer patients. I hurried along to find her standing with a red face beside the seated officer. 'What's the trouble,' I asked her.

Before she could answer the patient, a Royal Artillery lieutenant, interrupted loudly. 'I was offered a menu, and I chose prosciutto for my breakfast. Now this person tells me I can't have it.' He pointed to the blushing sister, who explained to me in an undertone that the ward orderly had given him the wrong menu.

'I'm afraid she's quite correct, sir,' I said with a smile. 'Our rations don't extend to such delicacies. You can have tinned bacon and fried egg, or just boiled egg. That's all we can offer.'

'Who are you, a mere private, to tell me what I can or can't have? I demand to see your officer at once.'

'Somebody asking for me?' came Captain Price's voice as he entered the ward. 'Just what's the trouble, Lieutenant?'

'I was offered a menu, and I indicated my choice, and now this woman,' he waved an angry arm towards Sister Vincenza, 'and this English private are trying to fob me off with frizzled bacon or hard-boiled eggs, and I demand to be given what I've chosen.' By now his voice had risen to a shout.

'Do you mind just stepping into the nursing sisters' office, please?' said Captain Price calmly, though I could detect a steely glint in his eyes. With a angry shrug of his shoulders the lieutenant followed him in and the captain firmly closed the door. What was said I have no way of knowing, but within five minutes the lieutenant's angry bluster had disappeared and he was hanging his head in embarrassment when they came out of the office. Captain Price said briskly to Sister Vincenza, 'The officer will be content to accept whatever food you're able to offer him.' He turned and left the ward as the lieutenant sat down beside his bed, head down and glancing neither right nor left.

With a little smile Sister Vincenza thanked me, and I walked back to our mess room to find Captain Price talking to the others.

'Thank you for sorting him out, sir,' I said.

'That's all right. I've come across him before. He was in the officers' club in Cairo one time, kicking up a similar row in there. He ended up being barred, so I reminded him politely of the incident. I think I quite upset him,' he added, with the nearest thing to a grin we had ever seen on his face.

* * *

It was two more days before we reached Tripoli, during which time we suffered no more upsets or difficulties. The transformation that had taken place since we were last there was amazing. Apart from the sunken wreck, the whole harbour area had been cleaned up and the damaged cranes were repaired and working. The *Toscana* moved up to the quayside immediately after lunch, and it took the whole afternoon to transfer our patients to the ambulances that were waiting to take them to the military hospital.

It was a relief to relax after our evening meal with the bottle of Kummel that Aldo had produced, announcing 'Compliments of Tedeschi'. It was quite potent and we ended up feeling rather light-headed. We were laughing like hyenas at one of Billy's bawdier jokes when Aldo popped his head round the door and hissed, 'Your capitano – he come to visit you.'

'Mesh, attenshun,' muttered Corporal Wallace, who had probably enjoyed a little more of the fiery liquid than the rest of us. We staggered to our feet as Captain Price entered. 'At ease, at ease,' he said. 'You appear to be having a relaxing evening. I came to tell you that I've received a radio signal asking me to go ashore tomorrow morning for a meeting with the senior medical officer at the hospital, and it occurred to me that you might like to come along too, as you spent some time on detachment there. Can I take it that you all wish to accompany me?' We all nodded our assent. 'Very good. As this vessel must anchor in the harbour, I'll request the captain to have us brought ashore in the ship's motor boat – and returned afterwards, of course. Be ready for an early start immediately after breakfast – even if some of you are suffering the after-effects.' He gave a little nod in the direction of our corporal as he departed.

I noticed that Alan seemed particularly pleased about this visit, and mentioned this to Arthur. He laughed. 'He worked in the same ward as Sister Davidson, and they got on very well together. I think he rather fancies her. He keeps on about her.'

At nine o'clock the following morning the motor boat was lowered and we followed Captain Price down the gangway, stepping gingerly across the dancing gap between the bottom of the steps and the deck of the tiny boat, which was bucking alarmingly. The crewman started the engine and we shot away, bouncing over the wavelets and throwing up clouds of spray. Minutes later we were climbing the jetty steps, and our captain turned to me. 'Tell our boatman he's to pick us up at twelve o'clock – and impress on him not to be late.'

I passed on the message, and the crewman saluted before roaring away.

'Right. How far to the hospital, Corporal?' asked Captain Price briskly.

'At least a mile, sir. It's a good long walk.'

'In that case I'll ring the hospital and ask for a car to collect us. We don't have time to waste in walking!' He strode across to the harbourmaster's office.

'Where are you lot from?' came a harsh voice behind us. We turned to see the burly figure of a Military Policeman, immaculately uniformed with his red cap on his head. 'Are you patients from that Italian hospital ship?'

Corporal Wallace stepped forward and explained rather sharply that far from being patients we were on special supervisory duty on that vessel. 'Our officer's in the harbourmaster's office, arranging transport down to the hospital,' he added.

Rather taken aback, the Military Policeman grunted, 'Staying overnight, then?'

'Very unlikely,' replied our corporal, 'since he's ordered the motor boat to pick us up at noon.'

A few minutes later a huge staff car drew up, the driver got out and took a step towards the office as our captain came out. 'You Captain Price, sir? Needin' a lift to the hospital?' He saluted.

'That is so, driver,' the captain answered primly, 'And I hope you can fit in these other chaps as well.'

The RASC driver looked rather taken aback at the sight of another six hefty passengers, but he shrugged his shoulders and muttered, 'I wondered why they insisted I brought the biggest car. Pile in.'

As he drove through the town it was obvious that much effort had gone into repair and restoration, now that the threat of air raids had diminished. Soon we were entering the courtyard that surrounded the hospital. 'What time do you want taking back to the harbour, sir?' asked the driver, halting beside the administrative block.

'Kindly pick us up at 11.45, driver,' Captain Price replied. He turned to us and said briskly, 'You all heard that. Off you go and meet your friends again, and make sure you're back here in time.'

We turned left, heading for the long corridor that led to the wards. The hospital seemed to be bursting at the seams, with occupied beds in every available inch of space, and patients sitting around in chairs, chatting. 'Let's go to Ward One and surprise Sister Davidson!' said Corporal Wallace. When we knocked on the door of the sister's office we heard her tired voice. 'If you're some more patients from that wretched Italian hospital ship, we're full up. I don't know what Reception are playing at. I rang them up and told them we already had more patients than beds.' Then she looked up, and her face registered amazement, followed by recognition. 'Oh, it's you lot from the One Five One.' She hesitated, lost for words, and her eyes lit up as she caught sight of Alan. 'I do hope you'll come and work with us again. I'm sorry I was so crotchety with you just now, but a hospital ship's brought a load of patients down that we can't possibly take in unless we get rid of some of our long-term and convalescent patients, and the ship to take them is in Alexandria.'

The door opened and Corporal Baxter, the senior RAMC orderly, entered. 'Oh, this is where you are! I've just come from the SMO's office. The officer in charge of these lads has been having a real set-to with him about these new patients. Don't worry,' he added, seeing her look of dismay, 'I think they've got a solution. You lot are going to rescue us again by taking the long-term patients off our hands.'

'What do you mean?' said Corporal Wallace.

The phone on the desk rang, and Sister Davidson picked it up. She turned to us. 'Captain Price needs you in the senior medical officers' room right away. It sounds urgent.'

Corporal Wallace hurried us along there and knocked on the door. We entered to find both officers, rather red of face and frowning. 'What's up, sir? What's this about more patients?' asked Corporal Wallace anxiously.

The SMO took over the conversation. 'It seems that timings have got a bit mixed up. Your DADMS knew that we intended to move quite a large proportion of our special needs patients down to the Delta region, but the normal hospital ship's been delayed, which has thrown the cat among the pigeons. After some frantic radio signalling we've agreed – not without some dismay on the part of your captain, I might add – that you'll do this one final trip down to Alexandria and back. I hope I can count on you fellows to help us out once more.'

Corporal Wallace turned to our officer again, who shrugged his shoulders and held out his hands. 'I'm afraid it's the only way out of complete chaos, Corporal. We've sent a radio signal to *Toscana*'s captain instructing him to up anchor and come in right away. I'll ask the staff car driver to take us back at once so we can sort everything out.'

We trooped back to the forecourt, where the staff car driver sat smoking and reading a magazine. 'You're early,' he said. 'I thought you said 11.45.'

'Change of plan,' said Captain Price as we clambered aboard, waving frantically to Alan who was saying a sad goodbye to Sister Davidson. The driver pulled away, and drove us swiftly back to the quay where the gangway had already been lowered, allowing us to hurry aboard. Instead of a relaxing hour or two with our friends at the hospital, therefore, we were back to the hurly-burly of loading up patients, rations and equipment before voyaging back to Alexandria.

We had been at sea for about twenty-four hours. The *Toscana* was ploughing steadily eastward, moving across the top of the Gulf of Sirte, with no further sighting of land expected until we passed the hump where Benghazi, Barce and Derna stood. The loading of our patients had been achieved very smoothly. Captain Price and Dottore Verrezi, and me as interpreter, seemed to have evolved a satisfactory system for speedily checking the patients and moving them into appropriate wards. The Italian nursing sisters and orderlies were getting used to the likes and dislikes of the 'inglesi soldati', and things were running smoothly. These patients, though still heavily bandaged and in some cases still in plaster casts, were coming to terms with their disabilities – having spent quite a bit of time in various treatment centres already, and were learning to make the best of things.

We had taken on board a fair selection of rations, including fresh vegetables and fruit, which allowed Fritz to improve the meals. He was assisted by three Italian helpers who nervously dashed around, carrying out the fat man's bawled instructions. Memories of the prosciutto incident on our earlier voyage had persuaded us that simple menus based on what rations we received would help to prevent any further misunderstanding, and after a rather heated session with Fritz we prepared some lists in English for the ship's office to type up.

The SMO had managed to organise the delivery of some comforts, playing cards, dominoes and some board games, which helped keep the patients from becoming too bored. In addition the Italian medical staff were picking up some words and expressions in our language, which eased the situation quite a lot.

Most of our patients behaved impeccably towards the Italian nursing sisters, but one day as I was going around one of the younger women called me into her office, and enquired shyly in Italian, 'Could you please tell me what certain words mean? One of the patients keeps whispering them to me with a funny look in his eyes.'

'Tell me the words, Sister Imelda.'

'They are "Shuf-ti C–".'

I held up my hand to stop her. 'I thought as much! It isn't English at all. It's a crude invitation in Arabic to display certain portions of your anatomy, often used in the bordellos of Cairo. I'll have a word with him and he won't trouble you any more.'

The colour rose in her cheeks. 'Thank you for being so considerate. In our language we also have certain words that a convent-educated lady learns to close her ears to.'

As I left the ward I stopped to speak to the patient. 'Just cut out the gutter Arabic,' I said. 'These are caring and dedicated young ladies. The last thing they need is the unwelcome attentions of some sex-starved lout. Do I make myself clear?'

'If you say so, I suppose,' grunted the patient, shamefacedly scowling. 'You RAMC blokes seem to be bosses round here.'

'Has it not occurred to you,' I continued, 'that she may be related to one of the *Toscana*'s naval officers? I'm sure you're aware how sensitive the Italians are to threats to their womenfolk.'

I left him looking rather anxious.

A day later Sister Imelda attracted my attention once more. 'What's the matter, Sister?' I enquired. 'Has he been troubling you again?'

'Oh, no, just the opposite. He's now very polite and helpful. Whatever did you say to him?'

'I just had a little talk about brotherly love,' I replied with a smile.

The only other problem arose on the ward where Billy was supervising. One of the patients, an RASC driver with his leg in plaster, threw the paperback magazines that had arrived with the 'comforts' at Tripoli all over the floor, grunting angrily, 'This ruddy hospital ship. I bet you RAMC blokes pick out all the best books and comforts for yourselves. You lot have no idea what real action's about.'

'And you would, of course, having been in this region for a long time,' said Billy gently.

'Let me tell you, mate,' said the patient, warming to his theme. 'I've been in Monty's lot in the desert since just before the battle of El-Alamein an' I know what it's all about – drivin' hundreds of miles on them roads, in the open desert too. If you blokes had to suffer half of what we went through it'd open you eyes, I tell you.'

'And did you experience the earlier campaigns under Auchinlech and Wavell?'

'Well, no, but they were only skirmishes.'

'The battles to relieve Tobruk, Sidi Rezegh , El Adem . . .' continued Billy relentlessly.

'No . . .' mumbled the driver.

'Then it's high time you shut up and stopped moaning,' said Billy. 'We hospital blokes have been involved in every desert campaign as nursing orderlies with a light field ambulance, right up among the rough stuff and the first to treat wounded servicemen. We happen to be in charge of this ship because we were asked to help move fellows like you out of harm's way as quickly as possible – to give you a better chance of recovery. If you find travelling on this ship so distressing it's a pity you didn't try the alternative route.'

'What alternative route?' stammered the driver, subdued.

'I'd have thought that you ought to be familiar with the overland route back to Egypt. Had you not been enduring a few days of boredom, in comfort, eating well-prepared meals, you could have been bumping and rattling down those battle-scarred coast roads – you know what a hot, tiring, dusty affair that is, even for people who aren't injured, to say nothing of the constant flies, chlorinated drinking water and bully and biscuits to eat.'

Billy related this story to us in the mess room later. 'There was total silence for a few moments,' he said, 'then all the patients clapped and burst out laughing. I've never heard a word of complaint from him since – nor any of the others, for that matter.'

It was the morning of the fifth day since leaving Tripoli, and I knew exactly where we were. I was taking a breather on deck and Alan was beside me. 'That's it, for sure,' I said, 'no mistaking it!'

Alan sniffed. 'I couldn't agree more.'

'What are you two idiots on about?' asked Corporal Wallace, who had come up behind us. 'Have you been at the brandy bottle?'

'No. I'm just saying we'll be docking in Alexandria later today,' I said. 'It's the stench of the tannery. Once you've experienced it you never forget it. It's a better warning signal than a lighthouse. Didn't you manage to get a leave in Alex?'

'No. I had an attack of gyppy tummy, and we moved again before I was fit to go.'

Later that day the *Toscana* steamed quietly into Alexandria, once almost on the battle front. Now the massed naval escorts were missing and the barrage balloons were no longer floating in the sky. There were just a couple of small naval craft, and the occupants of the wharves were Merchant Navy vessels. We eased gently into position alongside the quay, under the guidance of the Egyptian naval pilot who had come aboard while we were still a couple of miles from the harbour. Ambulances lined the quay, partnered by the sleeker, more streamlined American Society of Friends vehicles that were waiting patiently for the gangway to be lowered. Our patients, all keenly anticipating their disembarkation, sat beside or lay on their beds, all clutching the large buff envelopes that contained full details of their disabilities and treatment to date.

At three o'clock the first stretcher carriers came up the gangway and into the first ward. 'All right, you lads,' said the leading bearer, 'we'll soon have you safely out of the hands of these foreigners. I bet you'll be glad to get back to civilisation.'

'You can cut that out for a start,' said the first patient. 'We've never been better looked after nor more comfortable. I don't want to hear one word of criticism about these nurses, and I reckon that goes for the rest of us.' A rumble of assent echoed around the ward.

By 5.30 all the patients had been taken away, and a sense of calm settled over the ship. We saw that two Military Policemen had taken up their stance at the foot of the gangway.

The *Toscana*'s first mate, a huge heavily built man with a face like a battered boxer and a voice like a corncrake, came seeking me. 'Why policemen?' he asked. 'Do they think we'll run away to this land of camel dung and deserts? I want only my dear wife and family in Naples. But what I ask about now is the coal for our boilers. The bunkers are bare and we can go no further until we replenish our stocks. Will you please ask your little capitan to do something about it?'

I promised that I would ask Captain Price about the fuel situation right away.

'I listen to the radio every night, Signor Giorgio, and pray your troops may have freed Napoli from the clutches of the Tedeschi,' the first mate said, gazing at me with imploring spaniel eyes.

'It won't be long before that happens, Bruno, so do not despair.'

I walked along to Captain Price's cabin and knocked on the door, entering to his invitation. 'Ah, Private Hill. I'm just completing my report to the Director of Medical Services Middle East Region about our work here. What can I do for you?'

I told him about the first mate's desperate plea for more coal.

'You can tell him that I'm going to visit the Director of Medical Services first thing tomorrow, and I'll stress the fact that it's imperative the *Toscana* is refuelled immediately, so we can return to our own unit without delay. Oh yes, I've also made arrangements for a Pay Corps officer to come aboard and pay you all. He'll be here shortly after nine o'clock tomorrow morning, so please have your pay books ready.'

'Thank you, sir,' I said, turning to go.

'Hang on a moment. I want you all to call in at the Forces Welfare Depot and see if you can sort out suitable comforts for the *Toscana*'s patients.'

Thanking him again, I retired to my cabin and to a well-earned sleep.

CHAPTER

21

The next morning I was washed, shaved and dressed in the smartest of my khaki drill slacks and shirts when Aldo brought our morning tea. Though I had been tired out the previous evening, I managed to pass on to Corporal Wallace the details of my meeting with Captain Price before falling asleep, and he had made them known to the other four. They were delighted at the prospect of pay and a trip into Alexandria – and especially the chance to get our very untidy hair professionally cut.

We were also looking forward to visiting the welfare depot, and finding books, magazines, writing paper and envelopes. This made me realise that I hadn't written to Edna for quite a while. We hadn't received any mail from home since landing in Sicily, though by now there could be quite a pile waiting for us back at our unit.

At nine o'clock a staff car drew up at the gangway, and a second lieutenant and a corporal wearing Pay Corps badges climbed up on deck. 'I think we'd better go along to my cabin,' said Captain Price, 'rather than attending to our financial affairs on deck.'

As the Pay Corps officer handed out our money in Egyptian currency, he chuckled to his corporal, 'They must be a bit strapped for cash up in the combat zone if these lads needed to commandeer an Italian ship in order to get paid!'

'It wasn't that, sir,' said Billy, his face a picture of innocence. 'We missed our bully and dry biscuits. It's all tins of stewed steak, fresh vegetables and fruit up there now.'

'Can't put one over on these Eighth Army blokes,' the officer said with a grin as he closed his money case and handed it back to the corporal. 'I'm going back to HQ, Captain. That's where the Director of Medical Services has his office. Why don't I give you a lift? I'm sorry there isn't room for the rest of you chaps, but I don't doubt you can find your way around.'

Captain Price gladly accepted the offer of a lift and the staff car shot away in a cloud of dust, leaving us to stroll after it in a leisurely fashion.

'Why not take a gharry?' suggested Alan, as the clip-clop of a horse's feet echoed in the street behind us. We waved the driver over, and after haggling we climbed aboard and ordered him to take us to the Forces Club. The smell of horse manure and old leather assailed our nostrils, kindling memories of our earlier visit as the horse drew us along at a steady pace, ignoring the honking, roaring and rushing motor traffic on every side.

'Forces Club, sirs. Fifty piastre, pliz,' said the driver as he drew up outside the large building.

'We agreed on twenty-five,' growled Corporal Wallace fiercely, 'and not one piastre more will you get.'

We crowded round, adding our displeasure, and the driver finally agreed. 'Me very poor man – many children – need money.' He grabbed the twenty-five piastres and drove away scowling.

'Poor man indeed,' said John. 'Did you see all those gold rings on his fingers? He must be worth a fortune!'

Corporal Wallace suggested that he and I should go the short distance to the address we had been given for the Forces Welfare Office, as the others went into the barber's shop at the Forces Club, rather than all of us sitting in a queue to have our hair cut. We walked down the street to find the welfare depot's door locked. The view through the windows was of a completely empty room

'Number fifty-two: that was the number our captain gave me,' said Corporal Wallace.

When we saw a Military Policeman approaching, I said, 'If you want to know the way, ask a policeman.'

We did just that, and he laughed. 'Do you know, this is the tenth time I've answered that question today. They moved a couple of days ago to the other side of the street and a little further along – number seventy-one. Just make sure you don't go too far, or you'll stray into the red light area.'

With difficulty we made our way across the busy road, and eventually reached number seventy-one. A tiny metal plate on the door bore the inscription 'British Combined Forces Welfare Unit'. We opened the door to find a passage leading to a flight of stairs, at the top of which was a long half-glazed wooden partition, with frosted glass panes. A small sliding window bore the legend 'Please ring and wait'. On the ledge below was a turnkey bell, and the corporal gave its little handle a tweak. As the tinkling ceased we stood and waited. 'You have a go, George. See if you have better luck.' I picked up the bell and kept on turning its key, making a fearful racket.

'All right – ALL RIGHT! That'll do,' came a sharp female voice from inside. 'For goodness sake stop. I'll be with you in a moment.' After a long pause the window was drawn back to reveal a young woman clad in WRNS uniform. Noting our faded and worn KD uniforms, she snapped, 'Yes? What do you want?'

'It's not so much what we want – more what we need,' said Corporal Wallace, smiling.

The young woman backed away in alarm. 'It's no use you coming in pestering me about that sort of thing,' she exclaimed haughtily, the colour mounting in her cheeks. 'This is the Forces Welfare Unit, not one of those places they have further down the road.'

'Just hang on a moment, young lady,' snorted the corporal, the colour in his cheeks matching hers. 'Whatever you imagine we're after, we're here to choose comfort items for the hospital ship that's alongside the quay. I suggest you ring the Director of Medical Services, who'll confirm what I've just said.'

The young Wren gazed at us, unsure what to do.

'Go on,' I said. 'Do what the corporal suggests. Ring the DMS's office, and ask if Corporal Wallace and Private Hill from the *Toscana* can collect any items of patients' comforts they think are suitable.'

She hesitated again, then murmured, 'All right. Just wait there a moment.' She moved away from the window and we heard her on the phone, her tones becoming more apologetic. 'Yes, sir, yes sir, certainly sir.' When she opened the door her cheeks were still flushed but her haughty manner had vanished. 'I'm so sorry,' she said, 'but since we moved over here a couple of days ago I've had one or two servicemen wandering in with some very unsavoury requests. I thought you two were the same. Do come in, please. Have a look at what we've got, and I'll arrange for our RASC driver to deliver everything to the quay.' She led us through the office into a store room, where rows of shelves were stacked with cardboard boxes. 'Nowadays it's mainly the military hospitals in this area who draw comforts from us. Just go ahead – pile everything you need on this table.'

The pile grew as we selected sets of draughts, dominoes, board games like Monopoly and Scrabble, dartboards and darts, bats, balls and nets for table tennis, and of course stacks of writing paper, envelopes, pens and bottles of ink. The Wren, who had introduced herself as June, proved, now that we were not under suspicion, to have a keen sense of humour. When we had chosen all our 'goodies' and were preparing to leave, Corporal Wallace asked, 'Why don't you join us all for a bite of lunch at the Forces Club?'

'I'd be delighted,' June answered, 'but please can my fiancé come as well? I'd arranged to meet him.'

We agreed, suggesting that 12.30 would be a good time.

After another perilous road crossing we made a beeline for the barber's shop just as the others were coming out, looking very smart with their shampooed and tidily trimmed locks. 'Don't have anything to do with these two scruffy blokes,' said Billy as we approached. 'They look like a couple of deserters on the run to me!'

We explained about lunch with June and her fiancé, and arranged to meet again at the Forces Club restaurant. They went on their way, leaving me and Corporal Wallace to join the queue of servicemen in the barber's shop.

We got to the restaurant just before 12.30, to find the others waiting. When we went in we found June and a young man in a pale grey suit already seated at a table large enough to accommodate us all. We introduced ourselves, and June said, 'This is David Eskull, my fiancé.'

I took one look at him. 'Your face looks familiar. I'm sure I've seen you before.'

He grinned. 'Yes, I believe you have. Only the last time you were chasing me out of a big canvas shelter in the Western Desert, up near Sidi Rezegh, shouting rude Arabic words at me. You see, I was dressed like a wandering Arab. In the Long Range Desert Group we liked to try out our disguises now and then by wandering into our Army camps. If we got sworn at in Arabic and chased out we knew our cover was good!'

So what's with the fancy suit?' I asked.

June took up the tale. 'He managed to get himself blown up, and since he recovered he's attended an officer training course. Now he's Second Lieutenant Eskull of the Intelligence Corps. He's on a special mission – but we don't discuss that!'

We enjoyed a lovely meal of fresh salad and cooked meats followed by a very fancy ice cream concoction, but most of all we savoured huge glasses of ice cold lager. We chatted about local news, and David brought us up to date with how things were progressing on the various war fronts. We were delighted to learn that in Russia, where the Germans had seemed to be unstoppable, they were now being forced back.

Corporal Wallace suddenly glanced at his watch. 'Look at the time – we ought to be back by now. Captain Price will have steam coming out of his ears!'

We stood up, saying our goodbyes, and called for the bill, but the former desert trooper waved us to put our money away. 'Don't worry – it's on my account.'

We rushed back to the welfare depot, where the driver of a fifteen hundredweight truck loaded with boxes was waiting impatiently. 'You lads like cutting it fine, don't you?' he said. 'Jump aboard and let's be off before your officer sends out a search party. He's already telephoned twice.'

We scrambled aboard, and drove off with a mighty roar, the driver manoeuvring the tiny truck through the crowded streets like a racing ace, finally coming to a halt at the foot of the *Toscana*'s gangway. At the top of it stood Captain Price, his little moustache bristling with impatience. 'Come on you chaps,' he said testily. 'I thought I was going to have to get the Military Police to chase you back here.'

'Why? Are we on our way back to the unit right away, sir?' asked Corporal Wallace eagerly, a gleam of hope lighting his eyes.

'Not precisely, Corporal,' murmured the officer. 'First of all we must make haste to the coal wharf, where they're waiting to load us with sufficient fuel for us to reach – hmm – Algiers.'

'Algiers!' snorted our corporal, looking as if he was about to explode. 'You promised us that we'd be returning to our unit. Why aren't we going to Taranto?'

'For a start our unit's moved up way beyond there, and if this ship went to Taranto there's no more coal there so it couldn't go any further. I've been told there's an abundance of coal near Algiers, and I've agreed that we'll take twenty-five badly injured and convalescing British soldiers there, on the first stage of their journey back to Blighty.'

'Don't suppose there's any danger of us taking them all the way back to Blighty, sir?' asked Billy, hopefully.

'Afraid not. Apparently our unit CO's been raising Cain with the brass hats about our return, so from Algiers it really is back to the One Five One – even if we have to swim it.'

We had been ploughing for five days westwards in the calm waters of the Mediterranean. Bruno, the first mate, complained that the 'carbone' was 'sporchissimo' – the coal was the dirtiest ever to be used on his ship. If the clouds of thick black smoke issuing from the funnel were anything to go by, this was the truth.

Before picking up the coal we had hurriedly carried the comforts aboard, stowing them in a lockable cupboard adjacent to our mess room, and had issued some of them to the wards. On this voyage only two of the wards were being used, one for the patients with major disabilities, some of which might be permanent, and the other one holding those who were expected to become reasonably mobile again after rehabilitation. They had all survived the need for intensive care, and were now able to play card games and board games to dispel boredom while they looked forward to the eventual return to their home country. The voyage was the quietest we had experienced so far. The Italian nursing staff were accustomed now to the laughing banter of the troops, who in turn were enjoying the care of the nurses and the well-prepared meals. Those not able to move about took advantage of the varied selection of books we had collected.

One of the boxes we had received looked unfamiliar, and when we opened it we were delighted to discover some brown glass bottles bearing the Stella beer label and a note that read, 'All the best, from one Desert Rat to some others. Good luck, and a speedy return home. David Eskull.'

Days went by, with the African coastline plainly visible on our port side and no interference from enemy aircraft or vessels. Quite suddenly we saw the white minarets and towers of Algiers gleaming in the sunlight. A long sleek grey shape with a stars and stripes flag fluttering in the breeze went gliding past out to sea, signal lamps flashing as it went by. Slowly our ship eased its way to the quay, guided by the pilot officer who had come aboard an hour before.

'Are the patients all ready to be collected?' asked Corporal Wallace.

'You should know by now that with Sister Vincenza in charge everything will be going like clockwork, Corp,' chuckled Billy. 'They've been ready since breakfast.'

As the gangway was lowered Captain Price came bustling down from the upper deck. 'Morning, men. The sooner we get our patients off the sooner we can prepare for our return to the One Five One.' Even as he spoke the ambulances, their red crosses on white backgrounds gleaming in the sun, began to line up on the quay. As there were only twenty-five patients they were soon collected.

'What did you mean when you said about preparing for our journey back to the unit, sir?' said Billy, anxiously. 'What do we need to do?'

'For a start you need new uniforms,' said Captain Price. 'Proper woollen khaki uniforms like you wore in England. I know you have your old ones in your kitbags back in the unit, but it's moved up a fair way and you'll find the weather very cold after being in North Africa again – there's even snow on the high ground, I'm told. Anyway, I have to visit the Director of Medical Services North Africa later today, and I'll request that we're all kitted out to suit conditions there before we set out. I think I'll be able to arrange it in the next two or three days.'

'What do we do in the meantime? Just sit around, sir?' I asked.

'By no means. I've arranged for a Pay Corps officer to come aboard later this morning to change our Egyptian piastres into local money, so you'll be able to spend a little time ashore.'

As Aldo served our lunch he said, 'I think you leave us soon, Signor Giorgio. Our ship's engineer, he tell me we need big work doing to our engines before we voyage much further, and we wait here while that work is being done, but your Capitan he makes the arrangement for you to go some other way. Is this so?'

'First I've heard of it, but I might find out when our captain comes back from his visit to the Director of Medical Services later today.'

Because Aldo had spoken to me quietly in Italian, the others had no idea what he was talking about, and I decided to say nothing until our own officer came back – besides which, it would avoid them mithering on at me about it during our afternoon visit to Algiers.

Before he left for his meeting our captain had stressed that we must return to the *Toscana* before 4.30, because she had to move away from the quay and drop anchor in the harbour. Directly after lunch, therefore, we all trooped down the gangway, intent on exploring this exotic North African port which had featured in many of the films we had seen in cinemas before the war. As soon as we reached the shopping centre we realised that Algeria was part of the French dominion: all the street names, directions and shop window notices were in French alongside the squiggly Arabic versions that were double dutch to us. Most of us had learnt a little French at school, so by searching our memories we managed to get by. The purchase of necessities like shaving cream, razor blades and toilet soap presented no difficulty: we just pointed at them and held up the French franc notes we had received. Anyway, many of the shop assistants spoke a little English.

The streets seemed cleaner and more free from litter than their Egyptian counterparts, and the Middle Eastern street smells were not so nose-turning. Having purchased our necessities, we looked around for little gifts to send home to our loved ones, as Christmas was not far away. Finally we spotted a shop window where various items of pure silk were on display. When we entered, a haughty lady assistant, well beyond the bloom of youth, gave our worn and faded KD uniforms a disdainful glance before launching into a French tirade that none of us could decipher. We enquired by sign language if we could purchase presents and have them posted to our homes in England, as had been possible in Egypt, but our efforts were in vain, and her face was far from welcoming as she pressed a button by the counter. There was the shrill ringing of a bell and an elderly grey-haired gentleman rushed out, his face bearing an agitated expression.

'Do you speak English?' Corporal Wallace said, slowly, loudly and clearly.

The look of alarm disappeared from his face, and with a relieved smile the man replied, 'But of course, Monsieur. How can I help you?'

We explained, and he said that it would be his pleasure to help. He also asked us to forgive the unwelcoming attitude of his daughter, who had suffered an 'unfortunate experience' with a foreign soldier. I chose a silk nightdress that I knew would delight Edna, and the others opted for dainty silk handkerchiefs. We filled in the necessary forms, giving the addresses to which the gifts should be posted, paid, and left the shop quite pleased with ourselves.

We realised that it was fast approaching 4.30, and hurried back to our ship. Captain Price was standing by the gangway, peering anxiously out towards the busy streets. 'You very nearly had to swim out,' he said with a frown. 'I know it's a shade early but they're wanting us to move out to anchor right now.' As we stood on the deck we felt the throbbing of the engines, and some of the crew began to raise the gangway.

'Any fresh news about returning to the unit, sir?' asked Billy, as the ship's anchor was lowered again.

'You'll never rest until you get a final answer, will you?' said our captain. 'All right. The DMS was very pleased with our efforts, and he's coming out to inspect this ship with a view to using it further. Don't look so alarmed: he doesn't mean with us – he says his signal equipment is red hot with constant pleas for our return. He's heard that some engine repairs are due, but he'll talk to *Toscana*'s captain about that tomorrow morning, when he comes out here. Now for the important bit! With him will be an ordnance sergeant who'll bring your new uniforms to be tried on *in situ*. He'll note any minor alterations needed and will take them back with him. They'll be ready for collection the following day, when we finally say farewell to the *Toscana*.'

'How are we getting back, sir? On another ship?' asked Corporal Wallace.

'No, Corporal. A truck will collect us from the quay with all our kit, then take us to the ordnance depot for your uniforms, and on to the railway station where we'll board a train . . .'

'A train, sir?' we interrupted in unison.

'If you'll allow me to finish, a train that'll transport us to Constantine, about two hundred miles distant, where there's the largest military airfield in the region. There's a huge storage depot nearby, and a transit camp where passengers can wait for vacant seats on the Douglas Dakota transport planes that take off daily for Bari in Italy. Our unit's sixty miles north of Bari at a place named Foggia. Does that answer all your questions?'

Our hearts leapt at the message we had wanted to hear for many days.

On the following morning, as promised, a small motor boat approached and the DMS and an ordnance sergeant climbed the lowered gangway.

'Squad, shun!' called Corporal Wallace in his best military style, presenting an immaculate salute as the senior officer reached us.

'At ease, men. Been hearing what a good job you chaps have done – not easy taking over and running a foreign hospital ship like this. Want you to know I appreciate your efforts.' He turned as Captain Price came down from the upper deck. 'There you are, Captain – better go on our tour of inspection, hey?'

I'll take you to the *Toscana*'s captain first, sir. He speaks a little English, so we should be all right.'

As they disappeared towards the bridge the ordnance sergeant, carrying a large case, followed us down to our mess room and handed out the new uniforms, after a quick sizing glance at each of us. We put them on and stood as he checked and made notes, which he pinned to the appropriate clothing as we handed it back. 'Right. I'll make sure they're ready tomorrow morning, even as far as sewing on your corporal's stripes,' he added, nodding to our NCO.

Next morning, after a magnificent breakfast prepared by Fritz and tearful farewells from Sister Vincenza and the other nursing sisters and orderlies, and much shaking of hands with the rest of the crew, Captain Price and the rest of us boarded the little motor boat that was waiting for us. The driver of a small fifteen hundredweight truck waved us aboard, and took us to the ordnance depot as planned. We dashed inside where the altered uniforms were handed to us. Putting them on, and pleased to discover they were a perfect fit, we climbed aboard once more and found ourselves only moments later at the railway station. So this was it. Goodbye *Toscana*, goodbye Algiers – but what next?

It was quite late in the afternoon when the train – a steam engine pulling a collection of rather ancient coaches – finally halted at Constantine station, just a couple of concrete platforms that passengers had to climb down the carriage steps to reach. The journey had been hot and dry, so we were glad we had filled our water bottles before leaving the Toscana, and grateful for the bully beef sandwiches that Fritz had insisted we take with us. The train seats, though worn, had some padding, but the noise of the steel wheels on the track created such a racket that conversation was extremely difficult. But now, as we stepped out, the only sound was the hiss and crackle of escaping steam from the engine.

Alan sniffed the air and wrinkled his nose. 'Typical North African stink. Hope it's not too long before we can get our lift. You did say it was organised, sir?'

'You lads aren't going to rest until we're in the sky, are you?' said the captain with a wry smile. 'There should be someone turning up any minute to transport us either to the airport or the transit camp, depending on what seats are available.' As if in confirmation of his words a RASC driver came hurrying up to us.

'Captain Price, sir, needing transport to the camp?'

'That's correct. All of us – either to the airport or the transit camp.'

'Sorry, sir. I don't transport Other Ranks in this car unless I've been officially ordered to do so by an officer.'

'Well, I'm an officer and I officially order you to take us all!' said Captain Price, his patience wearing thin.

The driver was not one to give in easily. 'Can't do that, sir, because the officers' camp is that way,' he pointed to his right, 'and the Other Ranks are that way,' he pointed to his left. 'And anyway, Other Ranks generally have to march it.'

Captain Price had a steely glint in his eye. 'What I'm ordering you to do, driver, is to take us all to the Other Ranks Camp, where I'll officially dismiss my men after I've made sure there's suitable accommodation for them, and then I shall order you to drive me to the officers' camp. Is that understood?'

The driver looked as though he would like to argue further but, realising he did not have a leg to stand on, mumbled 'Yes, sir' and led us to his car.

After a short drive east, beyond the huge storage compound, the driver turned off the main road and climbed a steep gradient: the surface was more like a dusty cart track than a road. Clouds of dust rose up as we bumped and rattled over the uneven surface. Through a wire fence we saw rows of white tents. He drove through an open gateway to halt outside a wooden hut that displayed the notices 'Constantine Transit Camp' and 'All Other Ranks Report Here'.

The driver spoke to Corporal Wallace, squashed in the rear with us. 'This is it, Corp. Just march your men in there to the duty sergeant. He'll sort you out.' He turned to Captain Price. 'And I'll be off to the officers' quarters with you, sir.'

'Not so fast, driver! I told you I intended to see my men accommodated satisfactorily. Another five minutes won't hurt you, so just hang around until I've accompanied them into this office.' The captain's lips curled in a prim smile at the driver's obvious discomfiture.

Inside the office a sergeant sat at a wooden table, writing in a ledger. Without looking up, he grumbled, 'What's the idea – turning up in the evening like this? All new intakes are supposed to arrive between 1.30 and 4p.m. You can't just come along at any old time and expect to be fed and given a bed. Against camp regulations, that . . .' He looked up, and his jaw dropped when he saw Captain Price. 'Ooh – er – awfully sorry, sir – I didn't realise it was an officer, sir.' He lapsed into embarrassed silence.

'That's quite obvious, Sergeant,' said our captain primly. 'First of all, I want to make it quite clear that these "new intakes", as you call them, are travelling along with me, and we'll be boarding a flight to Italy the moment the paperwork is completed. As you so rightly concluded they need a meal and beds for the night. I take it you're able to provide those facilities, at least for one night?'

I awakened the next morning after an uneasy and uncomfortable night, frequently recalling that we were no longer on board ship where our cabin beds had provided superb comfort. We were now wrapped in our blankets on those woven cane box-like bases as used at Qassassin, still six to a tent. We had been directed to our tent after giving our name, rank and number to the reception sergeant, and had managed to persuade the corporal cook to supply us with a warmed-up meal in the mess tent. Then we had explored the camp, to find that there were no NAAFI facilities or mobile canteens, or indeed a 'Shafto's Shufti', so we had retired to our tent. I glanced at my watch to find that it was almost seven o'clock. The other five were stirring as well: the corporal cook had informed us that breakfast was served at 7.30 sharp.

Corporal Wallace threw off his blanket and yawned. 'We'd better get to the ablutions for a wash and shave if we want to be in time for the food.' He didn't actually say it, but we knew he was thinking that we were not particularly welcome.

We found the ablutions easily. They were in the open air, which encouraged us to not waste any time.

After a breakfast of lumpy porridge, overheated tinned bacon and a hard-boiled egg, we retired to our tent wondering what would happen next. We did not have long to wait before a Service Corps corporal whom we had not met before shouted outside our tent. 'Come on, you lot – I've got a long list of fatigues to keep you chaps busy.' We went outside. When he saw Corporal Wallace, he said, 'Not you, Corp. Just these lazy layabouts,' and pointed at the rest of us, 'I've been told to make sure they don't get bored.' Our corporal tried to explain that we were expecting to catch a flight very shortly, but he just laughed. 'Officers, yes – but Other Ranks usually have to hang about for at least a week before getting away.'

As the NCO began to march us away Billy muttered, 'I knew something like this would happen. We seem fated!'

We had not gone more than a few yards when we saw Captain Price approaching accompanied by a service corps lieutenant, who said, 'Where are you taking these RAMC men, Corporal Smith?'

'Just to do one or two little tasks, sir.'

'Oh no you're not! I have a vehicle waiting to rush these men and their corporal, along with their captain here, over to the airfield. A Dakota's waiting to take off.'

'Oooer!' exclaimed Alan as the aircraft dropped beneath us like a stone, only to rise again just as rapidly.

'Sorry about that, gents,' sang out the pilot. 'We often meet a bit of turbulence round here. I hope nobody lost their breakfast.'

It was one of the older-style Dakotas, mainly used to carry urgent stores and equipment from North Africa to the battle area. They had a couple of long inward-facing wooden seats just behind the pilot, capable of holding twelve passengers at the most, and this was where we were sitting. The rest of the space was taken up by metal crates and wooden containers.

CHAPTER 22

After what seemed like a very long time in the air, although it was only about seven hours, we thumped on to the concrete runway at Bari Airport in southern Italy, where we taxied to a halt outside a cluster of small buildings. A sign printed in English, covering the original Italian one, proclaimed 'Transit Officer – all military arrivals report here'. We gathered in the reception room, and Captain Price disappeared to organise the next stage of our journey – sixty miles to Foggia.

Our captain eventually returned with the light of triumph in his eyes. 'Fine tale,' he barked. 'Might not be any available transport for a day or two. But I told them it wasn't good enough – that we were carrying out the DADMS's strict order to return to our unit immediately, if not sooner!'

'So when do we go, sir?' asked Corporal Wallace.

'Now. Straight away. Well, almost. We have to be at the railway depot in an hour's time, when a train's departing for Foggia. I'm afraid it's just a goods train with no seated carriages, so we might have a slow and bumpy ride, but at least we should get there by tomorrow morning. In the meantime I've arranged for us to have a meal in the canteen, where our troops in charge here have theirs.' This was welcome news: our captain had managed to obtain several packs of sandwiches and a vacuum flask of tea from the officers' quarters before we left Constantine, and we had been very grateful for these *en route*. But now evening was approaching and we were beginning to feel peckish again.

★ ★ ★

The rattling goods train, crammed with armaments, munitions, rations and other stores and travelling towards Foggia in the pitch darkness, could hardly be termed Pullman standard. We had managed to locate a load of blankets in rolls, which provided a softer surface to recline upon, but sleep was not an easy prospect. It was a nightmare of sudden stops and equally sudden starts, each stop making the buffers on the wagons collide with a fearful clang and each start being accompanied by a jolt and an ear-shattering hiss of steam.

Billy stirred for the umpteenth time, moaning as he prised himself upwards to try to see out of the tiny thick glass window just below the roof. 'Black as pitch,' he growled.

'Shut up, Billy,' I said, rather crossly. 'I'd just managed to drop off.' I must have been tired out, because the next time I dragged my eyes open silence reigned – apart from the stertorous breathing of my comrades. For a moment I was at a loss to recall where I was and why, but as memory came flooding back I realised that the sliding door was open and it was daylight outside.

Corporal Wallace was the next to stir. 'What's happened to Captain Price? He was here next to me – but now we seem to have lost the boss.'

'No you haven't, Corporal,' came our officer's voice from outside. 'It's high time you men stirred yourselves.' First the head then the rest of our captain appeared as he struggled to climb up into the truck, looking as dapper as usual. 'We're in a siding at Foggia station. I got up early – some of us do, you know – and rousted out the RT officer here at the station to contact our unit and organise some transport. My driver's already on his way to take us the final two miles. He should be here any minute, so shake your feathers, my lads!'

We hurriedly put on the boots and webbing equipment we had removed for comfort during the night – not a moment too soon, as we saw a little truck draw up beside the railway line.

'Over here, Barker,' Captain Price called. 'Come and carry some of my kit, please. He heaved out his officer's valise to his driver, climbed carefully down and said to us, 'Come along, get a move on. We want to be home in time for breakfast.'

After a very short journey beyond the small war-shattered town, the driver halted in a small paved square around which stood a cluster of single-storey buildings. The door of one of them bore a notice, 'Orderly Office', and standing outside was Captain Pomfret, his face wreathed in smiles. Quickly we scrambled down as Corporal Wallace rapped out

'Squad – Attention', accompanied by an immaculate salute.

Captain Pomfret acknowledged the salute. 'Welcome back, lads. For a time we thought we'd lost you.'

'Not much chance of that,' said Captain Price, stepping down from the cab. 'They've been pestering me to make sure we returned to the One Five One ever since we first sailed away in the *Toscana*.'

Leaving our kit inside the orderly room, we went off to the cookhouse in search of some breakfast while Captain Pomfret escorted our captain to the officers' mess. The corporal cook heard us enter, and without looking up said officiously, 'You're too late – breakfast finished ten minutes ago.'

'That's not a very friendly welcome for six weary travellers from distant lands,' said Corporal Wallace.

The corporal cook's head shot up. 'Hey, weelcome back! We thought you'd gone for good. Sit down and we'll cook up a feast for you.'

'That was certainly a meal worth waiting for,' smiled Alan, wiping the very last vestige of bacon dip, egg yolk and baked bean gravy from his plate with a crust of bread, as the rest of us swallowed the final dregs of our mugs of hot, sweet tea.

'You certainly deserved it,' came the voice of Captain Pomfret. 'No, don't get up,' as we tried to struggle to our feet. 'I've been hearing from Captain Price about your exploits, and I want to see you all in the orderly room in an hour's time. Don't worry, you're not in trouble,' he added, grinning at our alarmed expressions. 'We can safely assume you're back to stay this time.'

At precisely ten o'clock Corporal Wallace paraded us outside the orderly office, all of us feeling refreshed and brighter after a good wash, shave and change of underclothing.

'Squad – Squad attention,' he ordered as Captain Pomfret came out of the door.

'Stand easy,' said the captain. 'Now listen, Corporal, you're to march them into the CO's office – and be prepared for a few surprises.'

As we arrived, Major Forsythe was standing behind the desk with a smile of welcome lighting up his face 'Right you are, stand easy. You'll see there have been a few changes in our unit since you chaps went off on your somewhat extended "one trip only" hospital ship venture.

Captain Price has already given me a full account of your activities, about which, incidentally, I've received glowing reports. In case you're wondering what I'm doing at this desk, Lieutenant-Colonel Thompson has taken over command of a new casualty clearing station now operating at Taranto, and I , with promotion to acting lieutenant-colonel, am now in charge of the One Five One with Captain Pomfret as our new adjutant. Your return could not have come at a more opportune moment, as it appears that a minor epidemic of rubella – German measles – has struck down our fellow Polish Corps troops. The only way to prevent it becoming a major epidemic is for the infected men to be nursed back to health in an isolation environment. Because enemy resistance on the defence line from just north of here to Monte Cassino in the west has held back our progress, there are a lot of Allied units around here, and our other ADSs are scattered around doing sick parades and treatments – except Captain Clark's lot, who are in Yugoslavia with Tito's partisans. So you're the right people in the right place at the right time.' I glanced at Captain Pomfret, and the twinkle in his eye confirmed my suspicion that he recalled using those very words many months previously. 'To sum up, I've commandeered a deserted school building where two of the large rooms will provide excellent isolation wards. Captain Price is in command, Corporal Wallace in charge of daytime nursing carried out by you nursing orderlies – but not by you, Private Hill, whom I now promote to the rank of lance-corporal. You'll be in sole charge of the nightshift. Transport has been laid on to take you down to the school, which is a quarter of a mile from here and has all the equipment necessary. Gather your kit together and away you go. I hope the patients will recover in a short time, but please remember that "isolation" means no contact with the rest of the unit.'

I lay on my bed – a wooden one with spring wire base like all the others in our staff bedrooms and the two wards at the opposite end of the single-storey block. We had been transported down to find that everything – medical equipment, crockery, bedside cupboards – had somehow been located and installed. After lunch at the unit we were back, ready to receive our first influx of patients around teatime. I retired to my bed in the staff room, hoping to manage an hour or two of sleep before night duty commenced. As I lay there, finding sleep elusive, I pondered how our little group seemed to lurch from one emergency to another with little time for boredom. My eyelids drooped . . .

'Come on, George,' came Corporal Wallace's voice. 'It's nearly time for you to take over. We've saved your tea for you.'

I crawled out and put on my uniform as quickly as possible, had a wash and shave, then sat down in the little room we had claimed as our mess to eat the egg sandwiches and drink the mug of tea brought down from our unit cookhouse.

Corporal Wallace came in. 'We've had a fairly busy evening so far,' he said. Number one ward is three parts full, and I don't expect there'll be any more before morning. As you can see, the electric lights are working and we've put up the blinds in the occupied ward. There's a small kitchen complete with electric water heaters and a warming oven. One of our unit trucks will deliver prepared meals for us and the patients. They'll be deposited in the open-ended shed at our end of the building, and we pick them up when the driver's gone.'

'How did you manage about the language?'

The corporal laughed. 'No problem. They've all picked up enough of our language to get by. The accent's a bit funny and you have to listen carefully, but we communicated all right.'

'Thank goodness for that,' I murmured,' because Polish is one language I know nothing about.'

'If you're ready come along to the ward now. Captain Price will run through the patients' details with you and then I'll show you where everything is.' I followed him towards the wards, with the single stripe I had carefully sewed onto each arm of my tunic proclaiming my status as a lance-corporal. I was about to start my first night in sole control of the isolation wards.

I was sitting at a small desk with a heavily shaded table lamp throwing enough light to allow me to plough through all the mail that was waiting for me in our orderly office. I had scanned through it quickly before retiring for my afternoon sleep. It was all from Edna, and as I read the letters it was plain that she was becoming more and more anxious about not hearing from me for several weeks. She made no mention of the silk nightdress that I had ordered and paid for in Algiers. To ease her mind, I had obtained an aerograph form from the orderly office to transmit a telegram home, using certain numbers to represent pre-determined short phrases. I chose the numbers for 'All well', 'Letter follows' and 'All my love', filled in our home address and handed it to the sergeant clerk, who promised to see that it was dealt with right away.

Whiling away the hours of darkness on my first night in charge of the isolation ward, I only had the uneasy stirrings, the murmurings and snoring of the patients as company. Their treatment consisted mainly of fever-reducing drugs, calamine lotion on particularly irritated areas, plenty of fluid to drink, and Mother Nature.

Caught up as I was in my nightly duties, with patients coming and going and both wards in constant use, Christmas came and went with me hardly noticing. As Captain Price pronounced each patient to be free from infection and released him back to his unit, another arrived to take his place. I seemed to lose track of time, and five or six weeks, must have gone by before Corporal Wallace aroused me from my daily slumbers to inform me that the last rubella patient had been discharged.

During this time the Allied Forces in Italy had mounted several attacks in an effort to penetrate the 'Gustav Line', as the German stronghold had been christened, and two very costly attempts to dislodge the enemy from fortifications around Monte Cassino had come to nothing. An uneasy deadlock seemed to hang over the whole region.

With the epidemic of rubella finally overcome, our little isolation team was able to return to the main unit, having not become infected. The building we had used was to be thoroughly fumigated and cleansed by the Pioneer Corps and then kept in reserve in case of further need. For the time being we took over sick parade duties for the unit itself, and for a small REME detachment close by. I had just finished giving one of their men a gargle for his sore throat when Captain Pomfret entered the treatment room, and with a twinkle in his eye said, 'I want a word with you, Lance-Corporal Hill!'

I stared at him with a sense of unease. 'Why is it that I get a shiver down my spine when you say things like that, sir?'

'No need to panic. I just thought that after all your voyaging and the long spell on night duty you might benefit from a day or two in the lovely fresh air of the mountains – you and Private Wright here.'

Alan overheard his name and came over. 'What's all this about mountains, sir?'

'Spot called Campobasso. It's more or less on a mountain top halfway between here and Monte Cassino, and there's a special Royal Signals detachment located there. They need temporary replacements for their RAMC corporal and orderly who've had an accident and have been sent down to the CCS to recover. Just a few days, that's all, away from all this hustle and bustle. It'll do you both a world of good.'

'What'll we be doing, sir?' I asked.

'Oh, just keeping your eye on general hygiene arrangements and carrying out the odd treatment as and when required. Piece of cake for two experienced chaps like you.'

Alan and I had been travelling for the best part of two hours in the rear of the signal unit's stores truck, which the driver informed us made the journey down from Campobasso every day to collect necessary equipment, rations and so on. He advised us to put on our greatcoats, saying 'Things are a bit icy up there!' It seemed as if we were now reaching the 'ice belt', as patches of soft white slush began to appear on the ground around the constantly rising rough road. The higher we rose the more snow there was, and we understood why the truck was fitted with heavily treaded tyres. Eventually the driver halted within a small cluster of single-storey buildings, having just passed a road sign marked Campobasso. 'Watch your step when you jump out,' he said. 'There's ice everywhere. That's how our own two medics came to grief – one fractured his wrist and the other damaged his ankle.'

At the very top of the mountain, a hundred yards or so further on, there was a small castle-type tumble-down building. The driver indicated a small door marked 'MI Room'. Entering, we found a small room where shelves and a table were stocked with all the medical equipment needed for most day-to-day treatments and ailments, and against the far wall stood a washbasin. Another door led into what must have been the former medics' quarters.

'Ah, so you've come to help us out.' A very young-looking second lieutenant in Royal Signals uniform entered. 'Welcome to Campobasso, although it's not a frightfully attractive location at the moment. I'm Lieutenant Barry. The reason we're here is that mountain peak over there.' He wiped a rime of frost from the window and pointed to a distant peak, even higher than the one we were on, 'It's Monte Cassino.

So far the Germans have beaten off all attempts to dislodge them. In our little ruin here we've got some special radio equipment for covert eavesdropping on the enemy signals, which we pass by landline to our military HQ. Our American allies have established a rather precarious bridgehead at Anzio on the west coast, and we can contact them as well. We've fitted a generator down in the cellars, so we have power to run the show. The only problem at the moment is the water, which keeps on freezing – and that affects the toilets!'

We took our kit through to the staff room, where a couple of iron bedsteads with wire frames, blankets and pillows offered a place to rest, and ate lunch in the small cookhouse-cum-messroom, introducing ourselves to the rest of the Royal Signals troops. Then we waited to carry out the job we had been sent to do.

Alan and I had been at Campobasso a little over a month, during which time the freezing conditions had eased as warmer weather approached. We had been able to solve the problem with the frozen toilets – which were the primitive 'hole in the floor' type. Pouring down a liberal amount of warm and heavily salted water had been completely successful.

As the ration truck arrived one morning two RAMC men, a corporal and a private, jumped out and hurried into the treatment room. 'Hi there, Corp,' said the orderly. 'We're back. We're the blokes who were here before. If you hurry up and grab your kit the "ration express" will give you a lift back to your unit.'

'I hope you haven't busted up all our stuff,' said the corporal with a grin.

'It's you who should be thanking us for hanging on during the freeze, while you went for a warm-up,' said Alan, grinning even more widely.

Back at the One Five One we found everything pretty much as we had left it. Sick parades for nearby units were still going on, but there was an air of expectancy as if something big was brewing. Our expectations were justified: suddenly the battlefront erupted again as the Allies managed to break through the Gustav Line, and Polish troops fought inch by inch to the monastery at Cassino.

CHAPTER

23

On 4 June 1944 the American Ninth Army, having broken out of their Anzio bridgehead and forced the Germans to withdraw north of Rome, entered the city to a tremendous welcome by the relieved citizens. Having passed through the open city, the Allied troops continued to pursue the fleeing German forces, who were hoping to establish a line of resistance in the Arrezo–Florence area.

With the battle for Italy by no means at its end, the long-awaited invasion of northern Europe was launched. On the night of 5/6 June American Airborne troops were parachuted into Normandy, followed in the morning light by the landing of British and American troops on the beaches. That day would for ever more be known as D-Day.

Meanwhile, we RAMC men of the One Five One Light Field Ambulance waited with everything packed into our trucks for further movement orders. We clustered round the canteen truck, listening eagerly to the news about the landings in France. When our order came it was to move up to a position seven miles south-east of Rome – not a town, nor even a village, merely a stretch of flat, open grassland with a view of a crumbling viaduct.

'That viaduct doesn't look too safe for trains,' murmured Billy.

A new officer named Captain Lederer, who had been posted to our unit when Captain Pomfret became adjutant and did not yet fully appreciate Billy's outrageous jokes, shook his head sadly. 'That's an ancient and historic Roman aquaduct, Private Hough.' We all nodded wisely, but did not enlighten him.

Behind us there was a large section of high wall damaged by shellfire which had been whitewashed; a message had been hastily daubed upon it. 'What's it say?' asked Arthur. 'I can't make it out.'

'It's in German, that's why,' I said. 'It says, "English soldier – beware! Today you may chase us, but tomorrow our weapons will hang over London".'

'Typical German propaganda,' snorted John.

But those scrawled words proved prophetic. Later that month German flying bombs – doodle-bugs as they came to be known – started falling on London, still suffering from the Blitz two years previously.

Our unit was ordered to put up its shelters and act as sick bay and sick parade provision for the many units nearby. By now the area adjacent to us had been allocated to a company of the Fourth Indian Division and they were moving in. They had distinguished themselves in the desert battles as part of the Eighth Army, and were held in high respect. At one end of the area they were occupying stood a large earthen mound covered in dry scrub and weeds. On the second morning after they moved in they piled a lot of dry branches and sun-scorched weeds on it and set them alight. Thick black smoke swirled up from the fire.

Billy, having collected breakfast in his mess tin from our cookhouse, which was near the Indian encampment, had only gone a few yards when an almighty explosion rent the air. Bits of smouldering scrub flew up and a chunk of jagged metal whizzed past his face, missing his nose by inches. He yelled in alarm, his arms flew up, the tea in his mug splashed over his head and his food fell to the grass as he threw himself to the ground, convinced we were under attack. More bangs followed, but nothing more seemed to be aimed at him, and when he realised all the clamour was coming from the fire he scrambled to his feet and made a dash for our shelter.

'Is it a raid?' cried John.

'No – it's that blasted fire the Indians have lit,' said Billy. 'There's something queer under that lump.'

Captain Pomfret came dashing around with his steel helmet on. 'Tin hats on, lads! It seems our Indian neighbours have lit a bonfire on top of an abandoned ammunition dump, and nobody knows what's in there.'

'A piece of shrapnel nearly put Hough's nose out of joint, sir,' I said, 'as well as making him spill all his breakfast.'

'Right – so be prepared to cope with any injuries. Captain Lederer will come along shortly, as Captain Price is away. The fire could be out soon, because they've formed a human chain to douse the flames with water from a storage tank.'

During the next half-hour the flames spluttered out as bucket after bucket of water was thrown over the mound. Finally, after another quarter of an hour, there was another huge bang, throwing lumps of steaming, blackened earth into the air, then ceased totally as if the final explosion had literally blown out the fire.

We crouched there a minute or two longer, for fear there might be another flare-up, but the smoke cleared and calm returned.

Captain Pomfret strolled back, now wearing his normal officer's hat. 'It's out now. Apparently the first big bang and the last were the only two large artillery shells in the dump. The rest was just small arms stuff. Oh, and you're not the only one to have a near miss, Private Hough. Lieutenant-Colonel Forsythe had a metal splinter through his last bottle of Glenlivet, and he's not at all amused.' That raised a sympathetic laugh all round. 'He wants us over by the orderly office tent in ten minutes for a little chat.'

'This shows why we must all take extra care when dealing with unusual objects,' our CO said, 'particularly in areas where a conflict's taken place. Fortunately no one was hurt – at least not physically,' he added with a wry smile. 'And now I've some more information. Our unit is to remain in reserve for the time being, doing the usual sick parades. I've obtained permission for one of our trucks to take a different party of ten into Rome each morning, leaving here at nine o'clock and returning from there at seven in the evening.'

When our turn came to see the sights of this wonderful city, we climbed aboard the three ton truck and off we went. It was an easy ride on roads that had escaped the damage we had come to expect, and the only delay was caused by our own military vehicles. As we reached the outskirts of Rome Corporal Wallace was jiggling about in excitement. 'Isn't it great to see these beautiful buildings? They haven't been knocked to bits by shellfire . . .'

'Give it a rest, Corp,' muttered a RASC mechanic who was travelling with us. 'They're only buildings.'

'Yes, but just look at the beauty and design: utterly fantastic. And look at the women, dressed in the height of fashion – and so pretty . . .'

'Steady on, Corp,' chuckled Billy. 'Simmer down a bit or you'll be bringing yourself out in a rash, and we forgot to bring the calamine lotion.'

As our truck bowled along, the trees that lined both sides of the road seemed to become taller and greener, the buildings more ornate and the roadside flowers more colourful. We turned into a wide straight road heading for the city centre. 'The Appian Way,' said John.

'How do you know? Have you been here before?' asked Billy.

'No, but we had a Latin teacher at school who was always going on about Ancient Rome. There was this bloke about 300 BC called Appius Claudius who had this road built to link Rome with southern Italy.'

'And did it make him any 'appier'?' chuckled Billy, grinning as he dodged the pack of sandwiches hurled at him.

By now we had reached the centre of the city, and I pointed at a great mound of rough boulders, bearing a statue on a stone leaf gazing down at a small pond, where clear water rippled in the sunlight. 'Any idea what that is, John?'

'I think it's the Trevi fountain. It certainly looks like the place my teacher mentioned. Before any of you ask,' he said, as our truck crossed a bridge, 'that was the river Tiber, and straight ahead of you is the Great Dome of the Basilica of Saint Peter, with the square named after him in front of it.'

'You missed your vocation, Johnny boy,' laughed Corporal Wallace. 'You should have been a tour guide.'

'Right, lads, this is where you get out,' called our driver. 'Don't forget that I'm picking you up here at 6.45 this evening. Don't be late.'

By late afternoon, footsore and rather weary, we had wandered around the wonderful city, explored the basilica, and climbed to the Gallery of the Dome, admiring the fantastic view over the surrounding countryside. We had marvelled at the grandeur and beauty of the paintings, sculptures and artefacts. We had trudged to the ruins of the Colosseum, and now we were on our way back to St Peter's Square. We had long since eaten our sandwiches, along with cups of frothy coffee we had purchased from an open air stand, and when we espied the towering column in the distance we ambled slowly in that direction. 'My feet are killing me,' said Alan wearily.

'Mine too,' I said, 'and we've only seen a fraction of this place. Perhaps we'll get the chance to come here again.'

It had been a wonderful day, but as we made our way slowly to the square we were thankful to see the truck waiting for us.

CHAPTER

24

It was August, and the American forces in the west of Italy and the British Eighth Army in the Eastern sector had continued a slow progress northward, overcoming one defence line after another, until finally coming up against the German 'Gothic Line', which the enemy was convinced was totally impregnable.

The One Five One was still in position beside the old aqueduct, and Corporal Wallace, Arthur Copley and I were listening to the radio in the canteen truck where we heard that the Allied Forces in Normandy had finally achieved a breakout through the long contested bridgehead and the Germans were falling back towards the east. The bulletin was interrupted by a newsflash, telling how an American and a Free French force had made a landing on the Mediterranean coast of southern France against little opposition and were racing northward to link up with the American forces advancing through Normandy.

Some days later another newsflash announced that in Italy, after a very fierce fight, our troops had managed to penetrate the Gothic Line, and the enemy had fallen back across the river Po. This was a piece of news too tantalising for Billy's sense of humour to ignore. 'If the Germans are on the Po, doesn't that mean we'll soon see some movement?' he asked wit an angelic expression. We all threw something at him – but it turned out that he was right. A couple of days later (it was now well into September) our unit was ordered to move up as far as Perugia in central Italy, but not to set up for action as everything was fairly fluid.

After several days of kicking our heels we were ordered to move to Ancona on the east coast road, continue north through Pesaro and

Rimini, then north-west to a small town by the name of Forli. Here a set of buildings was allocated to us, where the unit was to establish a treatment centre and small hospital in order to serve the high number of troops in that region. The buildings had originally been barracks for Italian soldiers, so the accommodation was good – and undamaged. Our unit men and the hospital section were equipped with proper beds, and there was a fully fitted kitchen and cookhouse. All in all, it was a very pleasant change from the constant stop-start movement of recent months.

The news from our home country was not too good. Instead of the doodle-bugs, Hitler had now ordered the firing of V1 rockets on London. They were fired upwards in a huge parabola of immense speed, taking no more than three minutes from launch from hidden sites beyond the reach of our forces in France and other countries to explosion with no warning and terrifying force in London. Our air forces made round-the-clock raids on the well-disguised launching sites and our land forces in northern France made every effort to reach them and wipe them out.

In northern Italy the Germans were depleted by the need to reinforce their troops in the east, where the Russians had now completely turned the tables on them – advancing nearer and nearer to Germany's eastern border every day.

By mid-November rumours were flying around that leave to 'Blighty' was being considered. 'No chance,' said Billy. 'You know very well we've got to serve abroad for four and a half years to qualify for repatriation under the Python scheme. They wouldn't let us go on leave now if we were going to go back home in July, when we'll have done our time.' This seemed a reasonable assumption, and we thought no more about it until a notice appeared on the board outside the orderly office. It was headed LILOP.

I joined the crowd that had gathered to read it. When I got near enough I saw that LILOP stood for 'Leave in lieu of Python'. The notice stated that a small number of men from each unit could receive an immediate leave of one month over the Christmas period in the United Kingdom, providing they agreed to forego their entitlement to repatriation after four and a half years. A footnote was added by Lieutenant-Colonel Forsythe, saying that the names of those who applied would be put into a hat and three lucky names would be drawn out.

'There you are,' said Billy. 'They want you to sign away your chance of a permanent return to the UK in exchange for a four week break now, with a chance of being sent anywhere in the world when you return. No thank you!'

'I don't like the sound of it,' said Arthur. 'There's not even a guarantee you'll come back to your own unit.'

While the idea of spending a whole month with Edna was intensely attractive, I could not argue with my friends' sentiments. Even so, I suggested that we put our names forward on the proviso that if one of us was chosen he could turn the leave down if he chose. We handed in our names and later that day three names were published on the noticeboard. None of us was included.

In the evening when I was on my own in the treatment room when Captain Pomfret called by. 'Have those three blokes opted to go on Christmas leave, sir?'

'No – they all turned it down. It's this business of signing away the more permanent return six months later. Would you have gone if your name had come up?'

'I just don't know, sir. I can think of nothing I'd like better than a chance to spend Christmas with my dear wife, but then . . .'

Next morning the orderly room clerk came racing over to the treatment room. 'Lance-Corporal Hill – the adjutant wants to see you right away.'

I wondered what I had done to merit this sudden summons, and I hurried across, knocked on his door and entered his office. He was sitting at his desk with a smile on his face. 'How about going on Christmas leave, Lance-Corporal Hill?'

'I thought the LILOP list was closed, sir.'

'So it is, Hill, so it is, but you must be one of the luckiest people alive. The LILOP scheme's just been superseded by the LIAP scheme – Leave In Addition to Python – and there's one vacancy left. You have your Christmas leave now, and you can still apply for repatriation next July. How about that?'

My head was in a whirl. 'What – er – what do you advise, sir?'

'Grab it, man – grab it with both hands! I only wish I had the choice. Unfortunately this scheme doesn't apply to officers, or you wouldn't see my, er, rear for dust. You're a married man and you haven't seen your wife for over four years. Go and enjoy Christmas with her. Just make sure you're back here on time, that's all. Don't worry about your Python application: I'll see that goes through at the appropriate time. Now go and get your ruddy kit, man. There's a truck waiting to take you down to the railway station, and I'll have your leave documents ready before you leave.'

Stuttering my thanks, I dashed away to collect my belongings.

I huddled on the hard floor of the railway goods van, which was crowded with other servicemen, all intent on getting to Naples, where the leave boat would be waiting to take us to Blighty. The fact that it was the usual uncomfortable transport mattered not one whit. We were all light-headed and excited at the prospect of spending Christmas at home.

'You only just made it, Corp,' bawled a REME man sprawled at my side.

'I got held up,' I shouted back. It was the truth.

I had joined the queue of excited leave-takers outside the RTO's office at Forli station, and when I reached the officer who was examining the travel documents he had taken one look at mine before shaking his head. 'You wait here.' Once the rest of the queue had passed and stepped aboard the waiting train, he motioned me to produce my travel documents once more. With a horrible sinking feeling I handed them over. 'This paper says LIAP not LILOP, like the rest of them. I might have to hold you back.'

Frantically I told him about the new scheme that my adjutant officer had told me about. I was just about to give up hope when he said, 'Hold on – some new bumf came this morning, and I haven't had time to open it yet.' He disappeared inside his office, to reappear moments later with a sheet of paper in his hand and a smile on his face. 'Good job I remembered that,' he said, stamping my documents and handing them back. It had been only just in time, because as I scrambled aboard the engine had emitted a gush of steam and a piercing whistle and moved off.

All day we bumped and rattled southwards, making occasional halts at which Military Policemen handed out packs of sandwiches and mugs of tea, while allowing time for us to answer the calls of nature. As one Military Policeman said, 'If you hear three toots on the engine's whistle get back on board sharpish, even if your trousers are round your ankles.'

'Do you think we'll make it to Naples today, Corp?' my REME companion asked.

'Not if we keep stopping so many times and travelling so slowly.'

I was right, and we spent the night trying to snatch a wink or two of sleep as we trundled on. But what did it matter – we were on our way home.

It was fully daylight the next morning before we spotted the tall cranes at the port of Naples. The train pulled into the sidings on the dock and stopped with a clanging of buffers. We scrambled out, having seen a small ship moored further along with a queue of men in Army uniform moving slowly past a Military Policeman who was scrutinising their documents before allowing them to continue up the gangway. We called out, 'Is this the Blighty leave ship?' to which we received a rousing chorus of 'Not half, mate!' – although one comedian shouted, 'No, it's the *Mayflower* setting out to discover America.'

Our ship was tossed about in quite a lively manner as we ploughed northward through the Bay of Biscay. Some of the men on the lower decks were looking decidedly green about the gills, but after my fairly lengthy spells 'on the ocean wave' the rough sea caused me no discomfort. It was not a large ship, and most of us found it easier to sleep on our deck floor. As one fellow said, 'I'd even sleep standing up for this chance to be at home for Christmas.'

Having completed the voyage up the west coast of Britain, we steered into the Clyde estuary, where we berthed at Glasgow Docks. Impatiently we clustered at the ship's rail, having risen, washed and shaved, put on our uniforms and eaten our breakfast. Wearing our greatcoats in the chill morning breeze, we waited for the lowering of the gangway and the appearance of the Military Police to steer us through the checking and documentation necessary before we could go home.

It was nearly midnight in the huge storage hall adjacent to the docks. We had spent the day transferring from one queue to another, showing our documents again and again, answering questions about where we were going by train, queueing for meals, and queueing for fresh uniforms if they were very worn. Finally the tannoy up in the roof announced that we should retire to the benches around the hall to get some rest.

When we heard our name, rank and number called out we were to go to the RTO office to collect our individual UK leave pass, ration cards and train tickets, together with information about the time at which our train would depart and from which platform, and full details of the date and time of our journey back to Glasgow for re-embarkation. My REME companion of the goods train journey to Naples, who was resting on the next bench to me, murmured dryly, 'It's a wonder they don't give us a list of what we can and can't do when we get home.'

I told him with a laugh that I thought we could work that out for ourselves.

Constant tannoy announcements interrupted any chance of sleep. Eventually my call came, and I stumbled to the office half-asleep to collect all the bits and pieces of paper. We were to board a special train from the platform next to the hall at 6.00a.m. which would travel down the length of the country.

I knocked hard on the door of my home. There was no answer, so I knocked louder and tried the door. It was locked. 'This is a fine carry-on,' I muttered to myself. 'Come all this way, only to find myself locked out.' Then I realised that in the rush and excitement I had forgotten to send word home. I lifted the letterbox, put my ear to the aperture and thought I could detect a sound from the bathroom. I put my mouth to the letterbox and bawled 'Hello!'

This time Edna cried out, 'Who's there?'

'It's me,' I shouted, my voice hoarse with excitement.

'Who's "me"?'

'Me – George – your husband! For goodness sake open the door and let me in!'

The door was unlocked and thrown open to reveal my wife clad in a dressing gown, face pink, moist and devoid of make-up. The look of astonishment on her face turned to one of sheer joy. 'Ooh, George! It really is you!' She laughed. 'I was just having a bath. I thought it was Jehovah's Witnesses, and I wasn't going to get out of the bath for them.' A sudden look of fear filled her eyes. 'You aren't injured or anything are you?' she asked anxiously.

'No, I'm fine. I didn't have time to let you know I was coming, because I only found out at the last minute.'

'There was a bit on the wireless this morning about a scheme to let some servicemen in Italy come home for Christmas leave, but I never dared to hope you'd be one of them. My mother's gone shopping, my brother's out somewhere and my dad's working, so I thought I'd enjoy a long soak.'

'I'm sorry if I've spoiled it for you, love!'

'Don't talk so daft!' She grabbed me and kissed me with great fervour. 'This is the start of the most wonderful Christmas I've ever had, and you can start right now by scrubbing my back for me.' She took my hand and led me to the bathroom.

She was quite right: it was everything we could have hoped for. Although our home was still with her parents, we had a large room to ourselves, and her mother's clever way with the rations, augmented by the ration cards I had brought with me, allowed us to enjoy some wonderful meals. We had the added joy of visiting friends and family. Nevertheless it came as a shock when in mid-December we heard on the radio news that German troops had broken through in the Ardennes area of France. The American force had been taken completely by surprise, and the enemy column was racing northwards towards Antwerp, hoping to split our forces in half. It took several days of vicious attack and counter-attack before the marauding column was finally overcome, and the Allied advance towards the Siegfried Line was able to continue its slow progress. On the Russian front the Russians were virtually knocking on the door of Germany's eastern border, and it was becoming obvious that with the failure of the Ardennes breakthrough the days of Hitler's Germany were numbered.

All in all it was a fantastic leave – but, like all good things, it had to end, and all too soon I found myself kicking my heels on the platform of Skipton station, waiting for the connecting train to Glasgow at the start of my journey back to Italy and my comrades. It was a great wrench to leave, and we agreed to say our farewells at home rather than on draughty railway platforms. The return journey was marked only by its complete uneventfulness, although the Italian train that carried me north was a proper passenger train with cushioned seats, which offered a little comfort to ease my gloom. Back with the unit I found everything much the same as when I had departed, and our daily routine continued.

* * *

In February 1945 we learned from the canteen radio that a meeting had taken place between Churchill, Roosevelt and Stalin at a place somewhere in Eastern Europe called Yalta, where the final plans for defeating the enemy had been hammered out.

Hitler had insisted that a fairly large force of his crack troops should be maintained in northern Italy, in the belief that this would prevent the Allies from gaining access to the south-eastern European oilfields, but even these well-trained German troops were pushed slowly back, mile by mile.

The Allied forces facing the Siegfried Line continued to push steadily forward, with some small penetrations on 13 February, and on the 23rd, following intense and sustained bombing raids, a major breakthrough was achieved. On 6 March American forces entered Cologne. By the 24th our Allied forces were well inside Germany, and the Russian army had entered East Prussia.

In March our unit received the order to leave the Forli Medical Centre, which we had operated since before Christmas, and move nearer to the River Po, which was where most of the action was taking place. After an hour or two of driving along roads damaged by fierce fighting, we were instructed to pull off and await further orders. We parked there with nothing to do for days, which was extremely boring for a unit that was usually kept fully occupied.

One morning, after a sleepless night thanks to the continuous heavy rumble of distant artillery, I decided that a short stroll in the fresh morning air might brighten me up. There was a small river – more like a large stream – nearby, so I set off, keeping our unit in sight as I walked along the bank. The water was a shade muddy and slow-moving. Suddenly the path gave way, and I was pitched into a deeper part of the river. It was so unexpected that I involuntarily swallowed a mouthful of the muddy water. Unhurt, I scrambled out and hurried back to our section truck, to be met with my colleagues' caustic comments that if I washed my clothes I was supposed to take them off first. I changed into dry clothing and thought no more about it.

The next day, though, I began to feel quite poorly, and by late afternoon Corporal Wallace decided to call in Captain Federer because I had developed a raging temperature and was becoming delirious. My friends told him about my unfortunate dip in the nearby river, and after a quick examination he filled in the necessary forms and ordered one of our ambulances to get me to the nearest military hospital, forty miles down the line, as rapidly as he could. I was entirely unaware of this, having lapsed into a comatose state. Weird dreams and strange visions filled my mind, and I saw people dressed in white floating gently by. My weary mind speculated that I must have died, and these were angels coming to escort me hence.

Some ten days later my fever had abated, and I began to take notice of my surroundings once more. I realised that I was in a ward bed and, believing I was still in our unit at Forli, I looked around for some of my colleagues. It was a strange medical officer who answered my call. 'So – you've decided to rejoin the land of the living! We thought we were losing you. That was a very nasty infection you picked up. Luckily for you we received a delivery of a new drug called sulphonamide. In desperation we tried it out – and it worked!' Memory flooding back, I told him how I'd fallen into the stream. He nodded. 'That'll be it – full of all sorts of horrible sewage, I'm sure.'

'Can I go back to my unit now, sir?' I asked weakly.

'You most certainly can not,' he snorted. 'You're not fit to stand on your own feet yet, and you need lots of rest and recuperation before we even think of discharging you.'

Unwillingly I had to accept his ruling. When I tried to stand up everything whirled around, and I had to sit down before I fell.

After a fortnight of enforced idleness and proper meals I began to feel like my normal self again, and I was delighted when the medical officer who had just examined me said, 'Lance-Corporal Hill, you'll be very pleased to hear that I propose to get rid of you. Incidentally, sulphonamide was discovered by a German. Luckily for you our lot got hold of the formula!'

'So when am I going back to my unit, sir!'

'I never mentioned going back to your unit. Since you've been enjoying our hospitality the whole battle zone in northern Italy has erupted and Jerry has been practically driven out. We tried to trace your unit, but everyone's moved and we haven't a clue where they are. It's the transit camp for you. Don't worry – they'll sort things out.'

Very disappointed, I collected my kit – which had fortunately been put on the ambulance that had brought me down, and went with a few other recovered patients to a transit camp a quarter of an hour away.

Unhappily, I settled into the routine of morning parades, where the names of those who had to report to the camp office to be told where they were being posted were read out each day. I shared a tent with a forty-year-old RAMC private named Reg Jackson whose unit had also moved out of contact range. He had only moved abroad in the last few months, and said that at his age he was prepared to take things as they came and not worry. He was certainly a calming influence on me as I became more and more uneasy about where we would end up. 'There's nowt good got wi' worrying, Corp,' he said.

Ten days later both mine and Private Jackson's names were called out on the morning parade, so I hurried to the office with Reg ambling along behind. 'Lance-Corporal Hill, sir. My name was on your list.'

The young lieutenant looked up wearily. 'Ah yes, You're the chap who's kept pestering my sergeant about returning to the One Five One Light Field Ambulance. What's the matter? Don't you like our transit camp?'

'It's just that I want to get back to doing the work I trained to do, sir.'

'We've tried to trace your unit, but they've left this region altogether and so far we can't find out there whereabouts.' He was interrupted by the tardy arrival of Reg, who saluted and gave his name. 'I'm glad you've turned up as well, because I'm transferring you both to the One Hundred and Eleventh Light Field Ambulance. There's an ambulance waiting, so take this form, put your kit aboard the ambulance and report to your new unit.'

I was about to argue, but Reg nudged me and shook his head. 'Why did you do that?' I said as we went to the ambulance.

'Just think about it, Corp. We're joining a mob with little or no experience of action, and you as a seasoned Desert Rat will be able to run rings round 'em. They'll treat you with respect!'

Reg and I managed to settle in with this new and comparatively inexperienced unit, which was currently not giving medical treatments, but awaiting further movement orders. We had been drafted in to replace two of their men who had fallen out of a moving truck and suffered serious fractures. Reg's prediction that my lengthy desert travels would earn me respect proved correct. Now, aged twenty-seven, I was senior in age to most of the RAMC men in the unit, who liked me to retell some of the hair-raising situations I had been involved in. I must admit

I laid it on a bit thick at times with my tales about snakes, scorpions, tarantula and black widow spiders, and of course the ever-present flies; I had them gaping in awe.

Meanwhile, news of the bitter fighting in the very far north of Italy spoke of massive Allied aerial bombardments and slow though steady advancement – and then quite suddenly the opposition started to crumble as our Allied troops pushed forward and the Russians in the east advanced closer and closer to Berlin.

On 30 April the radio announced the unexpected and incredible news of the suicide of Hitler and his mistress in the bunker beneath Berlin's Nazi headquarters, as the Russians bombarded the city with artillery fire.

In northern Italy the new German commander who had just taken over realised that his situation was impossible, and he ordered his troops to lay down their arms. Almost a million tired, weary and disillusioned Axis troops in northern Italy and Austria surrendered to the advancing Allies on 2 May 1945.

Within hours the One One One Light Field Hospital was ordered to move to Austria, to a tiny town called Neumarkt. After a scenic journey over towering mountain passes and tortuous descents into deep valleys, we reached our destination. Up a hill outside the town, on the edge of a wood of tall fir trees, stood a large hostel – used until recently as a maternity centre for young girls who had obeyed Hitler's command to consort with the noble German soldaten, with predictable results. Now it was unoccupied, and it was a pleasant surprise to find it equipped with all the equipment necessary to run a small hospital, including a fully automatic laundry and a kitchen equipped with electric cooking ranges and masses of utensils. Our quarters were fully furnished, and the place was ideal for the small short-term illness and minor injury centre we were to run.

On 7 May the Germans signed an unconditional surrender on Luneberg Heath. The war in Europe was over.

The next day was declared Victory in Europe Day, a public holiday, and King George V addressed a message to the nation proclaiming our victory. All over Europe a great sigh of relief marked the cessation of bombing, shelling and ruinous destruction. But the Far Eastern war was still not over!

CHAPTER

25

Despite the cessation of hostilities in Europe there still remained a tremendous amount of clearing up to be done, and although conditions in the hostel at Neumarkt were very comfortable compared with earlier days, I grew daily more concerned about my Python repatriation due in late July. I had mentioned this to the adjutant of my new unit, explaining that quite a large proportion of the One Five One would become eligible at that time and I did not wish to miss out. He promised to look into the matter for me, so I left it at that. When mid-July arrived without any response I was beginning to think it was a hopeless que~~ in spite of my daily nattering to the sergeant clerk. Then one mo~ with barely a week left in the month, the orderly room clerk ~ find me. 'You're wanted in the office now – I think your re~ have come through.'

Not wasting a second, I dashed to the office, and wond~ it was true. The original application had been put thro~ Pomfret in January, which was what he had prom~ came the news that one of the unit medical office~ to Milan in his staff car and was happy to give ~ officer supplied me with a railway warrant to kit, bumping down to the Naples transit camp, from where my papers in glee. a UK-bound ship.

I dashed to the room I shared with Rencle, who was in the into him on the way. 'It's arrived!' I exclaieep yer 'ead down, and

'Didn't I tell you it would be OK? last war, used to say "When the m~

you'll come up smelling o' roses". Good luck, Corp. Maybe we'll meet again some day.'

Down in the Naples transit camp, at which I arrived in the evening of the same day, having caught an express train direct from Milan, I entered the camp office. 'It must be your lucky day,' said the sergeant on duty. 'There's a ship leaving for the UK tomorrow, and there's room for you on that. Some of the blokes in this camp have been waiting over a week.'

Coming down the ship's gangway at Liverpool after a calm and comfortable voyage, my heart was swelling with joy at the prospect of spending another month with my dear wife and the rest of my family. I followed the queue that had formed outside the repatriation office, and when my turn came I handed my papers to the Military Police clerk on duty. He took them away, and returned moments later with an extra one. 'Here you are, Lance-Corporal Hill – a railway warrant for you to travel to RAMC Base Depot in Fleet.'

'Do you mean to tell me that I have to go all the way down to Hampshire before I can go home on leave to Yorkshire?'

'Sorry, but that's the way it goes. Repats must go through their own base depot. You'd better hurry: your train goes in half an hour!'

Here we go again, I thought – back to the old red tape. I had no option but to obey, so I hurried to the platform and boarded the waiting train.

Into the platform of the tiny station that served the country I started walking down the road to RAMC Base Depot. Calm heard was the click of leather on wood, and I looked her I had a cricket match in progress. I knew beyond all doubt that days, then carrie on the way, I sent a telegram to Edna telling England and hoped to be with her in a few RAMC HQ, a large two-storey building in a fenced compound. The guard at the gatehouse waved me onwards after a quick glance at my documents. 'Straight through the main door there.' I followed his instructions and found myself in a vast reception area with wooden benches and a desk, at which sat a corporal clerk. I waited until he was free, and then handed over my papers.

'Repat, eh? Not many of them coming through yet – apart from returning POWs and badly injured men. You don't look like either of them.'

The answer suddenly dawned on me. 'No, I'm not injured, but when I was with the One Five One Light Field Ambulance in northern Italy I fell into a river and swallowed some of the water. I ended up delirious and with a high fever in hospital. They managed to cure me, but it was several weeks before I was discharged. Because my former unit had moved on I was eventually sent to join One One One Field Hospital.'

'That explains it,' said the corporal, who had pulled a file out of the desk, and was leafing through it. 'One Five One Light Field Ambulance – long service in the North African Desert – most men now due for repatriation. They're now in Venice, and will be brought home when Trieste can accommodate a ship for them. You seem to be one jump ahead!'

'So when do I get to go home on leave?'

'Tomorrow morning. Give us time to sort out the necessary paperwork. In the meantime go to the men's messroom. They'll feed you, and then you can go to the barrack room to stack your kit and sleep for the night. Make sure you're here at this desk for 9.00a.m. sharp tomorrow, or you'll miss your train for London.'

It was the first week in August, and Edna and I had decided we would spend a week of my month's leave in Morecambe – a Lancashire coastal resort that we both loved – as a delayed honeymoon. We were welcomed at the guest-house where we had stayed with Edna's family before the war, and luxuriated in the joy of being together in the sunshine and the gentle sea breezes. We were relaxing in the sitting room after our evening meal when a radio news flash reported that in the early hours of the morning an American aircraft had dropped the first of the newly developed atomic bombs on the Japanese city of Hiroshima, and went on to describe the awful, unbelievable destruction and loss of life it had caused – estimated at ninety-two thousand killed and thirty-two thousand injured. The war against the Japanese in the Far East had gone on and on, with the Americans particularly anxious to exact revenge on the Japanese for their massive attack on the American fleet in Pearl Harbor in December 1941. Since the war in Europe had ended Allied forces had redoubled their efforts to defeat the Japanese, but it was a very slow process.

'This bomb will surely make a big difference,' I said. 'Destroying a whole city with just one bomb – nobody can withstand that.'

Three days later the American air force dropped a second atomic bomb, this time on Nagasaki, which resulted in almost twenty-four thousand deaths and forty-three thousand injured. This was indeed enough to make a difference. Five days later Emperor Hirohito agreed to accept the Allied surrender terms, and ordered his fighting forces to lay down their arms. His order prevailed, and the agreement was signed.

Edna and I, back at our home in Thornton, listened constantly to the news on the radio for fear of missing some further announcement, and finally it came, late on 15 August. The whole war was finally over, and the following day was declared a public holiday in Britain and designated VJ Day – Victory in Japan.

'Does this mean that you won't have to report back to that RAMC place?' asked Edna.

'I'm afraid not,' I said with a wry smile. 'I'm still a member of the armed forces until I receive my discharge papers and get fitted out with one of those demob suits. Try and be patient, love: it could be quite a while before I'm a full-blown "civvy" again.'

Far too soon my month of leave was over, and I had to catch the train back to Hampshire.

'You're a day late,' grumbled the corporal clerk.

'I don't think so. There was an announcement on the radio that any military personnel on leave on VJ Day were entitled to an extra day.'

'So it did, but it didn't say right away! Oh well, I don't suppose it really matters – there isn't a war on any more, and in any case it's the military hospital at Shaftesbury in Dorset who'll be complaining. I was supposed to send you there today.'

'So what do I do now?' I asked.

'Don't worry – I'll give them a ring to say there was a delay on the railway and you'll be with them tomorrow,' he replied with a grin. 'You know where the cookhouse is and the barrack room, so be our guest for the night again – but don't you dare miss that train in the morning.' Gratefully I collected my travel warrant and my documents.

At Shaftesbury military hospital I was welcomed with open arms, because they were overworked and understaffed. Being a first class nursing orderly as well as an NCO I was put to work straight away on night duty, in charge of three medical wards. I found it hard going at first, particularly the adjustment to daytime sleeping. I found it difficult to sleep deeply, and began to feel very weary. Three full wards meant that I had to be on the move all night, and eating a warmed-up dinner in the early hours did not make my digestion at all happy.

One morning, coming off duty after a particularly busy night, the medical officer in charge of the wards waved to me and said 'Lance-Corporal Hill, I'd like a word with you, please.'

I tried to think if I had made any mistakes while on duty, but nothing came to mind. 'What can I do for you, sir?'

The officer, whose name was Captain Prescott, smiled. 'Don't look so worried. You do come from Bradford, don't you?'

'Yes, that's right, sir,' I replied, completely mystified.

'I think you could do with a break. You look tired out. I need someone to accompany a patient who's recovering from tuberculosis to her home near Bradford. She'll need to spend a little time in a TB recovery centre there. She's a QAIMNS nursing sister and still feeling rather frail, and I've said she can only travel if someone's with her. How do you feel about escorting her? An ambulance will be laid on for transit from Waterloo to King's Cross, and from the Bradford terminus to Clayton Recovery Centre. When you've seen her safely there you can go to your own home for the night and the next day before coming back. How does that sound?'

'It sounds like a very, very good idea, sir!'

'Right. I'll arrange for you to be wakened in time for a noon departure, when all the necessary documentation and travel warrants will have been seen to. All you need to do is carry your patient's case and give her a hand climbing in and out of the various transports.'

I hurried to my bed and fell asleep instantly, sleeping like a log until one of the day shift orderlies shook me awake. 'Lucky so and so you are,' he said, 'getting time off and a trip home as well.'

After a lightning wash and shave and a quick snack from the cookhouse, I joined the ambulance. Captain Prescott was talking to a young lady dressed in a QAIMNS uniform. He introduced us. 'Just you make sure you get her there safely, Corporal!'

After a completely untroubled and uneventful journey, I said farewell to the nurse at Clayton.

It was 10.30 in the evening when I arrived at the door of our home, a small terraced house five minutes' walk away from Edna's parents' house, which my wife had managed to rent since my repatriation leave. It was in complete darkness. I hammered on the door and waited. After an anxious moment or two I knocked again, even louder. The bedroom window was opened about an inch. 'Who's that knocking at this time of night?' Edna's sleepy voice grumbled.

'It's me. Let me in – it's perishing out here.'

She gave a little scream of delight. 'George! George! Whatever are you doing here?'

'If you let me in I'll explain, love.'

Sitting in front of the fire, which we had encouraged back to life, I told her the story – and that I didn't need to return until the day after tomorrow. As an afterthought, I remarked, 'I was a bit surprised to find you in bed. You usually like to stay up till eleven.'

'Well – I've not been feeling too well lately. I've been feeling awfully sick, especially in the mornings.' I saw the colour rising in her cheeks, and suddenly the penny dropped.

'Morning sickness! Are you . . .?'

'I think I must be,' she said softly. 'I've got all the signs. I've not been to the doctor's yet, but I'm pretty certain. Do you mind?'

'Mind, my darling? I'm over the moon! It's the most wonderful thing that's ever happened to us. Are you sure you can manage all right? Is there anything I can do for you? Shouldn't you be putting your feet up or something?'

'Stop fussing, love,' she murmured. 'It's all perfectly normal: you should know that with all your medical training.'

'What I do know is that all I want is my demobilisation, so we can start living a normal married life together, raising our family.'

'Do you hope it's a boy or would you rather have a girl?'

'I don't mind, as long as everything goes all right.'

Back again at Shaftesbury's military hospital, I found there had been some re-arranging of night shift staffing, with the continuous night duty organised so that I alternated a week on days and a week on nights, which gave me a chance to catch up on lost sleep and also to meet some of the day staff who had never served anywhere else. They were regular soldiers in their thirties who would carry on there until they retired. When I was asked about some of my scarier experiences in the desert I obliged, making things sound as dramatic as I could.

Two days before Christmas a notice appeared to the effect that some RAMC personnel were to be allowed five days' Christmas leave. I didn't think for a moment that it would apply to me, as I was on the verge of being released, and it was with delight and astonishment that I read my name. I certainly wasn't going to look the gift horse in the mouth, and joined the others hurrying down to the station. I even managed to ring Edna's brother, who worked at Thornton Co-operative Society, from King's Cross, asking him to let her know I was on my way home.

'Oh, George, I wish you didn't have to go,' sighed Edna as the day came for me to return.

'Don't worry,' I assured her. 'It can't be long now.' And I showed her the morning paper, where an article announced the proposed demobilisation of a large number of long-term servicemen in January. 'Let's hope with all our hearts.' I kissed her, and hurried to the station.

It was the morning of 5 January 1946, and I was on my way to start the last day of my week on daytime duty when the staff nurse in charge of our section of wards, a mature lady who had a great sense of humour, caught my arm. 'Lance-Corporal Hill, I've just seen your name on a list of those who are going to be demobilised tomorrow. Before you think of going on duty you ought to go and see what it's all about.'

A huge surge of joy filled me, but I knew her sense of humour. 'You really shouldn't make jokes like that, Staff Nurse.'

'I'm not joking – it's true! Go and find out for yourself.'

I raced to the office, and . . . it really was true.

I spent the rest of the day handing in items of equipment that had served me for many a long day, and collecting an array of official documents that related to more than six years of active service, including a quite surprisingly glowing testimonial about my character, army pay for a month to cover the period of my demob leave, and finally a form to present to my local labour exchange when my leave expired.

Next morning I was up with the lark, all trace of tiredness banished. I said goodbye to the new friends I had made at Shaftesbury Hospital, and walked jauntily to the station

After a journey that seemed to take a lifetime but was in fact less than an hour I arrived at Taunton's military dispersal unit. The place was heaving with queuing, bustling, chattering and laughing demobbers being measured for and supplied with new suits, shirts, shoes and all the paraphernalia of civilian clothing. I joined the queue that had my surname initial displayed above it. An hour or so later, following the complicated measuring and trying on, and finally satisfied with the fit, style and colouring of the clothes, which were packed into a huge carrier bag for me, I was dressed once more in my uniform and greatcoat – which I was allowed to keep.

I was beginning to feel decidedly hungry and made my way to the canteen, where a huge selection of sandwiches and buttered scones were available, as well as huge mugs of sweet tea. Much refreshed, I returned to the office to queue for the most important document of all – the Soldiers Release Book Class 'A'. I stepped out at last, gleefully clutching the release book and my carrier bag. I was out – in Civvy Street once more.

Feeling like a new man, I boarded the train for London. With a carriage to myself, I went over the many life-changing things that had occurred in the last six and a quarter years, and the lessons that I had learned. First of all, I was not going back to my home life – I was going forward. Life is a path that we must all follow, and the only way is forward. There is no going back. As we travel on we meet friends whose pathway runs beside ours, although they may veer away to be seen no more. Then there are our loved ones and our families, whose paths will run alongside ours to the end of life's journey. The lessons we learn help us through the difficult bits.

Although Arthur Copley, Alan Wright, Billy Hough, John Hill, Corporal Arthur Wallace and I were now moving in different directions, there was no reason to doubt that we would all meet again some day.

I pulled my mind back as the train ground to a halt at Bradford station. Half an hour later I got off the Thornton trolley-bus, climbed the three steps to our front garden and clasped Edna in my arms as we began our joint journey forward – along with our imminent baby daughter.

Chronology

1939
September
On the 2nd Hitler launches 'Blitzkrieg' attack against Poland, breaking his earlier promise to Prime Minister Neville Chamberlain – who supported Poland. On the 3rd Britain and France declare war against Germany. The British Expeditionary Force is sent to France to help guard the country's frontier. The calling-up of young men into the British armed forces is greatly accelerated.

October
On the 4th George obeys his call-up papers and joins the 151st Cavalry Field Ambulance (which becomes the Light Field Ambulance) in Newcastle-upon-Tyne. Later in the month the 151 moves to Malton, North Yorkshire.

November
The 151 moves to Ludford, Lincolnshire.
Russian troops attack Finland, and heavy fighting continues there.

December
The 151 moves back to its original base in Newcastle-upon-Tyne, and there is Christmas leave.

1940
January
George and the 151 begin lectures and examinations to progress

from third-class to first-class nurses.

February
To Newcastle Royal Victoria Infirmary for six weeks of practical nursing experience.

March
George becomes part of a team operating a unit sick bay in which he also finds himself a patient – recovering in time to go home on a week's leave. To Scotland, to set up an advance dressing station.

May
The Germans have swooped into Belgium, Holland and Luxembourg. Chamberlain resigns and Winston Churchill takes over as prime minister, forming a coalition government. German forces surround the French army, and the British Expeditionary Force is forced to fall back to the coast. A pincer attack by General Rommel traps the British forces in a small area near Dunkirk. Hundreds of small British boats pick up the troops and ferry them to safety – despite constant air attacks.

June
The rescue is completed, but most equipment has been left behind. George rejoins his unit and moves to Melbourne, Yorkshire, where training and examinations continue.

August
Home leave for George – during which Bradford is bombed. By the end of the month his unit has moved to Warsop, Nottinghamshire.

December
Embarkation Leave notice is posted: George is in the first batch. On the 17th George and Edna marry, and two days later he returns to his unit.

1941
January
The 151 embarks on the SS *Northumberland* at Liverpool, but after engine failure in the Irish Sea the convoy continues without them. The unit waits in Greenock, Scotland, while the engine is repaired, then re-embarks, rejoining the original convoy at Freetown, on the west coast of Africa. From there they go round the Cape to Durban, and after time at Clarewood Camp they are taken on to Port Said, Egypt.

March
The 151 travels by train to Tahag Transit Camp, where they are rejoined by the RASC drivers and new vehicles.
April George, as part of an advance dressing station team, moves into the desert.
May
They join up with the forward troops.
June
Germany invades Russia. George's unit returns to a railhead west of Mersa Matruh. A few days' leave in Alexandria follow.
November
General Auchinlech takes over from General Wavel, launching Operation Crusader. George's unit comes under heavy fire and has to move quickly to avoid capture. They return to the railhead in Egypt to re-equip. The Japanese attack the American fleet at Pearl Harbour.

1942
January
Rommel breaks through, but the attack peters out. The 151 moves up again with the Seventh Armoured Division.
May
One of Rommel's pincer columns appears and fires on the unit – but George and his comrades escape. The 151 falls back through western Egypt, through the heavily defended El-Alamein minefields, and is sent back to Qassassin Camp, south of Cairo, for a refit.
August
Rommel's forces fail to penetrate the El-Alamein defences. Re-equipped, George's unit moves to rejoin the troops near El-Alamein
October
The Eighth Army moves into position ready for attack, and on the 23rd the Battle of El-Alamein begins. George is just a few miles behind the artillery.
November
The First Army begins to land in north-west Africa, sandwiching the Afrika Korps and Italian armour between two Allied forces. The Eighth Army chases the Axis Forces through Libya.

1943
January
The Highland Division enters Tripoli. George's advance into Tunisia continues

May
General von Arnim surrenders to the Allies, ending the North Africa conflict. The Russians have turned the tide at Stalingrad and are pushing the Germans westward.

July
American and British forces land on Sicily. George's unit is transported to Augusta, Sicily.

September
American and British forces have moved into the toe of Italy. The Italians sign an armistice with the Allies, but Germany vows to continue the fight. The 151 is ferried up to Taranto, where George and his colleagues are seconded to an Italian hospital ship which is transporting Allied troops to Sicily. One quick trip turns into three months of journeying up and down the Mediterranean.

December
George returns to his unit in Foggia. Medical duties resume.

1944
June
The Americans break through at Anzio. On the night of the 5th American and British troops begin landing in Normandy: D-Day is under way.

August
The Italian conflict continues. George moves north to Forli and, to his astonishment, is offered Christmas home leave.

1945
January
George is back in Forli.

March
The 151 moves up to the river Po. George falls into the river and catches a serious infection from the polluted water. When he recovers he discovers his unit has moved away, and is sent to a

field ambulance unit only recently arrived from England.

April
On the 30th Hitler commits suicide.

May
The Axis forces in Italy and Austria surrender. On the 7th Germany signs an unconditional surrender.

June
Under the Python scheme, George is due for repatriation to Britain. His papers turn up during the last week of the month, and he presents himself to a transit camp near Naples. He returns to Liverpool, and travels back home to Yorkshire – via the RAMC Base Depot at Fleet, Hampshire.

August
VJ-Day: the surrender of Japan and the end of the war. Although the war is over, George remains in the army. He returns to Fleet, after which he is posted to a military hospital in Shaftesbury, Dorset.

1946
January
George's demobilisation documents come through. As a civilian he returns to Edna in their new home.